ROUTLEDGE LIBRARY EDITIONS:
TRADE UNIONS

Volume 23

PARTIES, TRADE UNIONS AND SOCIETY IN EAST-CENTRAL EUROPE

PARTIES, TRADE UNIONS AND SOCIETY IN EAST-CENTRAL EUROPE

Edited by
MICHEAL WALLER and MARTIN MYANT

Routledge
Taylor & Francis Group

LONDON AND NEW YORK

First published in 1994 by Frank Cass & Co Ltd.

This edition first published in 2023
by Routledge
4 Park Square, Milton Park, Abingdon, Oxon OX14 4RN

and by Routledge
605 Third Avenue, New York, NY 10158

Routledge is an imprint of the Taylor & Francis Group, an informa business

British Library Cataloguing in Publication Data
A catalogue record for this book is available from the British Library

ISBN: 978-1-032-37553-3 (Set)
ISBN: 978-1-032-39648-4 (Volume 23) (hbk)
ISBN: 978-1-032-39663-7 (Volume 23) (pbk)
ISBN: 978-1-003-35077-4 (Volume 23) (ebk)

DOI: 10.4324/9781003350774

Publisher's Note
The publisher has gone to great lengths to ensure the quality of this reprint but points out that some imperfections in the original copies may be apparent.

Disclaimer
The publisher has made every effort to trace copyright holders and would welcome correspondence from those they have been unable to trace.

Parties, Trade Unions and Society in East-Central Europe

edited by

MICHAEL WALLER and MARTIN MYANT

FRANK CASS

First published 1994 in Great Britain by
FRANK CASS AND COMPANY LIMITED
Newbury House, 900 Eastern Avenue,
Ilford, Essex IG2 7HH, England

and in the United States by
FRANK CASS
c/o International Specialized Book Services Inc.
5804 N.E. Hassalo Street
Portland, OR 97213-3644

Copyright © 1994 Frank Cass & Co. Ltd

British Library Cataloguing in Publication Data

Parties, Trade Unions and Society in
East-central Europe. – (Special Issue of
the "Journal of Communist Studies", ISSN
0268-4535; Vol.9, No.4)
   I. Waller, Michael   II. Myant, M.R.
   III. Series
   324.247

   ISBN 0-7146-4583-4

Library of Congress Cataloging-in-Publication Data

Parties, trade unions, and society in East-Central Europe / edited by
   Michael Waller and Martin Myant.
       p.   cm.
     "This group of studies first appeared in a Special Issue . . . of
   The Journal of communist studies, Vol. 9, no. 4."
     Includes bibliographical references and index.
     ISBN 0-7146-4583-4 : £29.50
     1. Political parties—Europe. Eastern—Congresses. 2. Europe,
   Eastern—Politics and government—1989—Congresses. 3. Trade
   -unions—Europe, Eastern—Congresses. 4. Europe, Eastern—Social
   conditions—Congresses. I. Waller, Michael, 1934–   . II. Myant,
   M. R. (Martin R.) III. Journal of communist studies. Vol. 9, no. 4
   (Special Issue)
   JN96.A979P38   1994
   323.247'009'049—dc20   94-6312
                                                                      CIP

This group of studies first appeared in a Special Issue: Parties, Trade
Unions and Society in East-Central Europe of *The Journal of Communist
Studies*, Vol. 9, No. 4 published by Frank Cass & Co. Ltd.

Typeset by Vitaset, Paddock Wood, Kent
Printed in Great Britain by
Bookcraft (Bath) Ltd, Midsomer Norton

Contents

Introduction

It was hardly surprising that, in the first flush of the fall of communism in east-central Europe, comment and analysis should have focused particularly sharply on new political parties. As successors to the earlier movements of dissent they carried to power the heroes of the struggle against the communist regimes. The turn away from communism meant a move in the direction of pluralism, and this, too, thrust the formation of political parties into the limelight. Finally, as vehicles for individual advancement, the political parties acquired a high profile as their leading personalities, often very colourful, jockeyed and jostled in the power game. Nor was it surprising that, for largely the same reasons, it was particularly the newly-created parties that were at the point of focus. This was a process of change; communism and all its apparatus of power had declined, whilst the new formations and forces were in the ascendant.

The first free elections produced a mild surprise when the communist parties or their successors won a respectable portion of the poll. In Romania and Bulgaria their continuing presence, covert or overt, was very substantial. Even in the northern tier of countries, with between 10 and 14 per cent of the vote (16.3 in the GDR) it was clear that they could still be a factor of some weight in the political equation of the transition. Their strength could be attributed to support from pensioners, from former party workers, and from a countryside clientele attached to occasional popular leaders or held in place through various forms of persuasion – but also to the organizational capacity that the former communist parties had retained. These were, in fact, no mean resources with which to maintain a footing in the circumstances of flux that followed the events of 1989. They were sufficient to keep the renamed post-communist Socialist Party in Bulgaria either hovering on the brink of governmental power or actually exercising it. But it was with the addition of a further factor that the fortunes of the former communist parties, particularly those of the northern tier, really revived. This was popular disaffection caused by the rigour of the economic reforms. It was in September 1993 that the Polish Socialist Left Alliance, with at its core the post-communist Social Democracy of the Polish Republic, headed the poll in a national election, with a further post-communist party – the Polish Peasants' Party – coming in second place.

Meanwhile, organizational continuities from the communist past had from the very start of the transition process been extremely strong in an area less open to the gaze of external observers, but closer to the daily lives of the citizens of these countries than had been the ruling communist parties themselves, not to mention their squabbling successors. Subordinated to the power of the party in the communist period, and having little or no organizational autonomy, the trade unions had none the less played a central role in welfare distribution. Since their role was circumscribed in this way, and since they were associated in the popular mind with many of the good things available under the communist system – rest homes and sanatoria, summer camps for the children, holiday accommodation (including, in Bulgaria, some of the best skiing chalets), cinemas, clubs and leisure centres, in addition to maternity and sickness benefits – there was no reason why they should share all the opprobrium to which the communist parties themselves were exposed. Moreover, the autonomy that they had lacked became available after 1989. They took it, and they retained a membership base that still at the time of writing, in all the countries of the region, exceeds that of the new trade unions that formed in the more open and competitive political environment.

The evolution of relations between parties, governments and trade unions therefore merits attention, and it is the aim of this collection of studies to provide an analysis of it. Largely because of the considerations contained in the foregoing, the emphasis is on the trade union side of that relationship. The countries covered are Poland, the Czech Republic, Slovakia, Hungary, Bulgaria, and Russia. In the case of the last, the focus is almost exclusively on the trade unions, for the simple but very significant reason that the process of party formation in Russia can with reason be described as chaotic, and the contrast between the evolution of post-communist Russia and that of eastern Europe, with exception made for the disruptions of war in the former Yugoslavia, is both substantial and of crucial importance for comparative analysis.

The collection stems from a conference hosted by the Political Institute of the Hungarian Academy of Sciences in March 1993, but forming part of the programme of a research project on Regime Change in East-Central Europe: Political Parties and the Transition to Democratic Politics (Grant No. Y309 25 3056), a central part of the East–West Programme of the British Economic and Social Research Council. John Thirkell and Simon Clarke are each involved in other projects within that programme more directly concerned with trade union affairs.

The collection is divided into two parts. The first contains comparative or overarching analytical studies of the place of parties and groups in the process of regime change in eastern Europe, with the study by Sørensen situating that process in a wider perspective. The second part consists of case studies drawn from the experiences of the individual countries.

Part I

Civil Society and the Development of Political Parties in East-Central Europe

PAUL LEWIS

Following an influential tradition within western political thought, the new parties in east-central Europe have been viewed with suspicion and have experienced considerable difficulty in establishing themselves. But it is barely possible to conceive of a modern democracy operating without major inputs from reasonably developed and operationally effective political parties. Relatively little attention has, however, yet been paid to the functions they might be expected to perform in post-communist east-central Europe and, indeed, to the actual characteristics of a modern political party. There are alternative definitions of parties and contrasting views of their primary features. The contemporary east-central European context will also exercise a strong influence on development of the new parties. Among the relevant factors here will be the fate of the elements of civil society that contributed to the demise of the former communist regimes.

The Role of Parties

Political parties have not had a good press in post-communist eastern Europe. They have been seen as weak, framgented, barely capable of sustaining effective government and poor at presenting themselves to the electorate,[1] cliqueish, divorced from the mass of society, increasingly unrepresentative of public interests and generally under-developed,[2] divisive, self-seeking, antithetic to hopes of national recovery and harmful to state interests.[3] Neither has the idea of their emergence and development received much of a welcome as a feature of the post-communist political order. Diverse forms of social movement were instrumental in overthrowing the communist regime and they, with the institutions understood to be characteristic of civil society rather than political parties, were initially identified as the major vehicles of subsequent democratic development.[4] Parties tended to be seen by many as outmoded and largely irrelevant to modern processes of democratization. The existence of such views has not been restricted to the east, and major currents of modern democratic thought have by no means been sympathetic to the activities and functioning of the political party. Parties,

Paul Lewis is Senior Lecturer in Government at the Open University, UK.

never particularly welcomed by thinkers as diverse as Jean-Jacques Rousseau and George Washington,[5] became denigrated as agencies of manipulation and bureaucratized authority and often appeared to be increasingly marginalized within the political process as levels of membership declined and their role seemed to diminish.

But the importance of political parties for the emergence, consolidation and operation of democratic practices and the role they play in the overall processes of government in modern society are also well documented. Through the electoral process, the party system determines the possibility and level of citizen participation; party activities in electoral and legislative arenas exercise a major influence on the nature and stability of political leadership; and the dynamics of party systems can have an important impact on prospects for the emergence or subsequent control of social turmoil and political violence.[6] In terms of the consolidation of new democracies it has, too, been argued that parties play a particularly important role.[7] Not so much replacing or appearing to substitute for the institutions of civil society parties may more appropriately be seen as belonging neither to civil society nor to the state.[8] They are rather the essential link between civil society and the state and one of the key buckles that holds the major components of the body politic together.

The 'anti-politics' that had been associated with the resurgence of civil society in east-central Europe and characterized much of the opposition in the early 1980s was in some ways seen to be giving way to a process of party formation well before 1989.[9] Aspects of the recreation or formation of political parties entered into all three elements identified in the necessary process of 're-inventing' civil society after communism.[10] Under the conditions of post-communism it could be claimed that civil society as a concept of practical and theoretical analysis had very limited value in its own right except as an 'initial slogan for rallying those not tainted by involvement with a discredited state'. A more important question was what would now happen to the relationship between politics and state power – whether politics could be turned from a tool into a check.[11] Nevertheless, the actual functions performed by political parties, their role in relation to modern concepts of civil society and the precise nature of their contribution to the democratic order remains somewhat uncertain. The notion of function is itself quite a fuzzy one and, while many observers seem to experience few difficulties in itemizing the diverse aspects of the role that parties perform in the political system, it is by no means always clear that specific parties actually live up to these expectations in any particular situation.[12] But it is not difficult to formulate a broad view of party activities and the functions they perform in a modern democracy.

A general view of party functions can quite easily be developed – although the same view is by no means shared by every observer. According to Alan Ball one of the most important functions of parties is that of 'uniting, simplifying and stabilising the political process. Political parties tend to provide the highest common denominator. They . . . bring together sectional interests, overcome geographical interests, and provide coherence to sometimes divisive government structures'.[13] A more comprehensive list of six functions can be drawn up with relative ease. Political parties, following King:

(1) as one of their very basic functions, structure the vote in a modern democracy and often carry that process into broader processes of opinion structuring;
(2) integrate citizens into the broader community and mobilize the mass public for participation in the political process – from the simple activity of voting to more complex and dedicated forms of behaviour;
(3) facilitate the recruitment of political leaders – although the role of parties as institutions may well be quite variable in this respect;
(4) organize government – although, again, the role of parties as institutions and select groups of individuals who act within the framework of party organizations may well need to be distinguished;
(5) form public policy, primarily by influencing the content of public thought and discussion, formulating programmes which party leaders then feel constrained to implement once elected to office, or by bringing pressure to bear on the incumbent government;
(6) aggregate interests, a somewhat uncertain process which can range from activity which simply takes note of social interests to that capable of structuring behaviour designed to achieve the objectives they give rise to.

S. Neumann ascribes a somewhat more active role to parties, with particular implications for their functions in less developed countries and the fluid conditions pertaining in post-communist societies, in directing attention to their organization of the 'chaotic public will', the transformation of the private citizen into a 'political animal', formation of links between government and public opinion, and the selection of political leaders.[14] Alternative views, by no means unconvincing in an age of market logic and amidst appeals to individual interest, direct attention to the functions that parties perform for individual voters, political activists and party leaders.[15] As the boss of New York's Tammany Hall is reported to have put it, 'men ain't in politics for nothin'. They want to get somethin' out of it'.[16]

Precisely what a political party is also emerged as an early source of disagreement. A straightforward view, which accords well with a widespread popular conception, is that parties are best defined by their common aim and that they are organizations that 'seek political power either singly or in co-operation with other political parties'.[17] Political power is, however, by no means an unambiguous or uncontentious concept itself and others prefer a more behavioural definition, such as that of an 'organization which nominates candidates for election to a legislature'.[18] For some of the classic theorists, however, parties are seen as more complex entities and definitions that convey some impression of their various aspects and the diverse functions they perform are preferred.

Thus for Neumann the idea of party connotes the coexistence of different competing entities, with their characteristic features of partnership, separation and participation, as well as the inclusion of each separate group as a part of a greater whole. He therefore defines party as the

> articulate organization of society's active political agents, those who are concerned with the control of governmental power and who compete for popular support with another group or groups holding divergent views . . . the great intermediary which links social forces and ideologies to official governmental institutions and relates them to political action within the larger political community.[19]

Hardly a snappy definition but one which does build in the multi-faceted character of the modern party. Others are even more specific about the functions a political organization should perform if it is to be identified as a party – one, for example, that is 'locally articulated, that interacts with and seeks to attract the electoral support of the general public, that plays a direct and substantive role in political recruitment, and that is committed to the capture or maintenance of power, either alone or in coalition with others'.[20]

A major problem here is that such a specific definition may well rule out many of the organizations we would tend to identify as parties and postulate as characteristics features we might otherwise be inclined to regard as empirical variables. Nevertheless, the political activities and functions that are generally associated with the party seem to go some way beyond those concerned just with the acquisition of power or the nomination of candidates for a legislature. It is, clearly, important to distinguish between different types of parties, the circumstances of their emergence and the ways in which they operate under the diverse conditions of modern political life. All these features can exert a major influence on the capacity of a party to perform the functions outlined above. The paths that modern parties have taken in order to emerge on the political scene present themselves, not suprisingly, as a major differentiating factor in terms of the role and profile of contemporary parties.

The Origins of Parties

Processes of internal and external origination with respect to the legislature are one historical source of difference which has had a major effect on the nature and development of modern parties. Whether political parties were formed, essentially, by parliamentary elites seeking external support throughout society and establishing an organization capable of sustaining their position, or by social forces forging their own organization and then endeavouring to secure parliamentary representation has been one important factor in determining the character and form of contemporary parties.[21] There were, as most observers point out, no modern political parties in existence prior to 1850 outside the United States. Processes of modernization and the extension of popular suffrage appear, it is often agreed, to have been the critical factors in promoting this innovation. The progress of democracy and, in particular, the extension of popular suffrage and generalization of the ability to vote were here the central features.

The primary process, in Duverger's view, was the establishment of parliamentary groups in the legislative bodies that were becoming of increasing significance in the political processes of early modern societies. With the extension of the suffrage, local electoral committees were rapidly established and soon became a major part of the mechanism involved in mobilizing the support of broader social forces for the groups forming within the parliamentary institution. This did not occur in the same way in each country. In Britain, Registration Societies were established by both private citizens and candidates after the 1832 Act to facilitate the implementation of newly granted electoral rights. More significant, however, was the formation of the Conservative National Union following the more radical Reform Act of 1867. The particular point of the exercise here was, as Robert McKenzie emphasized, the gathering of electoral support without sacrificing the members' freedom of action within parliament.[22]

Electoral committees in the United States gained particular importance due to the fact that a large number of public posts were elective and that organized guidance was rapidly accepted to be a necessity. The holding of a single ballot for the presidency (making the avoidance of a split vote highly desirable), the influx of large numbers of immigrants with no experience of American (or probably any other) politics, and the establishment (from the time of Jackson) of a spoils system which awarded all civil service posts to the victorious party were also important factors. Others argue that the formation of the first American party system took place well in advance of the Jackson period during the 1830s and occurred before the end of the eighteenth century in the context of the relations that developed between the Federalists and Republicans.[23] It was, indeed, an ironic consequence of the insistence with which the Founding Fathers formulated a constitution that prevented the instruments of government falling into the hands of any one faction that parties developed so rapidly in the United States. The fragmented governmental structure swiftly evoked the processes of mediation and linkage that parties were able to claim as their particular prerogative.[24]

Once distinctive parliamentary groups and electoral committees were in existence it soon became necessary to establish permanent coordination between them – and thus the beginnings of a modern political party. Such are the outline processes of the 'internal' or parliamentary origins of the political party which, it was argued by Duverger, was the original mode of party formation and remained dominant until around 1900. The other main mode involved externally created parties and the formation of groups or the articulation of existing interests which sought parliamentary representation. The range and variety of those involved is well known, and the activity of trade unions is probably the most prominent in this respect. Somewhat less widespread, but also significant in central Europe, Scandinavia and the British Dominions, were agrarian unions and peasant co-operatives. 'Philosophical societies' and intellectual groups, free-masons[25] and church-based associations, and leagues of ex-servicemen were also major agencies of party formation. In the context of post-communist eastern Europe one might well add groups of businessmen and commercial interests which, unlike their counterparts under the conditions of early capitalism, also need to break into and establish themselves in the newly established parliamentary arena.

The difference between internal and external party origination does not just have historical significance. Different processes of party formation seem to have exerted a continuing influence on the structure and *modus operandi* of the developed organization. Externally originated parties tended, according to Duverger, to be more centralized than those arising within parliamentary and electoral circles – whose primary processes of formation originated with the actions of electoral committees at the grassroots. The influence of the parliamentary group is also considerably greater in the case of parties of parliamentary or electoral origin. Some, indeed, suggest further that the very development of externally created parties poses a major threat to the opération and survival of competitive party systems.[26] Others, on the other hand, point rather to the dangers of instability associated with the continuing dominance of internally originated 'committee' parties into the second half of the twentieth century.[27] Neither has the rather rigid distinction drawn by Duverger between the two forms of party gone uncontested.[28]

But the different types of party which Duverger suggests have appeared in a particular historical order, may also be located within a more clearly defined developmental sequence. Party development can thus be seen to pass through the different phases of factionalization, polarization, expansion and institutionalization.[29] If, as many argue, Hungary and Poland show strong signs of party factionalism it seems likely that the phase of institutionalized party activity in east-central Europe lies some way in the future. But such developmental views do not represent the only perspective on processes of party formation. Another approach places it in the context of a number of more general theoretical accounts – those drawing on institutional theories which direct attention to parliamentary development and the formation of parties on that basis, others that invoke the onset of historical crises and the tasks which confront the political system as parties develop, and developmental perspectives that locate processes of party formation in the broader framework of modernization.[30] The broad conclusion that emerges from this account is that the origin of political parties, while deeply associated with specific historical crises, is also closely bound up with the general process of modernization.

In terms of this more general interpretation, further, the way in which parties develop and the evolution of the political regime as a whole may be related to the degree of coincidence or disparity between political and economic developments. In the context of contemporary east-central Europe, where post-communist democratization is scheduled to coincide with rapid economic transformation, there may be considerable relevance in the argument that highly ideologized politics appears to be typical of societies in which 'political claims outstrip underlying socio-economic realities'.[31] Such features of modern political life, it is argued, have also been associated with cases such as the enduring alienation of sizeable sections of the French population rather than their integration in a responsive political system and a considerable disillusion amongst the French citizenry with politics as such. These conclusions lend support to Blondel's view that in countries that are not industrialized, or are only partially so developed, 'natural forces' will not by themselves lead to mass parties.[32] The history and lessons to be derived from the experience of what is generally regarded as an established political democracy (if not one that can be said to boast a mature party system) should not be lost on those interested in developments in contemporary east-central Europe. The degree to which Blondel's views on party developments in pre-industrial societies may apply to post-industrial or apparently de-industrializing systems also merits consideration in the east-central European context.

The variety in patterns of political development and outcomes in terms of party formation even in such a relatively homogeneous area as western Europe provides a warning of the complexity of the processes involved, the diversity of the impact of different kinds of socio-economic change on political structures and the dangers involved in over-enthusiastic generalization. This proviso must have even greater relevance to non-European systems and Third World countries – and also to post-communist countries facing analogous demands of simultaneous political development and economic transformation. The relevance of schemes evolved to systematize and help explain party development in the countries of early democratic development and advanced capitalism may well have limited significance outside those areas. As LaPalombara and Weiner suggested, it was hardly appropriate to apply Duverger's scheme of early party development in terms of the emergence of parliaments and electoral systems to most of the developing areas. There were, frequently, no authentic representative bodies under the colonial regime – and even where there were, nationalist movements often had little interest in working within the parliamentary system.

Parallels with east-central European social movements and forces of dissent can also be drawn. The broader context of historical crisis and political response may well be more relevant here – and of the three mentioned (legitimacy, integration and participation) that associated with the legitimacy deficit has provided the primary challenge. This tended to be the issue around which some of the earliest parties both in Europe and the developing areas were first created. It also appears clear that the onset of the post-communist transformation in east-central Europe came with the failure of the existing structure of authority and the beginning of a period of political upheaval and transition. As in some developing areas, the rapid emergence of an effective formula to promote stability – in the east-central European case, the end of Soviet domination and a revival of national sovereignty – seemed to provide an adequate political solution. Yet this was by no means equivalent to the establish-ment of a base for effective party development, when (as was noted in connection of earlier cases of legitimation crisis) 'the "parties" formed may not involve a broader public and may be more appropriately conceived of as incipient parties'.[33]

This, however, raises further questions of political development in terms of the failure of new parties to perform the functions that underpin their formal existence and safeguard their place in the developing political system. Legitimation crises, as in the French case, can be protracted affairs and formal independence by no means provides the blanket solution: indeed, 'many opposition leaders in modernizing nations regard the new government much as they did its colonial predecessors, that is, as illegitimate'.[34]

Party Development and Political Functions

Effective party development, it should be clear, has by no means been mainly or even primarily about representing the interests of mass publics and newly formed social constituencies but is also about the defence of established, probably economic interests. It was, for example, the British Conservative Party that took the lead in establishing a National Union and successfully forming a modern political party. According to one recent analysis, further, a critical function of parties in developing countries seems to be their capacity to act as a mediating mechanism and secure the accommodation of dominant classes to an incipient democratic order by the successful defence of existing elite interests.[35]

Views about the prime functions of parties are, of course, highly diverse and one promoted by Duverger, for example, links an emphasis on elites with another on representation in his argument that the 'deepest significance of political parties is that they tend to the creation of new elites, and this restores to the notion of representation its true meaning, the only real one'. It is a view similar to that expressed by Lipset, that the essence of modern democracy and the key role of political parties concerns less the acquisition and exercise of power than the establishment of the possibility of gaining access to it and definition of the conditions relating to that access. Such conditions include the securing of effective representation which, in turn, is primarily concerned with defining possible combinations of relations between parties and potential social bases – and thus the provision of effective democratic government.[36] These observations clearly reflect on the situation in east-central Europe where it is the tenuous nature of links between elites and the mass public and the low representative capability of parties that are characteristic of the contemporary political scene.

Questions of function and political objective are, not surprisingly, closely linked with those that direct attention to issues of party structure and organization. Duverger's work makes, once more, a classic contribution in this area. In keeping with the fundamental distinction he makes between internally and externally originated parties, he draws a primary contrast between the caucus-based, middle-class parties deriving from nineteenth-century experience and the branch-based structures associated with the subsequent development of socialist parties. A third major category is formed by the later, strictly centralized parties that accompanied the growth of communist and fascist movements. Other parties occupy a position between these three archetypes. These include Catholic and Christian Democrat parties, labour and agrarian parties and more traditional organizations associated with dominant individuals or clans. On this basis he conducts more extensive analysis in terms of party organization (direct and indirect structures, forms of articulation), membership (concepts and criteria, degree and nature of participation), and leadership (selection, degrees of oligarchy, authority and parliamentary representation).[37]

Party organization with respect to internal structure and external links with the rest of the polity is, further, closely associated with the particular objectives of the institution, its forms of social implantation, and the degree and nature of the changes sought by the party.[38] Organizational complexity and depth also, according to Huntington, follow on from the capacity of a party to survive the passing of its founder or the leader who first brought it to power as the second major characteristic of party strength (the third is the capacity of the party to engender sentiments of identification amongst supporters, activists and power seekers).[39] Such aspects of party development and forms of organizational differentiation have so far received relatively little attention in terms of east-central European post-communist experience, not just because of the short time-span involved but also because many of those actively involved in its politics were initially ill-disposed towards the establishment of political parties and reluctant to conduct their activity within the framework of a party system. Neither did much of the east-central European public show any degree of enthusiasm for party activity or, indeed, institutionalized political participation in general.

Combined with a general lack of resources (financial, organizational, personal), pressing problems of government and coalition-formation and -consolidation (run mostly on an individual basis and conducted on the grounds of personality), and a complex and weighty burden of governmental, political and social tasks party development was not much of a priority in the early stages of post-communist transition in east-central Europe. It has, nevertheless, slowly risen higher on the political agenda. Already, too, significant differences in the context and nature of party formation can be detected between the different countries. The process was launched earlier and more successfully in Hungary, where a growing political opposition combined with strengthening social movements and a resurgence of the historic parties to conduct in 1990 well-organized parliamentary elections which were relatively successful in terms of governmental outcome and the achievement of political stability.[40] Six parties took 375 of the 386 seats (97.2 per cent) in the Hungarian parliament and a relatively stable governmental coalition led by the Democratic Forum was formed on that basis. An argument could therefore be made for the relatively successful, if partial, restoration of the historical parliamentary order in Hungary and the stabilization of a post-communist party system on that basis.[41] In terms of the immediate transition from communism the new parties could therefore be seen as externally derived, although in a more distant sense links could be drawn so as to suggest the internal origination of some post-communist parties from an earlier parliamentary existence.

In Czechoslovakia the social movement, in the form of Public Against Violence and Civic Forum, gained considerable impetus during the final phase of communist rule and received extensive parliamentary representation following the elections held soon after in June 1990 having gathered, respectively, 33 per cent of votes in Slovakia and 53 per cent in the Czech Lands. Of 22 electoral contenders only eight parties actually won seats in the federal parliament, a slightly broader spectrum of party representation than that achieved in Hungary a few weeks previously. The process of party formation accelerated shortly afterwards, however, as the movements disintegrated and fragmentation of the hitherto dominant political bodies became evident – not least in national terms as electoral preferences took a decidedly different form in Slovakia and the Czech lands during the 1992 elections. The emergence and relative consolidation of a party system evident in Hungary during the final phase of communist rule was not apparent in Czechoslovakia, then, and it was the transitional form of the social movement that dominated the first, competitive post-communist elections. Its subsequent dissolution and the fragmentation of political forces therefore centred to a significant extent on existing parliamentary representation and provided a basis for the internal origination of a range of new parties.

The relationship between social movement and party formation, and the location of that relationship within the sequence of post-communist transition and the holding of initial competitive, founding elections was again different in Poland. The negotiated, semi-free elections held in Poland during June 1989 were, indeed, the trigger for the collapse of communism throughout eastern Europe and produced a signal political victory for Solidarity forces. They were, however, elections held in the absence of competitive, pluralist parties and it was only in the conflict that emerged during 1990 over the Polish presidency – that is, before fully competitive parliamentary elections were held in October 1991 – that the process of party development got under way. Unlike Czechoslovakia, where dissident groups like Charter 77 represented highly select and numerically restricted opposition forces and the rise of a mass movement was very much a last-minute phenomenon, Poland had seen the rise of a mass anti-communist movement in the form of Solidarity as far back as 1980. It had, however, been repressed under martial law and became, to a large extent, politically neutralized throughout the 1980s. Solidarity gained access to 35 per cent of seats in the main legislative chamber of the Polish parliament (all of which it won) as a result of the round-table negotiations concluded in April 1989 and, for more than two years following the collapse of communist rule, parliamentary composition continued to be determined by prior political contract rather than the less constrained play of political forces expressed through electoral competition.

To a large extent the formation of post-communist parties occurred within this contractual framework as conflicts broke out within the Solidarity movement, which had both an influential base in parliament (as well as dominating government) and a mass following throughout the country in its union organization – although the number, coherence and political inclinations of the latter body were becoming increasingly uncertain as the pace of political and socio-economic change accelerated. Party formation in Poland was, therefore, both internal and external to the parliamentary body – and in many ways it was the tensions between the different wings of the Solidarity movement that provided much of the force behind the impetus for change and the formation of new political organizations. It is the existence of such overlapping forms of representation and the combination of internal and external forms of party origination that make it difficult to accommodate east-central European processes of party formation with the typologies proposed by Duverger – in terms, for example, of the direct or indirect forms of participation which trade unions evolved with the relevant political parties. Reference here to any 'general sociological schema' or 'sociological law' in this area is clearly wide of the mark.[42] The dynamics of party formation in east-central Europe have, not surprisingly, been very different from the models presented in much of the literature, and this may shed light both on the functions they have been able (or have failed) to perform and the difficulties they have encountered in defining a role for themselves in the post-communist political system.

Conclusion

It may well be concluded, then, that party formation and the development of nation-wide democratic political organizations got off to a particularly slow start in Poland. Unlike Hungary, where a variety of parties emerged at the end of the 1980s and only a small number passed the test of competitive elections to enter parliament in early 1990, party formation did not occur with any speed and the process of sifting in terms of electoral competition did not really begin until October 1991. Polish experience, with the attachment to the Solidarity tradition extending back to 1980 and the avoidance of the critical electoral test until more than two years after the ending of the communist power monopoly, also differed from that in Czechoslovakia where a mass political movement arose in late 1989 and achieved electoral success within a matter of months. Diversification of political organization then occurred within a more clearly defined parliamentary context and was further clarified during further elections held only two years later.

The process of party formation and development in Poland was protracted and encountered more obstacles than in the other countries of east-central Europe. While the Solidarity tradition was a great advantage in terms of stiffening resistance to communist rule and forcing the existing establishment to compromise on the elections of 1989, its very success and deep social roots militated against the potential conflict and political separateness that party formation implied. Polish experience tends to confirm the observation that 'the way in which the cards are dealt out and the outcomes of the different rounds played out in the formative phase of an organization, continue in many ways to condition the life of the organization' – probably for decades afterwards.[43] The lengthy experience of Solidarity as a socio-political movement mostly under conditions of clandestinity, too, did not permit it the advantages of formal institutionalization or to develop the processes of personnel circulation and elite recruitment that are normally permitted to political parties. The dire condition of the Polish economy also encouraged the undertaking of radical measures that were hardly favourable to the articulation of reasoned policy alternatives or the expression of politically refined social interests that might ideally have been expected to underlie the process of party formation.

Party formation and development in Poland was therefore slow, in some ways unnaturally restricted and by no means generally conducive to formation of the conditions for the operation of an effective modern democracy. When, finally, general elections were held in October 1991 they produced a fragmented parliament which encountered considerable problems in producing a stable and effective government. In general terms, then, neither the Solidarity movement nor the political parties which gradually emerged from and around it were very successful in securing the conditions generally regarded as necessary for establishing the framework of a modern democracy or performing the functions necessary for its operation. Recollection of the functions enumerated by King would suggest that most still awaited the appropriate institutional vehicle for their performance in Poland – those concerning, for example, leadership recruitment, government organization, policy formation, interest aggregation and (by no means least) integration of the citizenry into the broader political community and their mobilization for the appropriate democratic political processes. This had, as Democratic Union vice-chairman Frasyniuk pointed out, further restrictive consequences for political life. As no proper mechanism had been created to promote and draw new people into public life, political processes remained very much restricted to the capital and those with a provincial base tended to disappear from public view.[44] While the low electoral turnout paralleled that in Hungary it was combined in Poland, too, with a much higher level of party fragmentation, which meant that party identification and consolidation of the political spectrum was considerably less advanced.

The Polish case demonstrates most clearly the problematic nature of the relationship that emerges between civil society, party development and democratization in east-central Europe. The country that had first seen the emergence of a strong social movement within the communist system seemed to experience the greatest difficulty in producing a viable party system and sustaining the basic processes of a democratic order. While appearing there in a strongly pronounced form such tendencies were by no means restricted to Poland.[45] But it was in that country that the 'specific pathology' of the turn towards civil society became apparent in the form of polarization which, in turn, could be construed as having led to an over-unification of civil society that helped impose a barrier to the development of societal and political pluralism.[46]

It is here that parties enter more clearly into the overall calculation, as it is the encouragement of political society that has eventually become a favoured solution to this critical problem. Yet this too may turn out to be a self-defeating strategy, if the turn towards *political* society and growing preoccupation with a dominantly electoral identity on the part of political forces merely has the effect of helping (predominantly, perhaps, in line with the intentions of reformist elements of the former establishment) to demobilize *civil* society. The critical role played by a formation based on a trade union on both sides of the formula in Poland suggests, further, the need for more thoroughgoing examination of the interface of civil society and market economy, and of analysis of the complex relations between all these different dimensions of the social whole.[47]

Several tendencies in Polish developments, notably the neo-corporatist proposals of the Suchocka government in combination with a policy of toughing out the strike wave of the summer of 1992, and the fact that the government's budget was only passed in early 1993 due to a split amongst the Solidarity group of parliamentary deputies, testified to the continuing centrality of the issue. The fact that the conditions for the downfall of the Suchocka government were set in place with the defection of the Peasant Alliance from the governing coalition, and the role played by Solidarity deputies in laying down the vote of no confidence that finally brought about the dissolution of parliament in May 1993 provided further confirmation of this view.

NOTES

1. F. Millard, 'The Polish Parliamentary Elections of October 1991', *Soviet Studies* Vol.44, No.5 (1992), p.849.
2. B. Racz, 'Political Pluralisation in Hungary: The 1990 Elections', *Soviet Studies*, Vol.43, No.1 (1991), p.130.
3. R.W. Orttung, 'The Russian Right and the Dilemmas of Party Organisation', *Soviet Studies*, Vol.44, No.3 (1992), p.445.
4. E. Kiss, 'Democracy without Parties?', *Dissent* (Spring 1992), p.228.
5. See respectively, M. Duverger, *Political Parties* (London: Methuen, 1964), p.261, and W.N. Chambers, 'Parties and Nation-building in America', in J. LaPalombara and M. Wiener (eds.), *Political Parties and Political Development* (Princeton NJ: Princeton University Press, 1969), p.100.
6. G.B. Powell, *Contemporary Democracies* (Cambridge, MA: Harvard University Press, 1982), p.7.
7. G. Pridham, 'Southern European Democracies on the Road to Consolidation: a comparative assessment of the role of political parties', in G. Pridham (ed.), *Securing Democracy: Political parties and democratic consolidation in southern Europe* (London: Routledge, 1990), p.22.
8. N. Bobbio, *Democracy and Dictatorship* (Cambridge: Polity Press, 1989), p.25.
9. K.E. Jorgensen, 'The End of Anti-Politics in Central Europe', in P. Lewis (ed.), *Democracy and Civil Society in Eastern Europe* (London: Macmillan, 1992), p.49.
10. G. Ekiert, 'Peculiarities of Post-Communist Politics: The case of Poland', *Studies in Comparative Communism*, Vol.25, No.4 (1992), p.349.
11. E. Kamenka and A. Tay, 'Communism, Civil Society and Freedom', in C. Kukathas *et al.* (eds), *The Transition From Socialism* (Melbourne: Longman Cheshire, 1991), pp.76, 78.
12. A. King, 'Political Parties in Western Democracies', in L.J. Cantor (ed.), *Comparative Political Systems*, (Boston, MA: Holbrook Press, 1974), pp.302–3.
13. *Modern Politics and Government* (London: Macmillan, 1988), p.75.
14. 'Toward a Comparative Study of Political Parties', in J. Blondel (ed.), *Comparative Government* (London: Macmillan, 1969), pp.71–3.
15. R.E. Dowse and J.A. Hughes *Political Sociology* (London: John Wiley, 1972), pp.357–8.
16. D. McKay, *American Politics and Society* (Oxford: Blackwell, 1985), p.87.
17. Ball, *Modern Politics*, p.73.

18. Dowse and Hughes, *Political Sociology*, p.340.
19. 'Toward a Comparative Study', p.71.
20. J. LaPalombara and M. Wiener, 'The Origin and Development of Political Parties', in LaPalombara and Wiener, *Political Parties*, p.29.
21. Duverger, *Political Parties*, pp.xxiii–iv.
22. *British Political Parties* (London: Mercury, 1964), p.6.
23. Chambers, 'Parties and Nation-Building', p.80.
24. R. Maidment and A. McGrew, *The American Political Process* (London: Sage, 1986), p.108.
25. The particular significance of their role in French politics is emphasized by P. Avril in *Politics in France* (Harmondsworth: Penguin, 1969), p.75.
26. LaPalombara and Wiener, 'Origin and Development', p.27.
27. J. Blondel, 'Mass Parties and Types of Modern Societies', in Blondel, *Comparative Government*, p.119.
28. Ibid., p.118.
29. S.P. Huntington, *Political Order in Changing Societies* (New Haven, CT: Yale University Press, 1968), p.412.
30. LaPalombara and Wiener, 'Origin and Development', p.7.
31. H. Daalder, 'Parties, Elites and Political Developments in Western Europe', in LaPalombara and Wiener, *Political Parties*, p.56.
32. 'Mass Parties and Types', p.135.
33. 'Origin and Development', pp.12, 17.
34. D.E. Apter, *The Politics of Modernization* (Chicago, IL: University of Chicago Press, 1967), p.193.
35. D. Rueschemeyer, E. Stephens, and J. Stephens, *Capitalist Development and Democracy* (Cambridge: Polity, 1992), pp.169, 287.
36. S.M. Lipset, 'Introduction', in R. Michels, *Political Parties*, (New York: Collier, 1962), p.34.
37. Duverger, *Political Parties*, Book 1.
38. J. Blondel, *Comparing Political Systems* (London: Weidenfeld & Nicolson, 1972), pp.90–91.
39. *Political Order*, pp.410–11.
40. P. Lewis, B. Lomax and G. Wightman, 'The Emergence of Multi-Party Systems', in G. Pridham and T. Vanhanen (eds.), *Rooting Fragile Democracies* (London: Routledge, 1994).
41. S. Gebethner, 'Political Institutions in the Process of Transition to a Postsocialist Formation', in W. Connor and P. Ploszajski (eds.), *Escape From Socialism* (Warsaw: IFiS, 1992), pp.248–9.
42. Duverger, *Political Parties*, p.16.
43. A. Panebianco, *Political Parties: Organization and Power* (Cambridge: Cambridge University Press, 1988), p.xiii.
44. *Rzeczpospolita*, 6 Nov. 1992.
45. Ekiert, op.cit., p.353.
46. J.L. Cohen and A. Arato, *Civil Society and Political Theory* (Cambridge, MA: MIT Press, 1992), p.67.
47. Ibid., pp.68, 77.

Political Actors and Political Roles in East-Central Europe

MICHAEL WALLER

The transition from the communist power monopoly to a system of competitive politics has seen the creation of new political organizations, but it has involved also an adjustment on the part of those already existing. It is a process in which the roles of organizations as political actors are becoming defined through the inter-relationships between them. A group analysis of the period since 1989 reveals: first, a lack of clarity in the distinctions between roles in the political process; secondly, strong organizational continuity from the communist period; thirdly, an influence of international factors on the internal relations between government and groups; and fourthly, a pull towards tripartite negotiations between government and employer and employee organizations. These last have a particular character that reflects the specific circumstances of the region, but they none the less vary from country to country.

The political parties and party systems that were generally expected to come into being in East-Central Europe after the collapse of the communist power monopoly had duly done so by October 1991, if with all the imperfections that have been fully recorded in the literature. The logic of an electoral system had done its work, and through that system, and through its results in producing the first post-communist governments, legitimacy had been transferred, and competitive politics had been installed in the place of a discredited monopoly.

It was natural that the attention of analysts should follow that of the political class in those countries in focusing sharply on this central arena constituted by parties, parliaments and electoral procedures, where power and the new legitimacy lay. This study fully endorses the centrality of political parties in the process of regime change in the region, but its principal aim is to present the broader context within which the process of party formation has taken place by adopting a group approach to the political systems that have emerged since 1989.

Political parties will be treated in this study as collective political actors in an arena in which competing forms of political action are in the process of defining themselves through their interrelationships. In this process

Michael Waller is Professor of Politics and Director of European Studies at Keele University, UK.

not only are the functional boundaries between forms of political action (between, as a simple example, party and pressure group) coming to be more clearly demarcated after being initially often quite indeterminate, but the relative salience of the various forms of political action has been evolving. In this evolution, what emerged from the communist period in organized form has retained its organizational strength; whilst what has been created since 1989 has had difficulty in acquiring organizational definition and, in many cases, an organizational base. To take the now over-familiar case of Solidarity, growing pressure after the round-table talks of 1989 for the party function to separate out from the trade union function led to differentiation between these roles as the original move-ment effectively dissolved. But the relationship between party and trade union developed further, and in this new relationship between govern-ment and organized interest group, the Solidarity trade union found itself functionally ranged with its old rival, the official 'mass organization' unions of the final years of communist rule – the All-Poland Trade Union Alliance (*Ogólno-Polskie Porozumenie Związków Zawodowych* – OPZZ). The extent to which co-operation between the two was possible was at that point raised, paralleling, though with important differences, proces-ses of coalition-forming between political parties. But these are then negotiations within increasingly discrete forms of political agency.

This study will first give reasons for stressing the value of a group approach to the consolidation of political roles in the process of transi-tion. Secondly, it will focus on the factors that are influencing the way in which new and existing political group actors are settling into their present and increasingly well-defined roles. Thirdly, it will make some tentative suggestions as to how the system that is composed by these interrelated roles might be characterized. The countries covered will be Poland, the Czech Republic, Slovakia, Hungary and Bulgaria.

Analysing Political Flux

Few would now doubt that the communist years have had a powerful effect on the emerging political systems of east-central Europe, and it will be argued in what follows that the organizational overhang from those years has been substantial. Equally clearly, however, the shift from a system characterized by monopoly to one characterized by competition is categorical. If space allowed, it would be illuminating to go further into the question of change and continuity, and to rehearse the arguments of those analysts of communist politics who, since the late 1960s and chiefly with reference to the Soviet Union, claimed to discern elements of plural-ism therein. Those views were sharply contested, and even some of those who were most insistent in discerning a group process of politics at work stopped short of attributing the label of pluralism to an admittedly changing communist world.[1]

The process of transition since 1989, however, has brought into the discussion organizing concepts of a different order such as might help to give perspective to the process of change. That process has, in fact, caused less political turbulence than was at first expected, as comparison with the Russian case makes clear. David Stark has traced some of the factors that have helped the transition on its way in east-central Europe in his presentation of 'path dependence'.[2] None the less, especially in the period between 1989 and October 1991, when the elections in Poland completed the series of the first fully free electoral contests in the region, the political scene in each of the countries involved was sufficiently fluid to make hazardous any simple application of the organizational categories of established democratic systems, or indeed of established systems *tout court*. In the new circumstances ushered in by laws establishing freedoms of speech, association and assembly political parties and interest associations formed, but the boundaries between what constituted a party and what an interest group was none too clear, nor, in those early days, was it easy to say what constituted an interest.[3] It was a situation that seemed to invite a view of politics such as that put forward in the early years of the century by Arthur Bentley in his seminal work *The Process of Government*, in which, it will be recalled, the attribution of labels is secondary to tracing the contours of groups, in all their variety and in all their mobile permutations.[4] Any society, on this view, is susceptible of analysis in group terms, from the most authoritarian to the most democratic. But it is a view that is particularly helpful in circumstances of political flux, and it is brought into the discussion here because of its heuristic value in analysing the mobile cirumstance of the transition in east-central Europe.

Bentley's views, of course, were given a particular twist by the development of later treatments of interest groups – treatments that reflected the settled universe of established political systems in which pressure groups and parties were attributed their familiar fixed and analytically distinct roles.[5] As concerns east-central Europe, those roles remarkably soon began to crystallize after the first free elections. The elections themselves were a determinant factor in this crystallization. With very important exceptions which in fact give the east-central European transition its specific character, parties came to play the role familiar in established liberal democracies (as they have not, for example, in Russia), and the middle levels of the political system filled with autonomous associations, the most substantial of which played roles recognizable, in terms of liberal democracy, as those of pressure groups.

None the less, the ghost of Bentley, as it were, hovers over these developments at the time of writing. The political parties, as parliamentary structures, tend to have only weak links to organized interests in society, or indeed to established and stable constituencies of any kind. Moreover, the fluidity of the political systems is still such that a given political collective actor can play different roles, or be undecided as to what role it is to invest in. Finally, new circumstances at times make strange bedfellows: a Solidarity born to contest the legitimacy of the official trade unions of the communist days can find itself ranged in a new struggle side by side with its former rival; and the Bulgarian Podkrepa, born likewise as a trade union engaged in the struggle against communism, can fall prey to the same logic. Moreover, as will be seen in other contributions to this collection, both Solidarity and Podkrepa have moved between the roles of party and pressure group.

Arguments that will be adduced in what follows make it essential to register the flux of the early transition period, but the main emphasis of this study will be on organization, and on the factors that are influencing the way in which the political systems of the region are taking shape as they emerge from their initial inevitable disorientation, on the collective actors that populate the political scene in east-central Europe, and on the role, or roles, that they play.

Interest Organization in the Post-Communist Period

The purpose of this study is to highlight certain features of the process of group formation since 1989 and the focus will be on the articulation of group interests close to or at the centre of the political system. Selecting that focus has meant deselecting other points of focus. The legislation enabling associations to form in east-central Europe led to an explosion of political organizations at all levels, and this should be recorded in outline before the discussion moves to a more precise focus.

Thus, the Scouts, the YMCA/YWCA, the Czechoslovak Sokol sporting association and a host of other cultural organizations reappeared. The monopolistic youth organizations of the communist period dissolved, giving place to a plethora of associations sponsored by religious denominations and the now plural political parties.[6]

In a further category one step closer to government were the professional representative bodies, which were now able to operate autonomously, examples being the Polish National Notary Council (organizing a now privatized professional category, and becoming a member of the International Commission for Co-operation among Notaries) and the

Association of Hungarian Judges (which likewise joined the International Association of Judges), whilst the Polish Medical Council found itself at the heart of a *cause célèbre* when its conflict with the Catholic Church over the abortion issue provided an illuminating example of a clash between rival groups over the interpretation of the law. It should be noted in passing that such professional groups, whilst they enable group interests to be fed into the policy-making process, can also serve as corporate channels for the application of governmental decisions if membership in such an organization is obligatory for anyone exercising that profession, and if the organization is made responsible, through legislation, for licensing members of the profession, for disciplinary procedures or for regulating the fixing of qualifications – a feature of such groups familiar in liberal democracies, and not confined to the corporate practices of communism, or of its aftermath.

Nor does this study attempt to cover institutional rivalries within the bureaucracy, nor the relative influence on government of these rival departmental interests, although it would be rewarding to seek for a continuation into the post-communist period of the examples of institutional group interests in the communist period mentioned in the foregoing.[7]

These avenues must be left for others to explore. I turn now to examine the organization of group actors and the evolution of group interests at the point where government encounters major social groups, whose aggregative power governments must take into account.

When the configuration of organization for political ends in east-central Europe is examined, the following features emerge particularly strongly.

First, there has been a *lack of clarity of roles*. A clear example is, as noted, the Polish Solidarity. There is no need to rehearse the way in which this social movement, which drew both its goal and its unity in pursuit of that goal from its role in contesting the communist system, dissolved after 1989 into a series of competitive discrete organizations under the pressure of the logic of electoral politics. That it should have provided a series of parties for a particularly fissiparous party system is less significant than the fact that even that segment of it that emerged as the 'Solidarity trade union' has been unwilling to invest solely in a trade union role, and contributed 27 deputies to the Sejm as a result of the 1991 election. Podkrepa in Bulgaria, which was formed, as noted, as a trade union, at first assimilated its role to that of the party-like components of the Union of Democratic Forces, but then left that organization. It has not fielded candidates in elections, but its colourful leader, Konstantin Trenchev, has engaged in autonomous discussions with international funding bodies as an informal representative of Bulgaria and not merely of his organization, he has conducted discussions also with the exiled monarch, whose return Podkrepa favours, and his organization went well beyond a conventional trade union role in putting pressure on the UDF government to divest itself of two particular ministers in 1992.

These are perhaps the most obvious examples of a confusion of roles, but the appearance of a number of specifically pro-business parties in the early elections illustrates it further. With time, no doubt, these cases will clarify, as abiding links between group interests and particular parties develop, and as the bureaucracies of the major groups settle into a specialized role. In the meantime, however, this lack of clarity over political roles must be taken into account in any final judgments on the character of the emerging political systems in the region.

A second prominent feature of the transition is the *organizational continuity* from the communist period. It was only to be expected that the novel formations that the new circumstances were enabling to come into being should occupy the forefront of the attention of analysts of the changes that were taking place. But the results of the first free elections revealed that, despite the opprobrium to which they were being subjected, the former (and by then mostly renamed) communist parties had retained considerable organizational strength, as had the previous 'bloc' parties, where they chose to capitalize on that strength. Subsequent elections served to confirm the advantages of this inherited organization, the 1993 elections in Poland providing a dramatic breakthrough in this respect, the former (but now renamed) communist party and a former bloc party – the agrarian PSL – occupying the two leading positions in the poll.

But the passing of time has revealed other cases of an organizational strength carried into the post-communist period. A number of factors – the prominence of Solidarity in the story of communism's last years; the attention naturally paid to the new parties of government, all of which were recent creations; the assumption that the institutions of communist rule had departed from the scene together with the communist monopoly of power; the emergence of a number of new trade union formations which, it was often assumed, had replaced the former communist unions – long served to distract attention from the fact that the trade unions of the communist period, now independent, had retained considerable organizational strength, and that they were, moreover, less encumbered with opprobrium than were their erstwhile political masters.

Four years after the fall of the communist parties, the Hungarian MSzOSz still retained a larger membership than either the League or the Workers' Councils – the two major new federations that came into being when the new freedom to associate had been enacted. Similarly, the

OPZZ in Poland still outnumbered Solidarity by approximately two to one, despite the latter's mythic status. In Czechoslovakia – the only case of those covered here where no major newly born confederation emerged to rival the former communist *protégé* – the Czech and Slovak Confederation of Trade Unions (as the old Revolutionary Trade Union Movement has been renamed) enroled, before the separation, some 80 per cent of the active work force.[8] In Bulgaria, the Confederation of Independent Trade Unions (CITUB) had two and a half million members at the time of the registration at the end of 1991, against the 700,000 claimed by Podkrepa, the other major federation.

A graphic illustration of the ability of the trade unions of the communist period to retain support in the new circumstances was provided in Hungary in the first elections held to elect trade union representatives to the boards that manage social security and pension funds. These elections were competitive as between the various trade union centres. They were held, incidentally, on 21 May 1993, the same day as a law was passed in parliament banning the display of the red star – the emblem, of course, of communist power. Some half of the votes were cast for the post-communist MSzOSz, whilst that organizations' chief rivals – the League and the Workers' Councils – were given close to ten per cent of the vote each.[9]

There are, of course, reasons for this continuity. If their political role was muted in the communist years, the social role of the trade unions was substantial. They were the chief distributors of welfare benefits, they provided vacations for employees and summer camps for their children, they ran libraries, cinemas, theatres and provided all manner of leisure activities. Whilst the new political arrangements were to divest them of these functions, the point is that they remained major organized bastions of employee representation at the moment when the first flush of enthusiasm for change was beginning to wear thin. They had played a social role which was close to the daily life of most working people and, despite – or perhaps because of – their enforced organizational dependence on the ruling communist parties, they were able to retain a degree of support that was denied to their earlier masters.

It should be noted, too, that their initial proclaimed independence from the former communist parties did not prevent their developing close links with them later on, in all cases except the Bulgarian. Meanwhile those parties, in a somewhat similar evolution, lost a substantial part of both their membership and their property, but retained their organizational strength.

The position of the former official trade unions is different from that of the former communist parties in certain important ways. The latter have been pulled in two contradictory directions. The primary concern of one tendency within them is to protect the privileged positions they have contrived to retain, collectively or individually, in the industrial and trading concerns and elsewhere, and in some cases also the personal liberty of individuals, whilst another tendency seeks to re-establish the party's socialist credentials. The former mass organization trade unions have not got this problem. They changed their leaderships, and even if they end up with former communists in charges, the latter are not just trying to protect themselves from prosecution.

Possibly even less frequently noted by commentators has been the continuity as concerns employer organizations. True, as with the trade unions, new bodies came into being to represent an entrepreneurial interest that was novel under the circumstances. Examples are the Union of Private Citizens' Initiatives in Bulgaria and the National Association of Entrepreneurs in Hungary. These associations speak chiefly for the owners and managers of small and medium-sized business concerns. But, as we all know, if the advent of pluralism in east-central Europe is dependent on the creation of a middle class of market-oriented, independent business people, together with the services they need (in banking, estate agenting, litigation, arbitration, communications and so on) there is still some way to go. This clearly has implications for the structuring of interest articulation. One obvious implication is that inputs into policy-making from a lobby of entrepreneurs will lack substance. Rather less obvious is the fact that since politics, like nature, abhors a vacuum, the voice of the entrepreneurial lobby is drowned out by that of representatives of another constituency – the managers of the state-owned enterprises which still, at the time of writing in 1993, constitute a substantial part of the industrial economy.

Particularly at the time they were coming into being, the view that the new entrepreneur associations took of their role in relation to government and the state differed markedly from that which underlay the relationship between the state and the various 'chambers' that represented the state-run enterprises. The attitude of the newly-born Hungarian National Association of Entrepeneurs (the VOSZ) in 1990 towards the proposed Bill on the Protection of Interests is illuminating in this regard. Fearing that a bill initiated by the existing business federations would enable 'executives of these organizations . . . "elected" or simply appointed according to the good old communist way' to cling to their positions, the VOSZ opposed the bill, discerning a distinction between, on the one hand, a 'chambers law' which would give chambers the right to regulate an obligatory membership, thus asserting the interest of the institution (and ultimately the state) against that of its members, and on the other hand a true 'protection of interests' law which would leave interest associations free to regulate their own affairs.[10]

Before leaving these two chief components of the employers and business lobby, it is important to recall that the strategy that the dynamic new entrepreneurial interest has adopted in relation to parliament and the party political arena has not so much been to invest in one or other of the major parties, but to set up parties of its own. Thus the Polish Party of the Friends of Beer ('Big Beer'), which began its life as a joke party, became a parliamentary representative of the entrepreneurial interest, until its failure to achieve representation as a result of the 1993 election. Examples elsewhere are the Business Bloc in Bulgaria and the Republican Party in Hungary. Whether this is to be interpreted as an example of the initially fluid boundaries between party and pressure group characteristic of the transition period, and as such destined to succumb to the aggregating logic of party competition, or whether these parties will themselves develop an aggregating role as privatization proceeds, remains to be seen.

It is worth adding – to adapt a comment of Bachrach and Baratz in relation to pluralism – that non-organizational continuity may be as important as organization itself.[11] That is, the members of these organizational overhangs from the communist period presumably perceive the organization, its political and social role, and their own contribution to that role in a manner shaped by modes of thought that equally owe their origin to the communist past. In Jerzy Hausner's words, 'the fact that [people] have rejected communism and communist government does not necessarily mean that they have abandoned the corporatist way of thinking or that they can express and defend their interests in other ways'.[12] Here again, as in the case of the blurred boundaries between party and pressure group, is material to be built into any final conclusion as to the present character of the political systems of east-central Europe.

A third feature of the transition that has very severe implications for the structure of group interests in east-central Europe, and for the efficacy of group pressures on government, varies very much in the manner of its incidence, but it is important across the region. It is a factor that affects especially those countries with a high foreign debt (that is, Poland, Hungary and Bulgaria), and is likely to give those countries a particular profile as concerns the structure of relations between government and the major interest groups (and indeed non-governing parties).

The claims made for dependence theory some two decades ago have since been contested, but there is no need to embrace dependence as a fully articulated theory to understand that *external funding bodies are having a strong impact on the internal politics of certain east-central European countries*. Crudely put, east-central Europe today is dependent on international finance and external know-how if it is to achieve its aim of being integrated economically into Europe, and desirably the EC itself. This argument has been developed, with evidence drawn from the Polish case, by Andreas Stadler.[13] Pointing out that 'the concept of dependence has to be adjusted for the study of east–west relations, since the classical "dependence" concept is not really adequate for this purpose', Stadler produces a version of the 'dependence triangle' to illustrate dependence in the east-central European context.

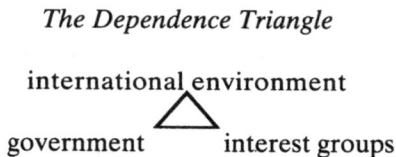

The Dependence Triangle

international environment

△

government   interest groups

Stadler comments:

> We can speak of dependence of the government on the international environment when socio-economic interest groups are either excluded from the triangle and play no part in the bargain, or are included to such a limited extent that the government's policies are mainly shaped by the international environment. Dependence can be measured by the distribution of power within the triangle.

This has proved to be a weapon of particular value to the populist leaders in the region. In June 1993 Vladimir Mečiar, the Slovak Prime Minister, and leader of the Movement for a Democratic Slovakia, claimed publicly that the West would cut its financial aid to Slovakia if the former communist Party of the Democratic Left were to call early elections, and were to win them.[14]

It is, however, a factor that can cut both ways. A government can use its obligations to the international funding bodies in order to bring recalcitrant trade unions or the home business lobby into line. But by the same token a powerful trade union federation, or a non-governing party with leverage in the parliament, can act independently to get its views across to international actors, and can give assurances to them of co-operation provided that those views are heard. As the Bulgarian Evgenia Ivanova put it: 'Only a president who has the full backing of the Movement for Rights and Freedoms and Podkrepa can offer the international community the kind of guarantees it requires.'[15]

The international factor, indeed, has influences on the structure of group representation and group pressures that extend well beyond the sphere of trade union, employer and governmental relations, and are particularly evident in matters concerning the environment. A substantial amount of Western aid to the region is earmarked for environmental projects. The combined influence of the funding bodies and other international agencies such as the International Atomic Energy Agency or the G24 Nuclear Safety Group in Brussels substantially circumscribes the independence of east-central European governments (in this case particularly Bulgaria, the Czech Republic and Slovakia, with Poland being unaffected). The EBRD and the PHARE programme are both spending substantial sums in restructuring Bulgaria's energy sector, and with the aid come advisers and technicians. Such aid is to be welcomed by anyone inside or outside Bulgaria concerned with nuclear safety, but it none the less represents an external factor that can influence the internal politics of the country.

The World Wildlife Fund itself intervenes quite substantially in the politics of the region, and the fact that this takes the form of cooperation only serves to cloak the effects of such initiatives on the internal political life of the countries concerned. The WWF, for example, is organizing a scheme to turn the land that once formed the iron curtain boundary into a conservation area. Whatever benefts this brings to the countries concerned, it none the less constitutes an intervention from outside those countries in their internal politics, adding to an already substantial amount of such intervention.

It is revealing that the WWF's Newsletter, which records its (environmentally very valuable) work in east-central Europe, contains a mass of information about other projects, which have nothing to do with the environment, but illustrate yet further the ramifications of external influences on the political life of east-central European countries. The Cutter Corporation's publicity for its journal *Environment Watch: East Europe, Russia and Eurasia* states that it is 'the *only* publication that reports in detail on developments in environmental regulation, law, enforcement, and prevention in the important region . . . describes and forecasts the impact of these developments on business . . . and provides direct, detailed business and funding leads'.[16]

But perhaps the most prominent feature of the group politics of the region – and it is one to which the other features themselves contribute – is the pull towards *'tripartite'*, *'social parnership'* negotiations and agreements. In all the countries covered in this study, but with Poland being very much the laggard, the period since 1989 has seen tripartite discussions set up, involving government, the trade unions and the employer organizations. Such was the National Tripartite Commission on Coordination of Social Interests set up in Bulgaria in 1990, and lasting until the Dimitrov government sent it packing in 1992. It is to be noted that this move by the UDF government had the effect of bringing the rival major trade union federations, CITUB and Podkrepa, closer together, and was to favour their support for the Berov government when it entered office at the end of 1992. Berov, indeed, a non-party figure, had been chairman of the Tripartite Commission during its two years of existence.

In Hungary a National Coordinating Council was set up in 1990 to bring together employers, private entrepreneurs, workers, trade unions and farmers. The inclusion of the farming interest here is worth noting, since the agricultural lobby and the agrarian political parties are a crucial part of the emerging systems.

In Czechoslovakia, an agreement was signed between the Czechoslovak Federation of Trade Unions and the federal government, which resulted in the setting up of a Council of Economic and Social Accord for negotiations among the government, the trade unions and employers's organizations. This was followed by the signing of separate agreements in the Czech Republic and Slovakia. This did not, however, prevent the government from omitting a number of provisions that had been agreed on in the Council when it drafted the subsequent Law on Employment and Collective Bargaining, and in its amendments to the Labour Code. All the trade unions could do was object after the event, just as they complained that they had not been consulted over price liberalization before that crucial reform was put into effect on 1 January 1991. On the other hand, when the three governments (federal and republican), the Czech and the Slovak Councils of Unions of Entrepreneurs, the Czecho-slovak Trade Union Federation and the Confederation of Art and Culture Unions signed a General Agreement for 1991 laying down the rules for collective bargaining, and fixing a minimum wage and rates of unemployment benefit, the bargaining was real enough for some of the agreement's provisions to be criticized by Václav Klaus. The Czechoslovak trade unions also made it clear on occasion that they were prepared to strike in defence of their claims.

Commenting on these various negotiations, László Bruszt writes:

> During the last year [1991 – MW] there were several general agreements between governments and trade unions in various Eastern European countries, in which usually wage-restraint and/ or strike-stop was exchanged for the extension of trade union rights and some form of less than 100 per cent wage indexation. In these agreements trade unions on the average gave the green light for but 3 to 12 months in which the government may proceed unchecked with the transformation of the economy. Examples for the shorter one are the agreements made between the Bulgarian

or Romanian trade unions and governments; for the longer, the
example is the one struck between labour and government in
Czechoslovakia.[17]

The pressures leading east-central European governments towards creating such tripartite bodies have been great. First and foremost, in a situation
where government parties have had, in most cases, a still unconsolidated
social base and where the neo-liberal policies that they have pursued have
made severe demands on the population, expediency suggested that the
political price of exclusion was higher than that of inclusion. Secondly,
not only do the governing parties lack a solid party organization and
established organizational links with the major interest groups, but, for a
number of very specific reasons, the left has been disadvantaged in the
development of the party systems. The former communist parties have
remained, with the exception of Bulgaria, removed from governmental
power whilst social-democratic parties have developed only slowly and
with difficulty. On the other side of the equation the new entrepreneurial
interest has, as noted, invested parliament in the form of new, small and
independent parties. Parliamentary oppositions, therefore, like the
governing parties and coalitions themselves, operate (as was said of the
parties of the French Fourth Republic) 'in a house without windows'. The
lack of organic links with society is clearly a factor urging governments in
the direction of negotiations with their social partners.

Thirdly, the trade unions, as noted, emerged from the communist
period with their already considerable numerical strength enhanced by
their new-found independence. Certainly in Poland, Bulgaria, and the
Czech Republic at least, trade unions – both those previously existing and
the newer creations – have the muscle to wreak havoc with a government's
plans. Particularly in the case of Solidarity in Poland, they identified with
the governing parties in the early stages of the transition, and were
prepared to 'hold an umbrella' over them. The governments of the region
could be excused for preferring to maintain negotiations with the trade
unions rather than to incur the possibly immense risks of exclusion. As
Jacek Kuroń was to say in March 1993, 'the trade unions are the only mass
organizations in Poland with any real power . . . We're pushing them to
the wall. It is only a matter of time before they revolt.'[18]

Conclusions

If the facts contained in the foregoing are substantially correct, and if the
selection of headings broadly reflects what is going on in east-central
Europe, they suggest the following conclusions.

The first, cautionary, conclusion is that it is difficult to generalize across the region, and is becoming more so.

Secondly, whilst the extreme flux of the months between the fall of the communist parties and the holding of the first free elections has moderated quite considerably, the new political systems of east-central Europe are still in the process of formation. The political parties in many cases (though not all) lack a solid implantation, their links with major interests have not yet become consolidated, there is still confusion of roles as between political parties and pressure groups. That said, all these features of the political life of east-central European countries at the time of writing are working themselves out in a direction which seems likely to accord (if – to use Whitehead's phrase – the transition stays on track) with the view of democracy that the political class of those countries shares with the political class of countries to their west. The slow process of privatization does not spell the absence of a business lobby. It spells the presence of an industrial lobby that is distinct from the newer entre-preneurial lobby, and which inflects the structure of interest group representation in a certain direction, but is none the less a valid player in an east-central European game – a game that is tending to a form of pluralism with corporatist features (on which more below).

Thirdly, external factors – the requirements of international funding bodies, but also the internationalization of environmental policies – seem certain, in the middle term at least, to have a strong influence on the relationship between government on the one hand, and non-govern-mental parties and the major pressure groups on the other. The final impact of this factor it is difficult to foresee, but in any case the short and middle term are likely to be decisive in many ways.

Fourthly, in circumstances where new political organization of any kind is necessarily experiencing difficulties concerning resources, the building of structures that are both stable and well-rooted, and the creation of an identity, organizations that have a continuity from the communist past have a valuable, and probably underestimated, durability. In the case of the former communist parties, this organizational strength has been discounted because of their current image; but the trade unions of the communist period do not suffer from this disability. Now independent, and flanked by other, less numerically powerful unions, they are likely to play an important role, again at least in the middle term.

Fifthly, the tendency of governments to accept to engage in tripartite negotiations with employer and employee interest organizations invites the suggestion that a form of corporatism is taking shape which might become consolidated. Those governments of the region that most favour policies which in western Europe would be termed 'Thatcherite' have the least chance of disposing of trade union power with the dispatch that Mrs Thatcher brought to that task. It seems at least likely that governments will choose accommodation in preference to exclusion.

Whether this spells corporatism is a matter of definition, and whatever definition is selected is likely to evoke debates and distinctions concerning the evolution of western European societies and of the welfare state in those societies, and use of the term is likely to lead to confusion. If the aim, however, is simply to be able to make comparisons, then the term might be used in a loose sense to indicate that east-central European societies seem to be falling into the category of those countries such as Germany, and until recently Sweden, that have favoured permanent and stable discussions between government, employers and trade union organizations. If, as Claus Offe has suggested, 'political systems can be more or less corporatist . . . depending on the extent to which public status is attributed to organized interest groups', then the east-central European societies are amongst the more corporatist.[19] But even this minimalist understanding of the term creates problems, which arise largely from the still provisional nature of the political systems.

NOTES

1. Jerry Hough's views on 'institutional pluralism' were a forthright example; see Jerry F. Hough, *The Soviet Union and Social Science Theory* (Cambridge MA: Harvard University Press, 1977). For a later and considerably nuanced presentation see his 'Pluralism, Corporatism and the Soviet Union' in Susan Gross Solomon (ed.), *Pluralism in the Soviet Union: Essays in Honour of H. Gordon Skilling* (London: Macmillan, 1983). For a group analysis of Soviet politics that stopped short of the pluralist attribution, see Gordon H. Skilling and Franklyn Griffiths (eds.), *Interest Groups in Soviet Politics* (Princeton, NJ: Princeton University Press, 1971); also H. Gordon Skilling, 'Interest Groups and Soviet Politics', *World Politics*, Vol.18, No.3 (1966). For a celebrated categorical rejection of the pluralist view of 'what was going on' in the Soviet Union, see Joseph LaPalombara, 'Monoliths or Plural Systems: Through Conceptual Lenses Darkly', *Studies in Comparative Communism*, Vol.8, No.3 (1975), p.325.
2. David Stark, 'Path Dependence and Privatization Strategies in East Central Europe', *East European Politics and Society*, Vol.6, No.1.
3. A. Przeworski, 'Some Problems in the Study of the Transition to Democracy', in G. O'Donnell, P. Schmitter and L. Whitehead (eds.), *Transitions from Authoritarian Rule*(Baltimore, MD: Johns Hopkins Press, 1986), pp.53–6.
4. Arthur F. Bentley, *The Process of Government*, edited by Peter H. Odegard (Cambridge, MA: Harvard University Press, 1967). The first edition was published in 1907.
5. It was with David Truman's *The Governmental Process* (New York: Alfred A. Knopf, 1951) that the study of groups in politics departed from the universalist character that Bentley had given it and, via in particular David Easton's work (*The Political System*, New York: Alfred A. Knopf, 1953, but also in others of his works) came to concentrate, in what can be claimed to constitute its mainstream, on relations between government and what S.E. Finer terms 'the lobby' (*Anonymous Empire: A Study of the Lobby in Great Britain*, London: Pall Mall, 1957).
6. See Jan Obrman, 'New Youth Groups and Movements', *Report on Eastern Europe*,

30 March 1990; Tom Yazdgerdi and Jan Obrman, 'The Disintegration of National Front Organizations', ibid., 3 Aug. 1990.

7. Those who wish to conduct this exploration in relation to the military may consult Dale R. Herspring, 'Civil–Military Relations in Post-Communist Eastern Europe: The Potential for Praetorianism', *Studies in Comparative Communism*, Vol.25, No.2 (1992).

8. According to László Bruszt: 'Transformative Politics: Social Costs and Social Peace in East-Central Europe', *East European Politics and Society*, Vol.6, No.1 (1992), p.64.

9. *Le Monde*, 22 May 1993.

10. 'The VOSZ Opinion on the Chambers Act', paper delivered to a conference on *Business Interest Associations in Eastern Europe and Russia*, University of Warwick, 1993.

11. P. Bachrach and M.S. Baratz, 'Two Faces of Power', *American Political Science Review*, Vol.56, No.4 (1962), pp.947–52.

12. Jerzy Hausner, 'From Socialist Pluralism to Societal Pluralism: Evolution of Interest Representation in Post-Socialist Society', paper presented to a conference on privatization, labour markets and social policy, Budapest, Oct. 1992, p.12.

13. Andreas Stadler, 'Problems of Dependent Modernization in Eastern Europe', in Michael Waller, Bruno Coppieters and Kris Deschouwer, *Social Democracy in a Post-Communist Europe* (London: Frank Cass, 1994). Stadler in turn bases his theoretical argument substantially on R.O Keohane and J.S. Nye, *Power and Interdependence: World Politics in Transition* (Boston, MA: Little, Brown, 1977), but also to an extent on Caparaso, Höll and Zimmerman.

14. RFE/RL News Briefs, 7–11 June 1993.

15. Evgenia Ivanova, 'Current Forces in Bulgarian Life and Politics', *East European Reporter* Vol.5, No.1 (1992),p.79.

16. Circular distributed to trial subscribers in 1992. Punctuation as in the original. Shiva has shown how, in the Third World too, the WWF plays an important political role which is not entirely compatible with its mission of 'resisting the patenting of life' (V. Shiva, 'Violating Peoples' Rights, Protecting Corporate Profits', *Third World Resurgence*, No.34, 1993, p.2).

17. Op. cit., p.59.

18. *The Economist*, 13 March 1993, p.4. For an assessment of the the trade unions' options in Poland see Piotr Marciniak, 'Polish Labour Unions: Can They Find a Way Out?', *Telos*, No.92 (1992).

19. Claus Offe, 'The Attribution of Public Status to Interest Groups: Observations on the German Case', in S. Berger (ed.), *Organizing Interests in Western Europe* (London: Cambridge University Press, 1981), p.136.

Social Forces and Changes of Political Regime: The Question of Democratic Development

CURT SØRENSEN

History provides many examples of the transformation of political regimes. Several classic studies suggest that democracy was only possible under very specific circumstances. Several point to an automatic causal link between capitalism and political democracy. More comprehensive historical analysis shows democracy to have emerged out of social forces and conflicts created during the development of capitalism, with the working class its most consistent supporter. It may be possible to relate these broad historical generalizations to changes of regime over short periods. The suggested framework follows four defining characteristics of regime types. The conclusion on the future of democracy throughout Europe is cautiously optimistic.

Over the last 15 to 20 years, a number of remarkable changes in the types of regime have taken place around the world, including parts of southern Europe, Latin America and now, more recently, eastern Europe and the former Soviet Union. These regime transformations are often seen as being part of a huge, irresistible and irreversible world-wide process of democratization. Optimism and expectations have been high with frequent references to a new 'democratic wave'.[1]

It should, however, be noted that sudden transformations of the political system are neither new nor unique. This century, for example, has experienced a number of changes of political system. Examples include the Russian revolutions in 1905 and 1917, the central European revolutions at the end of the First World War, the right-authoritarian or fascist changes of regime in central, eastern, and southern Europe in the inter-war period and the transformations of the political systems in many countries at the end of the Second World War.

Neither are attempts to establish democratic regimes something completely new and unique. At the end of the First World War there was an earlier 'democratic wave', but within a relatively short space of time these newly established democratic regimes broke down and were

Curt Sørensen teaches and conducts research in the Department of Political Science, Aarhus University.

replaced by right-authoritarian or fascist dictatorships. Juan Linz coined the concept 'break-down of democratic regimes' to describe this phenomenon, but perhaps it would be more appropriate to refer to failed attempts to establish and consolidate democracies.[2] The collapse of the Weimar Republic, for example, could be seen as an unsuccessful attempt to consolidate a democratic regime rather than as the 'break-down' of a well-established democracy.

Several attempts have been made to identify the historical-structural conditions for democracy.[3] These might suggest a rather pessimistic view of the possibilities of democratic development in the modern world. Thus democracy could appear to Karl de Shweinitz as something which developed under very specific circumstances at a certain moment in the course of western European and North American history. It depended on 'an unusual configuration of historical circumstances which cannot be repeated', so that, as far as other countries are concerned, 'the European–American route to democracy is closed'.[4] Barrington Moore, too, emphasizes, in his celebrated work on roads of modernization, the unique and special conditions for the constitution and implementation of 'the democratic road'. Again, they are conditions that are not to be repeated.

A similar conception of capitalist development and democracy was put forward at an early time not by Marx – who had a surprisingly optimistic view on capitalist development and democracy – but by the 'bourgeois Marx', Max Weber. As early as 1906 Weber's analysis of Russian development led to a highly pessimistic view on the possibilities of democratic development in that country and also of democratic development under advanced capitalism in general.[5] According to Weber, freedom and democracy were rooted in conditions characteristic of early capitalism, conditions which would never occur again.[6] There was, in Weber's view, no necessary connection between modern, advanced capitalism and democracy.

Against this can be set the 'optimistic' view, within which the relationship has been seen in straightforward terms, with capitalist economic development automatically producing both material affluence and democracy. Needless to say, this is the predominant conception at the present time. In a more sophisticated form this conception postulates capitalist development as a necessary, but not sufficient condition for democracy.[7] Concomitant with this general thesis is the assertion that a strong bourgeoisie – or middle class – is a precondition for democracy.[8]

The following section will take up these points with a consideration of the two interconnected notions of, first, an automatic causal link between the capitalist market economy and democracy and, secondly, the view of the bourgeoisie as the main historical agent for democracy. The sub-sequent section is intended to relate these general points to the study of the relationship between social forces and changes of political regime. That then provides a basis for a suggested theoretical framework for further research. The final, concluding section brings the argument together around some comments on the prospects for democracy in contemporary Europe.

Capitalism, Social Forces and Democracy

The extensive literature on the subject of capitalism, liberalism and democracy cannot be summarized fully here, but four general points can provide a basis for the discussion that follows.[9] First, neither in real historical developments nor in contemporary world events has there been any unambiguous and automatic connection between capitalism and democracy. The capitalist economic system has been, and still is, connected with widely different political systems, including restricted monarchies with limited suffrage, Bonapartist dictatorships, military dictatorships, right authoritarian dictatorships, fascism and democratic republics with universal suffrage.[10]

Secondly, even in those instances where capitalist development actually resulted in political democracy, or 'polyarchy', the process was never automatic and there was no immediate transmission from capitalist economy to political democracy. Despite the views of Weber and Barrington Moore, democracy need not be seen as the result of a unique historical situation. Nevertheless, its emergence can be attributed to social and political struggles within which different social classes and other social agents had different interests and played different roles. As Stephen and Rueschemeyer aptly put it:

> capitalist development is associated with democracy because it transforms the class struggle, strengthening the working and middle classes and weakening the landed upper class. It was not the capitalist market nor capitalists as the new dominant forces but rather the contradictions of capitalism that advanced democracy.[11]

Thirdly, as pointed out not only by socialist but also by several liberal scholars, there is in advanced capitalist societies an enormous concen-tration of economic power which is beyond effective democratic control. There is a strong tension, or even contradiction, between this and the endeavours to realize the democratic ideal of a social and political system with democratic participation and popular control.[12] This problem can be circumvented, at the theoretical level, by the famous redefinition of democracy as elite competition[13] or by making a sharp distinction between democracy proper and real existing 'polyarchies'.[14] Neither solution seems completely satisfactory.[15]

Fourthly, capitalist economic development itself was very different in different countries. The 'market' of the economic textbooks probably never existed and modern advanced capitalist economies are characterized by the existence of large corporations and a considerable measure of planning. Moreover, in all advanced capitalist countries, including even the United States, there is a complicated interplay between private enterprise and the state.[16]

Evidence from Sweden and Germany

Taken together these points suggest a complex relationship between political democracy and the market economy. Their significance can be illustrated at a simple level around the example of Sweden. At the turn of the century it was one of the poorest countries in Europe with a rather undemocratic structure, within which almost three-quarters of the adult male population did not have the right to vote.[17] In the years 1917–18 Sweden experienced a 'democratic breakthrough'. Under the impact of food riots, the threat of a general strike and signs of a collapse of morale in the armed forces, the conservative government and the landed aristocracy conceded universal suffrage and the principle of parliamentary responsibility. Over the following years the driving force in the development of Swedish democracy was the social-democratic labour movement.[18]

In the same period Sweden experienced an economic transformation, such that Sweden today is one of the richest countries in the world. Moreover, this development did not come about as the result of the interplay of forces on a 'free market'. On the contrary, the process was characterized by active political intervention and substantial cooperation between the state, capitalist enterprises and the main interest organizations. Moreover, this economic and political transformation coincided with the construction of the renowned Swedish welfare state.[19]

A more complex argument can be developed around the case of Germany. The prevailing interpretation of German history points to the failure of a genuine bourgeois revolution in 1848–49.[20] Its subsequent history has then been seen as a 'special case', a *Sonderweg*, compared to other countries. Imperial German society was characterized by the presence of strong pre-industrial, authoritarian values, attitudes and ideas and a power system within which the power and interests of the agrarian upper class, the Junkers, were dominant. This had serious consequences for subsequent German history leading to the weak foundations for democracy in the Weimar Republic and hence to its subsequent collapse.

This interpretation is in line with Barrington Moore's classical account as well as with newer research in which the agrarian aristocracy has been seen as the main social force opposing democracy.

This view, however, has recently been challenged by two British historians, David Blackbourn and Geoff Eley, who argue that Germany did in fact 'experience a successful bourgeois revolution in the nineteenth century',[21] and that the bourgeoisie in Imperial Germany was not weak at all. Wilhelmine Germany was not a backward society with an obsolete power structure, nor was society dominated by pre-industrial interests and values.

Their criticisms hinge on three points. First, if German development is to be defined as a 'Sonderweg', then it has to be set against a standard. In this context, they criticize the idealized picture of the 'British road' and the tacit assumption, widespread in modernization theories, of a normal road to modernization.

Secondly, they question the notion of 'bourgeois revolution' as a dramatic, spectacular act where a homogeneous and conscious bourgeois class, acting on its own, seizes power with one blow and after that event exercises all power. In this sense, they contend, there never was a 'bourgeois revolution' in any country. Instead they suggest a broad concept of 'bourgeois revolution' focusing on longer processes of structural change and adjustment.[22]

Thirdly, they too dispute the widespread assumption that there is some sort of automatic, unilinear link between capitalism, the bourgeoisie and liberalism, and democracy. They suggest that 'both the bourgeoisie's degree of liberalism and liberalism's degree of democracy depended in nineteenth century Europe on complex social configurations'. Within these, 'the mobilization and independent dynamism of subordinate classes like the peasantry, small property-owners, and the working class played an important, possibly decisive, role'.[23] Capitalism, furthermore, has been and can be associated with a variety of political systems. As they point out, 'capitalism has historically been able to survive and reproduce itself within varying state forms along a continuum from parliamentary democracy to radical fascism'.[24]

This would seem close to the Rueschemeyer–Stephens thesis which, like the old Barrington Moore position, stresses the role played by different social classes in the development of democracy. The contribution of the former, however, was to emphasize the role played by the European working class in this historical process, suggesting that 'it was the subordinate classes that fought for democracy', while 'the classes that benefit from the status quo nearly without exception resisted democracy'. Thus the bourgeoisie initially fought for its share of political participation from royal autocracy and aristocratic oligarchy, 'but it rarely fought for further extensions once its own place was secured', so that 'the working class was the most consistently pro-democratic force'.[25]

Blackbourn and Eley are on firm ground in their criticism of modernization theories, but their comments on the specific character of Imperial Germany require closer examination. Their thesis on the humble role of the Junker class is not fully convincing.[26] Moreover, a substantial body of evidence points to the fact that the agrarian elite in many European countries has been a major social force against democratization. This was probably the case – despite the contrary view of Blackbourn and Eley – in Germany and in other countries, including Italy, Spain, Hungary, Poland, Sweden and Denmark.[27] Moreover, other forces were also at work. In Norway, Sweden, Germany and Austria, for example, the bureaucratic elite was another strong force resisting democracy, while in such countries as Germany, Spain, Italy and Greece the military played a role as an anti-democratic force.

In both Germany and Austria the peasants and the petty bourgeoisie in the towns resisted democracy and in the late 1920s and the 1930s they went over to fascism.[28] In Denmark and Sweden, however, and to a certain extent also in Norway, part of the middle class and the peasantry turned to democracy, helping the Scandinavian countries along the social-democratic road. The bourgeoisie, however, has tended to waver, fighting against the old monarchy for constitutional government and rights, but generally resisting an extension of democratic rights to the lower classes. Moreover, especially in central Europe, there was strong sympathy for an authoritarian 'solution' in the late 1920s.[29]

The Working Class and Democratic Transformation

These observations suggest a basis for the beginnings of a more complete interpretation of the relationship between social forces and democracy. The assertion that a strong middle class is essential for political democracy is clearly open to question. In the Weimar Republic and in Austria's First Republic, the middle class turned to fascism and it was the workers who sustained political democracy. This is reflected in the strength of the political parties too. In Germany the Liberal Party (*Deutsche Demokratische Partei*) gained only about one per cent of the votes cast at the last two parliamentary elections of the Weimar Republic[30] and in the Austrian Republic a liberal party was simply absent from the political scene. Conversely, the social-democratic labour movement was the only strong and visible force supporting democracy and fighting fascism. In the Scandinavian countries, too, the main force for democracy was the social-democratic labour movement. This general picture, however, was modified by the presence in these countries of at least some liberal and peasant forces which also supported democracy and were willing to co-operate with the labour movement.

If the thesis on the working class as 'the most consistently pro-democratic force' is confirmed by historical facts, then we are left with a striking paradox. The general political debate, the mass media coverage and also a substantial body of scholarly work on transition processes in eastern Europe and the former Soviet Union, are all focusing on the question of how to create a bourgeoisie which can function as the main social base for democracy. At the same time, a substantial body of theoretical and empirical work on political development and regime changes is pointing to the working class as the main historical agent for the establishment and consolidation of democracy.

To some extent, however, the Rueschemeyer–Stephens thesis needs further clarification and a degree of modification around five main points. First, and most obviously, the working-class movement must be victorious or at least not defeated, as were the German and Austrian labour movements in the 1933–34 period. Secondly, insufficient attention is devoted to the importance of developing strong democratic political cultures based on popular movements (*folkrörelser* in Swedish). Such movements were essential for the development of democracy in the Scandinavian countries: the classic European working-class movement was not only a political but a cultural movement as well.[31]

Thirdly, it must be recognized that workers did not everywhere and in every situation fight for democracy. In Germany communist workers certainly fought against fascism, but they did not fight for democracy.[32] Another example is the working-class support for the Arrow Cross movement in Hungary in the 1930s.[33] This once again underlines the importance of the development of democratic traditions and of a popular democratic culture.

Fourthly, Rueschemeyer and Stephens pay little attention to the question of alliances between social forces although, as the examples mentioned earlier indicate, this was one of the decisive differences between Scandinavian and central European developments. To some extent this weakness can be corrected with reference to the work of Gregory M. Luebbert, for whom the question of alliances is a principal concern. He, however, suffers from 'super-structuralism'.

Luebbert seems almost to deny the importance of political action at all, maintaining that 'one of the cardinal lessons of the story I have told is that leadership and meaningful choice played no role in the outcome'.[34] Following this assertion, he pays little attention to the importance of political action and cultural struggle. This cannot provide the basis for a statisfactory explanation of the differences between northern and central Europe. Even if historical and structural conditions differed, a political struggle still took place in which some lost and some won, and this in turn determined the outcome.

Luebbert also leaves a number of further complicated issues unresolved. For example, he explains the different strengths of liberalism in different countries in terms of the existence or non-existence of cleavages within that trend. Where it was subdivided by many pre-industrial dimensions of conflict it remained weak. Where liberalism was homogeneous, and not internally divided by pre-industrial cleavages, it became strong. This in turn conditioned the different character and development of the labour movement in the different countries of Europe.

Luebbert, furthermore, studies the strength and behaviour of the labour movement in different countries in relation to the force and character of liberalism and to the attitudes and opinions of the peasants. This certainly is important, but the bunch of questions can be pushed further back to issues relating to the deeper historical reasons for cleavages within liberalism, its strength or weakness, different roads to modernization, the relationship between the agrarian sector and industrialization and so on. Thus the account needs to be brought into line with the analysis of the long-term trends within different paths of European history, of the kind associated with Barrington Moore.[35]

The fifth and last weakness in Rueschemeyer and Stephens', and also in Gregory Luebbert's, analysis is the inadequate treatment of international political and economic relations.[36] It seems obvious, for example, that German and Austrian political development in the present century cannot be explained without taking into account the effects of the outcome of two world wars. Similarly, as convincingly demonstrated by Andrew Janos, political development in Hungary can only be understood by taking into consideration the country's peripheral position in the general European context.

Despite these reservations, one main conclusion seems to stand out from the historical evidence. A strong and autonomous labour movement, including a free and strong trade-union movement, is one of the essentials for developing and maintaining democracy. This was recognized by Hitler as well as Stalin, neither of whom could tolerate the existence of free trade unions. Nevertheless, this very general point, derived from the analysis of very broad historical trends covering large time periods, requires amplification and clarification. The next section therefore looks at some of the theoretical problems involved in a more detailed study of the relationship between social forces and the transformation of political regimes.

Theoretical Approach and Conceptual Clarifications

Towards a New Framework

Recent changes of political regime in several European and Latin American countries have generated an extensive and growing literature.[37] In this literature attention has been directed towards the process of 'transition' and processes and problems in the subsequent period of 'consolidation'.[38] A principal focus is furthermore on the action of elites. There can be no doubt about the value of this approach, which has been used by such scholars as Juan Linz, Guillermo O'Donnell, Philippe Schmitter, Terry Karl, John Herz, Adam Przeworski and Giuseppe Di Palma.[39]

Nevertheless, this approach, if it stands alone, has the serious limitation of focusing on the 'now', the short span of time when the 'transition' takes place, neglecting historical conditions. Moreover, it analyses the processes of transition in terms of actors, abstracting from structural conditions and within that it focuses in a one-sided way on elites. In other words, it tends to abstract from the study of the long historical trends, historical preconditions and structural constraints which are the main focus in the work of Barrington Moore, Karl de Schweinitz, Theda Skocpol, Gregory M. Luebbert, and Stephens and Rueschemeyer.[40] This missing perspective is especially important when studying developments in eastern Europe precisely because it is so often forgotten, the main focus of attention being the spectacular recent changes.[41]

It should, however, be possible to combine the two approaches so as to embrace structural as well as behavioural elements of social reality.[42] There should be no need to make an either–or choice, as some authors appear to do on one side or the other side.[43] On the contrary, it can hardly be main-tained that social reality is either actors floating in empty space[44] or structures totally dominating and determining the behaviour of social actors, reducing them in this way to mere 'agents'.[45]

Unfortunately, as recognized by Charles Tilly, it is surprisingly difficult to combine the approach that focuses on the actor with the one that focuses on structural factors, especially when working at a high level of abstraction.[46] It ought to be possible to demonstrate in each concrete historical case the interdependence between structural conditions and social actions. That, however, points towards a pure historical study of quite unique situations and would risk losing the benefit of the broad generalizations derivable from comparative analysis.

No full solution can be suggested here, but it is possible to suggest a number of methodological pointers which could help bridge the gulf between the study of broad historical trends and the detailed study of the kinds of system transformation being experienced in eastern Europe today. The starting point is to define the differences between political regimes in such a way as to relate them to the social forces that can lead to their creation or transformation. The suggested framework is clearly an over-simplification, not least because it is impossible to detach social and political development completely from economic development.

Nevertheless, it could provide a basis for the incorporation of different time perspectives, for an incorporation of awareness of the importance of historical-structural conditions as well as recent actions, and for a recognition of the importance of taking account of a wide variety of social forces. The suggested framework concentrates on two core concepts, social forces and political regimes.

Social Forces and Political Regimes

The concept of social forces can be clarified with the help of a distinction made by Charles Tilly between 'social behaviour' and 'social action'.[47] In contrast to mere 'social behaviour', 'social action' entails an amount of conscious endeavour to realize some goal, an amount of organization, interest articulation and influence on the course of social events.

Many different social groupings can be engaged in 'social action'. To some extent, a distinction may be valid in which, in the long run, social classes and class constellations, as pointed out by Barrington Moore and Gregory M. Luebbert, can be seen as the most important social agents in political development and changes of regimes. In the short run, however, the actions of political elites, bureaucracies, the military and the like can be decisive.

A very good recent example is the transition from the previous type of political regime to the present type of regime in Hungary, and perhaps other east European countries too. This transformation process has been analysed notably by Elemér Hankiss, and his 'conversion of power thesis' can aptly be formulated in his own words:

> I have expressed my conviction that the ruling elite in Hungary gave up its coercive and bureaucratic power without too much resistance and took the risk of a radical transformation of the political system because it realized that it had a good chance of converting the power it had possessed in the old system into a new kind of power which would be relevant and workable in the new system.[48]

In this case the ruling elite transformed itself into a new ruling elite and its strategic decision and following actions were, following Hankiss, decisive for the recent transition in Hungary.

It can be argued that the former *nomenklatura* was not just an elite. Perhaps it would be more appropriate to consider it as a ruling class converting itself into another ruling class, especially if the concept of class is defined in terms of the real social control of the forces of production.[49] In this sense the *nomenklatura* in the former Soviet Union and in the eastern European Stalinist systems, for example, was a ruling class in the same sense as was the feudal nobility in feudal society, and as is the grand bourgeoisie in capitalist society.[50] This, however, does not affect the general argument.

It is worth stressing the familiar point that class organization, class consciousness and collective action do not follow in a unilinear and automatic way from given class positions. Classes in real societies are processes and the outcome of those processes can be different in different countries.[51] Classes are only active as agents in historical processes, as social movements developing organizations and ideologies. The Stephens–Rueschemeyer thesis can therefore be reformulated as follows: the organized European labour movement – and, as central in this general movement, a free trade-union movement – was the main social and political force in the development of democracy in Europe.

The process in the course of which a social category, group or class develops into an active social agent – the process of 'social mobilization' – is crucial for understanding the process of regime transformation. Social mobilization, in this context, refers to the development from an original, amorphous, not yet articulated position to a high degree of organization and ideology. The mobilizing social group, as a consequence of increasing social and political participation, will increasingly articulate interests, making demands on other groups in society or on the state apparatus.

The second core concept, the 'political regime', can be understood as the specific features of government, bureaucracy, parliaments or other kinds of assemblies, courts and the like, together with the way in which they are organized and their interrelations. In short, the concept refers to the specific character of what is usually called 'the state'. In addition to that, it is also legitimate to include within the concept of the 'political regime' the party system, the prevailing ideologies and the overall relations between the ruling elite and the population.[52]

Participation, Control, Pluralism and Ideology

It is possible to distinguish between democratic, authoritarian, fascist and Stalinist types of regime, in terms of their specific character in relation to the four variables of participation, control, pluralism, and ideology.[53] For the period and area in question this four-fold classification should suffice, although a more comprehensive framework may be needed for analysing all the types of regimes in Third World countries.[54]

In the fascist and Stalinist regime types, participation is a pseudo-participation. It is organized from above by the ruling elite and gives those 'participating' no real influence at all. In authoritarian regimes the ruling elites do not intend, or do not have the ability, to carry through the same kind of organized and forced mass participation as is the case in the fascist type. On the other hand, there is no genuine participation as in the democratic type either.[55]

Even in the democratic type, whilst participation is genuine the extent of it varies considerably. In the European countries electoral participation has usually been high. In the USA electoral participation has in recent years been rather low. Both in Europe and in the USA other forms of participation do occur, but they are usually weak.

The concept of 'control' has two dimensions, these being the extent of control of the government by the people and the extent of control of the people by the government. In the fascist type there is no control whatsoever of the government by the people but, conversely, there is extensive control of the people by the government. The same can be said of the Stalinist type. Elite-control of the population is somewhat weaker in the authoritarian type, in which the technique of mass-domination is less developed, but control of the political elite by the people is also absent. It is, however, a distinguishing feature of democratic government that the people to a certain extent do control government. It may be argued that democratic control 'from below' is in real life too weak, but it is none the less clearly much greater than under the fascist, Stalinist or authoritarian types of regime.

Pluralism in the fascist type is restricted to rivalry and the clash of interests between different sections of the ruling elite.[56] It is absent in society in general with all opposition activities illegal and persecuted by the ruling elite. This is also the case in the Stalinist type. Due to its looser character and inadequate, old-fashioned technique of domination, the authoritarian type will display a certain amount of pluralism, but not to the extent found in democratic systems.

Pluralism, however, is crucial in democratic systems. In many theories pluralism is presented as the outstanding characteristic of political democracy, often to the neglect of the equally important element of participation.[57] The older pluralist theory in particular often pictured existing political democracies as fair systems of balanced interests.[58] Opposing this, neo-pluralist theory has stressed the dominant position of corporate interest in Western society, especially the USA, and conversely the weak position of organized labour.[59]

Turning now to the fourth and last variable, a central feature of fascist systems is the presence of an all embracing ideology, monopolized and sustained by the state apparatus and the party. The same is the case in the

Stalinist type, although its dominant ideology is, of course, quite different. Moreover, in fascist systems there is a conformity between elitism in ideology and elitism in practice. In Stalinist systems there is a gross discrepancy between ideology and reality as far as mass participation and influence is concerned. Again the authoritarian type is a less efficient system of domination containing several uncoordinated dominant ideologies.

In democratic systems, finally, a plurality of ideologies is part of the overall system of pluralism. It is, however, clear that in real existing democracies some ideologies are propagated more powerfully than others. Antonio Gramsci's concept of hegemony is useful here as a conceptual device for investigating the ideological structure of real existing democracies, or 'polyarchies'.[60]

The distinction mentioned above between democratic, authoritarian and fascists forms of regime is only a preliminary one. Within each main type it is possible make further distinctions taking into account a variety of social political and cultural circumstances. American democracy in the 1930s, for example, was quite different from the Weimar Republic's democracy or the kind of democracy in the First Austrian Republic, just as it was also different from the Scandinavian democracies of the same period.

Regime Transformation

It is by affecting and changing these four central variables – participation, control, pluralism and ideology – that social forces can modify and eventually transform the political regimes within which they have developed. Participation, for example, was enormously extended during the nineteenth century and the first two decades of the twentieth century by the successive extensions of the suffrage across many European countries. A main social force fighting for universal suffrage was the European labour movement. The main social force pushing forward the extension of the control over government and pluralism was historically the bourgeoisie. And since the French and the industrial revolutions political ideologies such as liberalism, socialism, conservatism and fascism have played a major role in the political processes which transformed political regimes or kept them alive. These ideologies, of course, were not free-floating, but were articulated and sustained by different social forces.

This consideration of long-term trends must be related to the regime changes which occur over short periods of time. A recent example of an important and swift change is the abrupt transformation of ideology carried through by the ruling elite, or possibly class, in Hungary and other east European countries during the last few years. From Marxism-Leninism they have moved to a nineteenth-century *laissez faire* liberalism.[61] Another example is the sudden extension of pluralism in the same countries.

Conclusion

This discussion of the nature of political regimes, and of the social forces that can cause their transformation, has major implications for the understanding of democracy itself. Democracy should be seen as a political system with high and genuine political participation, universal suffrage being here a minimal and necessary condition. Another crucial element is pluralism and respect for human rights. There is no conflict between participation and pluralism, despite Tocqueville's old assertion to the contrary,[62] as long as self-determination and self-development are maintained as basic values and rights.[63]

Democracy in the sense given above does not, as yet, exist. As has already been argued, this difficulty can be resolved, following Robert A. Dahl, by making a distinction between democracy proper, which is seen as a purely theoretical construction, and actually existing 'polyarchies'.[64] Alternatively, democracy can be set as a goal to aim for. It does, however, seem awkward effectively to discard a term in such common use as 'democracy'. Therefore, if a given political system features a reasonable amount of participation and pluralism, it seems reasonable to describe it as 'democratic'.

One of the contributions of the classic European labour movement was to see the potential for an extension of 'actually existing' democracy.[65] Parliamentary democracy was to be maintained, including the usual catalogue of rights guaranteeing minority protection, but procedures and structures for democratic decision-making were to be developed within economic life too.[66] Democratic control by the democratically-elected parliament and economic democracy at the local level were in the European social-democratic tradition the two main vehicles for the process of democratization.

It is possible within this framework to strike a balance between the pessimistic and the optimistic view, mentioned in the introductory remarks, of the possibilities for democracy in the modern world. Democratic development must be conceived as a serious *problem*. The establishment, consolidation and further development of democracy is not impossible in today's world. There is, however, no strong case for accepting the optimistic and careless view that the world is safe for democracy from the moment the capitalist market economy is introduced.

Nevertheless, it should not be impossible to develop, in a distant future, political and social systems that are more democratic than the present democracies. It may be possible to close, or at least diminish, the gap between democracy and 'polyarchy'. It was not essential to accept the Fukuyama thesis of the 'end of history'.[67]

This, however, is a far-reaching perspective, which may not arrive on the agenda in any European country for the next 20 to 30 years. Especially in the eastern parts of Europe the great problem at the moment is to initiate capitalist development and to develop simple pluralist democracy. As indicated by past European history, both tasks can be accomplished in very different ways. Economic and social development need not assume the character of untamed, raw capitalism, a social-Darwinist nightmare,[68] and political democracy does not, of course, exclude democratic popular participation. A case can, in fact, be made for the thesis that even restricted democracy, 'polyarchy', was accomplished most successfully in those countries where free, popular participation was most developed.

Indeed, the major democratic question in the contemporary world is no longer universal suffrage. That has been settled. The main problem today relates to actual democratic, popular participation. Even the most restricted pluralist democracy presupposes a certain amount of popular participation and a basic democratic political culture. Moreover, if the democratic goal is supposed to be something more than only elite competition or 'polyarchy', then popular participation is essential.[69]

Democratic participation is precisely *the* problem in the east, but also in the west, of course.[70] Its weak development may be related to the historical defeats of European labour, and especially to the crushing of the central-European labour movement by fascism.[71] This was fatal for the labour movements in other European countries, too. The German and the Austrian labour movement had been politically and culturally the most advanced part of European labour movement. In southern Europe fascist or right-authoritarian types of regimes were victorious, too, and the same was the case in most east European countries, with Czechoslovakia as an important exception.[72] The old ideals and beliefs of European labour, its distinct culture built on such values as cooperation and solidarity, and its whole identity began to crumble away after the historical defeat by fascism and under the subsequent impact of the cold war.

It is often claimed that European class struggle has come to an end and that the working class has been well integrated, the reason for this being a general rise in the material standard of living.[73] However, neither historical nor current evidence confirms the thesis of a unilinear and automatic relationship between the material standard of living and working class radicalism.[74] It can furthermore be argued that the so-called 'integration' is based not on accomplished objectives and a higher standard of living, but on defeat, demoralization and apathy.

One of the consequences of the deterioration of the classic European labour movement, and of the weakening of working-class solidarity, could be the creation of a new situation, perhaps already emerging in several European countries. At the top of society there is an all powerful and unchallenged power elite of corporate interests, top politicians, top bureaucrats and mass media commanders. At the middle level of society an alliance is developing between the middle class and the better-off skilled workers, submissive to and admiring the power elite. At the bottom of society there is a new 'lumpen proletariat' of low income workers, the unemployed and social clients. This new 'sub-proletariat' is left without mutual social bonds, without identity and without self-esteem. It therefore lacks organization and the capacity to articulate and enforce its interests.

In eastern Europe new elites will emerge, or the old elites will be transformed. At the bottom of the east European societies will be the immobilized, unorganized, atomized masses. The great problem in the east is therefore precisely the problem of genuine popular participation and interest articulation, and of how to develop a popular democratic culture. Both the west and the east, then, are facing the same basic problem of creating and maintaining a democratic popular culture and mass participation. In the west the question is how to regenerate this sort of popular social movement. In the east the question is effectively how to create it from scratch.

NOTES

1. Samuel P. Huntington, *The Third Wave: Democratization in the Late Twentieth Century* (OK: University of Oklahoma Press, 1991).
2. Juan Linz and Alfred Stepan (eds.), *The Breakdown of Democratic Regimes: Crisis, Breakdown and Reequilibration* (Baltimore, MD: Johns Hopkins University Press, 1978).
3. See especially, Barrington Moore, *Social Origins of Dictatorship and Democracy* (Boston, MA: Beacon Press, 1966) and Karl Von Schweinitz, *Industrialization and Democracy: Economic Necessities and Political Possibilities* (New York: Free Press, 1964).
4. Schweinitz, *Industrialization*, pp.10–11.
5. Max Weber, 'Zur Lage der bürgerlichen Demokratie in Russland', in Johannes Winckelmann (ed.), *Max Weber. Gesammelte Politische Schriften* (Tübingen, 1980), pp.33–68, and Max Weber 'Russland. Übergang zum Scheinkonstitutionalismus', in Winckelmann, pp.69–111.
6. 'Niemals sich wiederholende Konstellationen', Weber, 'Zur Lage', p.64.
7. See S.M. Lipset, 'Some Social Requisites of Democracy: Economic Development and Political Legitimacy', *American Political Science Review*, Vol.53 (1959), Philips Cutwright and James Wiley, 'Modernization and Political Representation: 1927–1966', *Studies in Comparative International Development*, 1969, and Janos Kornai, *The Road to a Free Economy* (New York and London: W.W. Norton & Co., 1990).
8. Barrington Moore, *Social Origins*, p.418.

9. See, among others, Robert A. Dahl, *Polyarchy, Participation and Opposition* (New Haven, CT: Yale University Press, 1971), C.B. Macpherson, *The Life and Times of Liberal Democracy* (Oxford: Oxford University Press, 1977), Charles E. Lindblom, *Politics and Markets* (New York: Basic Books, 1977), Benjamin R. Barber, *Strong Democracy* (Berkeley, CA: University of California Press, 1984), John Hoffman, *State, Power and Democracy* (Brighton: Wheatsheaf, 1988), and Ellen Meiksins Wood, *The Retreat from Class*, (London: Verso, 1986).

10. See Reinhard Kühnl, *Formen bürgerlicher Herrschaft* (Hamburg: Rowohlt Verlag, 1971), Göran Therborn, 'The Rule of Capital and the Rise of Democracy', *New Left Review*, No.103 (1977), pp.3–41, and Dietrich Rueschemeyer, Evelyne H. Stephens and John D. Stephens, *Capitalist Development and Democracy* (Chicago, IL: University of Chicago Press, 1992).

11. Rueschemeyer *et al.*, *Capitalist*, p.7.

12. Cf. Lindblom, *Politics*, Macpherson, *The Life*, Robert A. Dahl, *A Preface to Economic Democracy* (Cambridge: Polity Press, 1985), Wood, *The Retreat*, Ralph Miliband, *The State in Capitalist Society* (London: Weidenfeld & Nicolson, 1969), and Göran Therborn, *What Does the Ruling Class Do When it Rules?* (London: NLB, 1978).

13. Joseph A. Schumpeter, *Capitalism, Socialism and Democracy* (London: George Allen & Unwin, 1943), pp.269 ff. See for the 'pluralist school' in general, David Held, *Models of Democracy* (Cambridge: Polity Press, 1987), Ch.6.

14. Dahl, *Polyarchy*.

15. See Macpherson, *The Life*, Carole Pateman, *Participation and Democratic Theory* (Cambridge: Cambridge University Press, 1970), and Carole Pateman, *The Problem of Political Obligation: A Critical Analysis of Liberal Theory* (Colchester: John Wiley, 1985).

16. See Lindblom, *Politics*, and John Kenneth Galbraith, *The New Industrial State* (London: Hamish Hamilton, 1967).

17. Gregory M. Luebbert, *Liberalism, Fascism or Social Democracy: Social Classes and the Political Origins of Regimes in Interwar Europe* (Oxford: Oxford University Press, 1991), p.129.

18. See Niels Elvander, *Skandinavisk arbetarrörelse* (Stockholm, 1980), Walter Korpi, *The Working Class in Welfare Capitalism* (London: Routledge & Kegan Paul, 1978), Walter Korpi, *The Democratic Class Struggle* (London: Routledge, 1983), and John Stephens, *The Transition from Capitalism to Socialism* (University of Illinois Press, 1986).

19. *Der Fischer Weltalmanach*, 1993, pp.183–6.

20. See Alexander Gerschenkron, *Bread and Democracy in Germany* (Berkeley, CA: University of California Press, 1943), Ralf Dahrendorf, *Society and Democracy in Germany* (New York: Doubleday, 1967), and Hans-Ulrich Wehler, *The German Empire 1871–1918* (Leamington Spa: Berg Publishers, 1985).

21. David Blackbourn and Geoff Eley, *The Peculiarities of German History* (Oxford: Oxford University Press, 1984).

22. Ibid., p.86.

23. Ibid., pp.18–19.

24. Ibid., p.26.

25. Rueschemeyer *et al.*, *Capitalist*, p.46, and p.8.

26. For a more realistic assesment of the position and influence of the German Junker class, see William Carr, *A History of Germany 1815–1985* (3rd edn., London: Edward Arnold, 1987), Gordon A. Craig, *Germany 1866–1945* (Oxford: Oxford University Press, 1978), Gerschenkron, *Bread*, Dahrendorf, *Society*, and Wehler, *The German*.

27. See Rueschemeyer *et al.*, *Capitalist*, Martin Clark, *Modern Italy 1871–1982* (London and New York: Longman, 1984), Raymond Carr, *Spain 1808–1975* (2nd edn., Oxford: Oxford University Press, 1982), Andrew Janos, *The Politics of Backwardness in Hungary 1825–1945* (Princeton, NJ: Princeton University Press, 1982), Hans Roos *A History of Modern Poland* (London: Eyre & Spottiswoode, 1966), Steven Koblik (ed.), *Sweden's Development from Poverty to Affluence 1750–1970* (Minneapolis, MN: University of Minnesota Press, 1975), Elis Håstad, *Sveriges historia under 1900-talet* (Stockholm,

1958), Vagn Dybdal *De nye Klasser 1870–1913* (Copenhagen, 1965), and Per Salomons-son (ed.), *Den politiske magtkamp 1866–1901* (Copenhagen, 1968).

28. Luebbert, *Liberalism*, William Sheridan Allen, *The Nazi Seizure of Power* (London: Eyre & Spottiswoode, 1966), Richard F. Hamilton, *Who voted for Hitler?* (Princeton, NJ: Princeton University Press, 1982), and Charles A. Gulick, *Austria from Habsburg to Hitler* (2 vols, Berkeley, CA: University of California Press, 1948).

29. See earlier references plus Curt Sørensen, 'Mellem Demokrati og Diktatur' (2 vols., dissertation, University of Aarhus, 1992).

30. Thomas T. Mackie and Richard Rose, *The International Almanac of Electoral History* (2nd edn., London: Macmillan, 1982), pp.154–5.

31. See 'Mellem', Helene Maimann (ed.), *Mit uns zieht die neue Zeit. Arbeiter-kultur in Österreich 1918–34* (Vienna: Habarta & Harbarta, 1981), Joseph Weiden-holzer, *Auf dem Weg zum neuen Menschen. Bildungs- und Kulturarbeit der öster-reichischen Sozialdemokratie in der ersten Republik* (Vienna: Europaverlag, 1981), and Niels Elvander, *Skandinavisk arbetarrörelse* (Stockholm, 1980).

32. See Ossip K. Flechtheim, *Die KPD in der Weimarer Republik* (Frankfurt a.M., 1969), and Hermann Weber, *Die Wandlung des deutschen Kommunismus. Die Stalinisierung der KPD in der Weimarer Republik* (2 vols, Frankfurt a.M., 1969).

33. For the working class support for the 'Arrow Cross' movement, see Janos, *The Politics* pp. 270–1.

34. Luebbert, *Liberalism*, p.306.

35. See also Daniel Chirot (ed.), *The Origins of Backwardness in Eastern Europe* (Berkeley: University of California Press, 1989).

36. For such a perspective and treatment, see Immanuel Wallerstein, *The Modern World System* (3 vols., New York, San Francisco and London: Academic Press, 1974–89).

37. See Guillermo O'Donnell and Philipe C. Schmitter, *Transition from Authoritarian Rule: Tentative Conclusions about Uncertain Democracies* (Baltimore, MD: Johns Hopkins University, 1986), Guillermo O'Donnell, Philippe C. Schmitter and Laurence Whitehead, *Transitions from Authoritarian Rule* (Baltimore, MD: Johns Hopkins University Press, 1986), and John H. Herz (ed.), *From Dictatorship to Democracy: Coping with the Legacies of Authoritarianism and Totalitarianism* (London: Greenwood Press, 1989).

38. See Philippe C. Schmitter, 'The Consolidation of Democracy and the Choice of Institutions' (typescript, Stanford University, 1991), and Philippe C. Schmitter, 'The Consolidation of Political Democracies: Processes, Rhythms, Sequences and Types' (typescript, Stanford University, 1991).

39. See earlier references to these authors and Giuseppe Di Palma, *To Craft Democracies* (Berkeley, CA: University of California Press, 1990).

40. See earlier references plus Theda Skocpol, *States and Social Revolutions* (Cambridge: Cambridge University Press, 1979).

41. It is, however, worth noting that at least some scholars do recognize the importance of long historical trends. See, for example, Janos *The Politics*, Chirot, *The Origins*, Stephen Fischer-Galati, 'Eastern Europe in the Twentieth Century: "Old wine in new bottles"', in Joseph Held (ed.), *The Columbia History of Eastern Europe in the Twentieth Century* (New York: Columbia University Press, 1992), pp.1–17, and George Schöpflin, 'The Political Traditions of Eastern Europe', *Daedalus*, Winter 1990, pp.55–91.

42. For this position, see Michael Taylor, 'Rationality and Revolutionary Collective Action', in Michael Taylor (ed.), *Rationality and Revolution* (Cambridge: Cambridge University Press, 1988), pp.63–97, and Anthony Giddens, *The Constitution of Society* (Cambridge: Polity Press, 1984). It was, of course also Marx's ambition to embrace structural as well as behavioural elements of social reality.

43. For one side of the argument, see the position of Skocpol (in *States*) who accuses all other theories on social revolutions of 'voluntarism'. Within the Marxist tradition Nicos Poulantzas has maintained a similar position in his *Political Power and Social Classes* (London: NLB, 1973). The alternative 'extreme' can be represented by Jon Elster, *Making Sense of Marx* (Cambridge: Cambridge University Press, 1985), and Jon

Elster, 'Marxism, Functionalism and Game Theory: The Case for Methodological Individualism', *Theory and Society*, Vol.11 (1982), pp.453–82.

44. For an example of this position, see Ernesto Laclau and Chantal Mouffe, *Hegemony and Socialist Strategy* (London: Verso, 1985).
45. Louis Althusser, *Pour Marx* (Paris: Maspéro, 1973), and Poulantzas, *Political*.
46. Charles Tilly, *From Mobilization to Revolution* (New York: Random House, 1978), p.6.
47. Ibid., pp.7 ff, and pp.84 ff.
48. Elemér Hankiss, *East European Alternatives* (Oxford: Oxford University Press, 1990), pp.253–4.
49. For the classic interpretations, see Milovan Djilas, *The New Class* (London: Thames & Hudson, 1957), and Tony Cliff, *State Capitalism in Russia* (London: Pluto Press, 1974). See also François Fejtö, *A History of the People's Democracies* (Harmondsworth: Pelican, 1974), pp.394 ff.
50. See Antonio Carlo, *Politische und Ökonomische Struktur der UdSSR* (Berlin, 1972).
51. Ira Katznelson and Aristide R. Zolberg, *Working Class Formation* (Princeton, NJ: Princeton University Press, 1986), and Wood, *The Retreat*.
52. For the concepts 'regime type' and 'regime form' and more generally for the study of regimes and the transformation of regime types, see Juan Linz, 'An Authoritarian Regime: Spain', in Erik Allardt and Stein Rokkan (eds.), *Mass Politics Studies in Political Sociology* (New York: The Free Press, 1970), pp.251–83, Linz, *The Breakdown*, O'Donnell and Schmitter, *Transition*, and Herz, *From Dictatorship*.
53. See Lene Bøgh Sørensen, 'En sammenlignende analyse af aktørhandlinger og strukturdeterminanter i de igangværende regimeformskift-processer i Sovjetunionen og Ungarn med særligt henblik på en fremdragelse af interaktionerne mellem politisk elite, bureaukrati og befolkning/civilsamfund' (Institute of Political Science, University of Aarhus, 1990).
54. For some new classic attempts to construct broader typologies, see Gabriel Almond and James S. Coleman, *The Politics of the Developing Areas* (Princeton, NJ: Princeton University Press, 1960), and Gabriel Almond and G.B. Powell, *Comparative Politics* (Boston, MA: Little, Brown, 1966).
55. See Linz, 'An Authoritarian', pp.251–83. For the Austrian case Everhard Holtmann, *Zwischen Unterdrückung und Befriedung. Sozialistische Arbeiterbewegung und autoritäres Regime in Österreich* (Munich: Oldenbourg Verlag, 1978), Franz West, *Die Linke im Ständestaat Österreich* (Vienna: Europaverlag, 1978).
56. Martin Broszat, *Der Staat Hitlers* (Munich: Deutscher Taschenbuch Verlag, 1979).
57. For a most competent exposition of prevailing theories, see Held, *Models*.
58. See, for example, David B. Truman, *The Governmental Process* (New York: Alfred A. Knopf, 1951).
59. See Dahl, *A Preface*, Galbraith, *The New*, Lindblom, *Politics*.
60. Antonio Gramsci, *Selections from the Prison Notebooks* (London: Lawrence & Wishart, 1971), pp.210–76.
61. For Hungary, see Hankiss, pp.247 ff.
62. Alexis de Toqueville, *Democracy in America* (New York: Harper & Row, 1966).
63. See Dahl, *A Preface*, C.B. Macpherson, *Democratic Theory: Essays in Retrieval* (Oxford: Clarendon Press, 1973), and Macpherson, *The Life*.
64. Dahl, *Polyarchy*.
65. A thorough documentation is given in Curt Sørensen, *Marxismen og den Sociale orden* (2 vols., Grenå, 1976), and Curt Sørensen, 'Mellem Demokrati og Diktatur' (2 vols, dissertation, Institute of Political Science, University of Aarhus 1992). See also Michael Harrington, *Socialism, Past and Future* (New York: Arcade Publishing, 1989).
66. See, for example, Rudolf Hilferding's programmatic speech at the 1927 conference of the SPD, *Sozialdemokratischer Parteitag 1927 in Kiel*, pp.165–84, and the Linz programme of the Austrian SDAP (*Protokoll des sozialdemokratischen Parteitages 1926 abgehalten in Linz vom 30. Oktober bis 3. November 1926*, pp.168–95).
67. Francis Fukuyama, *The End of History and the Last Man* (New York: Free Press, 1992).

68. See *Agenda 92 for Socio-Economic Reconstruction of Central and Eastern Europe* (Bologna, 1992).
69. See Macpherson, *The Life*, Barber, *Strong* and Hoffman, *State*.
70. For the case of Denmark, see Palle Svensson and Lise Togeby, *Politisk Opbrud. De nye mellemlags græsrodsdeltagelse* (Aarhus: Politika Forlag, 1986).
71. Sørensen, 'Mellem'.
72. The prevailing type of regime in the Baltic, in Eastern Europe and in the Balkans in the period between the two world wars was a right authoritarian or semi-fascist dictatorship. As mentioned, Czechoslovakia under Tomáš Masaryk and Eduard Beneš was the one famous exeption. See Martin Kitchen, *Europe Between the Wars* (London: Longman, 1988), Chapter 5, Hugh Seton-Watson, *Eastern Europe between the Wars* (Cambridge: Cambridge University Press, 1946), Anthony Polonsky, *The Little Dictators: The History of Eastern Europe since 1918* (London: Routledge & Kegan Paul, 1975), Joseph Rothschild, *East Central Europe Between the two World Wars* (Seattle: University of Washington Press, 1974), and Ingemar Glans, 'Östeuropas Fascistiska Förflutna' (unpublished typescript, Institute of Political Science, University of Aarhus). For the Czechoslovakian exception, see Victor S. Mamatey and Radomir Luza (eds.), *A History of the Czechoslovak Republic 1918–1948* (Princeton, NJ: Princeton University Press, 1973).
73. For some classic statements of this thesis see Reinhard Bendix, 'Transformations of Western European Societies since the Eighteenth Century', in Reinhard Bendix, *Nation-Building and Citizenship* (New York: John Wiley & Sons, 1969), pp.66–126, S.M. Lipset, 'The Changing Class Structure of Contemporary European Politics', in Mattei Dogan and Richard Rose (eds.), *European Politics: A Reader* (London, 1971), pp.146–59, Clark Kerr et al., *Industrialism and Industrial Man* (London: Heinemann, 1962), and Ferdynand Zweig, *The Worker in an Affluent Society* (London: Heinemann, 1961). For a more recent re-statement, see Patrick Dunleavy and Brendan O'Leary, *Theories of the State: The Politics of Liberal Democracy* (Basingstoke: Macmillan, 1987), pp.247 ff and pp.288 ff.
74. In the post-war period workers in northern Italy, for example, have been much more militant than workers in the poorer southern Italy. In Denmark some of the most militant trade unions have been the unions of better paid workers, whereas unions of lower-paid workers have often been much more moderate. The history of labour in almost all European countries suggests that workers living under bad social conditions and lacking traditions for union or political organization were certainly not very militant. The story of a 'Golden Age' of tremendous class struggle is a myth. For a discussion of the theses on 'the end of class struggle' and on 'embourgeoisification', see Dick Geary, *European Labour Protest 1848–1939* (London: Croom Helm, 1981), pp.107–33, Wood, *The Retreat*, and Sørensen, *Marxismen*, Vol.2, pp.495 ff.

Part II

Czech and Slovak Trade Unions

MARTIN MYANT

Unions in the past were subservient to the Communist power structure, but under-took a range of important welfare activities. The 'velvet revolution' of November 1989 led to the rapid transformation of the old unions. The new union centre has kept its distance from political involvement. Its strategy centres on negotiation with governments through tripartite structures. Unions have succeeded in retaining many legal rights in exchange for general support for governments' economic policies. There is persistent tension within the tripartite system, but union leader-ships have consistently rejected the alternative of a more militant, oppositionist stand. They have good reason to believe that such an approach would command inadequate public support and would destroy the unions' unity. As a result, trade unions have had little direct influence over political developments.

In our country trade unionists don't behave like trade unionists. There is absolutely no difference between the standpoint of citizens and of trade unionists . . . It is surprising that the great majority of citizens and trade unionists are content to tolerate the fall in living standards and the continual increase in the number of people who are either on the border, or already below the border of the existence minimum.

Richard Falbr, President of the Czech and Slovak Confederation of Trade Unions, *Rudé právo*, 12 February 1993.

One of the main tasks of the Czech and Slovak trade union movement is to defend our road to a democratic and legal state. Democracy however lies not only in the political sphere, but also in the economic and social areas. It therefore must not bring only unemployment, poverty and a continual decline in living standards. The mechanism which guarantees a solution to these problems is tripartite negotiation and dialogue, seeking and finding a consensus from all participating parties.

Roman Kováč, President of the Czech and Slovak Confederation of Trade Unions, at the Fifteenth World Congress of the International Confederation of Free Trade Unions, Caracas, 20 March 1992.

Martin Myant is Reader in the Department of Economics and Management, University of Paisley.

These two quotes from successive Presidents of the ČSKOS, the main force in Czechoslovak trade unionism from early 1990 until the break-up of the federation, broadly sum up the philosohy and dilemmas faced by leading trade unionists after the overthrow of communist power. In Falbr's words, they found themselves 'in a schizophrenic situation', supporting the economic transformation that was taking place, and wanting it to succeed, but also 'not agreeing with certain phenomena'. This schizophrenia was handled by accepting a narrow interpretation of the unions' role, with a concentraiton on negotiations within a tripartite structure. Although some union activists wanted to take a more definite stand against some government policies, that would not have been compatible with the continued loyalty of the membership or the degree of union unity.

This paper aims to show how this new union structure emerged out of the unions of the communist period, how it related to the emerging political parties as it worked out its immediate policies and tried to formulate clear programmatic principles, and how it retained its unity and dominance over rival union bodies. The emphasis on exerting influence almost exclusively through a tripartite structure may have led to favourable results in the development of social policy and employment law, but it left the initiative over all other issues firmly in the hands, first, of the newly-formed broad political movements and then, increasingly, of political parties. In terms of the broad transformation of society, trade unions were rather peripheral. This may change with the break-up of the federation, but the first months of independent Czech and Slovak republics suggest strong continuity from the old federation.

Unions under Communist Power

As in other Eastern European countries, unions had no independent political voice during the years of communist power. Their activities were clearly circumscribed within the existing economic and social system. Their primary role, as defined by law, was to help increase productivity through activities such as socialist competition, the organization of shop floor innovation movements and general commitments to reach plan targets. They were therefore clearly seen as linked to the existing power structure, but that did not mean that they were viewed with unqualified hostility by the bulk of the population. On the contrary, as elsewhere in Eastern Europe, they maintained almost universal membership among employees, thanks largely to a range of activities related to employee welfare.

These included a substantial range of cultural and recreational facilities for employees and their dependents, help to members in financial difficulty and various traditional activities such as presents to long-standing employees and help on the death of a family member. These were financed directly out of a union subscription, set at one per cent of an employee's salary. Unions also administered the Fund for Cultural and Social Consumption, an allocation equivalent to two per cent of the wage bill, which was made available to help employees both individually and collectively. It was even permissible to transfer some of this money directly into the union's account.

Unions were involved in signing collective agreements with management. These, however, were an obligatory part of the plan formulation process and had to contain commitments from the union to help in achieving plan targets alongside commitments from the employer to provide improvements in facilities for employees. Financial and investment resources for this, whether nominally financed by the Fund for Cultural and Social Consumption or directly by the enterprise as an additional contribution, had to be negotiated from higher levels in the planning hierarchy, and collective agreements were therefore dependent on approval from outside the enterprise. In fact, they were often little more than a reformulation of instructions approved at a higher level.[1] These, then, were in no sense voluntary agreements reached between independent partners. In so far as any real bargaining took place within a centrally-planned system, it was over plan targets, and in this both management and employees had a common interest in achieving the best terms from higher levels in the economic hierarchy.[2]

The Origins and Structure of the ČSKOS

Two competing groupings emerged out of the 'velvet revolution' of November 1989. One was based on a group of officials from the old central organization, while the other was based on a coordinating body formed out of the committees – estimated to number around 6,000 – that organized the short protest strikes that helped bring down communist power. Both groups had nominally the same programme – aimed at the creation of unions independent from the power structure – and each set about organizing a congress representing very much the same membership. An organizational split in the whole movement was avoided largely because the nascent new unions wanted to take over the assets of their predecessor.[3] They were therefore happy to seek election within the old constitutional structures and, backed up with demonstrations and strike threats from some big factories, they easily won the majority at a congress of the old trade union organization on 2 March 1990.

They then dissolved the old central body and created the Czech and Slovak Confederation of Trade Unions (Česká a slovenská konfederace odborových svazů – ČSKOS) as a loose coordinating body with representatives elected by individual unions. The centre was to have very limited powers – losing the right to half the revenue from membership dues – and certainly no authority over constituent bodies. Its activities centred around the formulation of a broad strategy, tripartite negotiations with the government and employers, and international contacts. The first two of these are taken up in detail later. International activities centred on the International Confederation of Free Trade Unions which accepted the ČSKOS affiliation on 9 May 1990: this has been judged an area of considerable success with the Czechoslovak unions earning widespread respect for their size, their moderation and their apparent success in creating structures for negotiating with their government.

There was no question of a more aggressive involvement in politics for at least three reasons. The first was that the initiative was clearly with Civic Forum which, even if it lacked a formal mass membership base, enjoyed enormous popular trust and prestige and had a clear and relevant programme: with social issues of less significance in the transition from communist power than in other Eastern European countries, it was the obvious focus for the revolutionary changes that were taking place. The second reason is that unions themselves were undergoing their own transformation, with considerable internal confusion, which prevented them from appearing as a credible leading force in society generally. The third reason is that the logical objective for changes within unions appeared to the newly-emerging activists to centre on 'depoliticization': links with parties were to be broken. The Communist Party was, of course, the only one readily available at the time and a major plank in the new union policy was that its organizations should be expelled from workplaces.

There was some reorganization within unions, with some representing employees in one republic only while others maintained a federal structure alongside separate Czech and Slovak executives. There were changes in some basic organizations with moves away from the 'one workplace one union' concept, which had been appropriate for the old role of unions as stimulators of higher productivity, to allow for separate representation of specific occupational groups. Generally, however, there was considerable organizational continuity from the past.

Up to 40 per cent of representatives and 60 per cent of the apparatus may have been inherited unchanged.[4] Very much the same welfare activities were maintained and appear to have been consuming the bulk of union organizations' budgets and local union officials' time.[5] The Fund for Cultural and Social Consumption has been continued in all state enterprises, and in private firms if unions and management can so agree. Survey evidence on how employees view their unions' activities is sparse, but one opinion poll covering 760 individuals in May 1993 indicated that over 40 per cent – roughly the same as the proportion of union members in the sample – were impressed with the unions' work in organizing culture, sport and children's recreation. Somewhat less were impressed with their work in checking the observance of labour law and few believed unions to have a substantial influence on how their workplaces were run.[6]

Continuity in organization and in activities were reflected in continuity in membership, with the ČSKOS claiming nearly seven million affiliated members at the end of 1990 – 80 per cent of the active labour force – falling to 6.4 million in the spring of 1992, grouped in 67 separate unions. Both of these membership figures may be exaggerated, reflecting an underestimation of the loss of membership, but union density is certainly high. A survey of 940 adults in 1991 showed 50.8 per cent belonging to ČSKOS affiliated unions while 5.2 per cent belonged to other unions and 44 per cent were unorganized. For manual workers and for other employees the percentages in ČSKOS-affiliated unions were 68 per cent and 76 per cent respectively.[7] A later survey suggested that only 25 per cent knew themselves to be in ČSKOS-affiliated unions, while three per cent knew they belonged to other unions and 19 per cent, although union members, knew nothing of their union's affiliation to any centre.[8]

The loss of membership is largely explained by the effects of privatization and structural change in the economy. Membership is very low in the new private sector, based on very small enterprises. Nevertheless, and despite the loss of rights enjoyed before – such as paid holidays and compensation for injuries – surveys do not suggest a high level of discontent among these employees.[9] Some union representatives have complained of encountering an obstructively anti-union stance from some employers and there have been cases of employers trying to insist on contracts of employment that exclude union membership,[10] but reports in the trade-union daily rather suggest that in many new private firms the issue of unionization has simply not arisen.[11] In some cases union organizations in formerly publicly-owned small enterprises willingly used up savings held in the Fund for Cultural and Social Consumption on a spate of foreign holidays, and dissolved their own organizations when a new private owner appeared.

Alternative unions have not become a significant force. The largest rival centre is the Confederation of Art and Culture (Konfederace umění a kultury – KUK) formed on 27 February 1990 with 22 affiliated organizations and a membership between 100,000 and 200,000. Its leadership claims to have a 'right' orientation, warning against 'social demogogy' and opposing minimum wages which, it argues, endanger jobs in culture. Its stated objective is to prevent preferential treatment for industry, but wage levels of its members are probably around 45 per cent below the average in industry. Despite a certain amount of rhetoric, KUK has cooperated on many issues with the ČSKOS.

This is not true of the Trade Union Association of Bohemia, Moravia and Slovakia, formed on 4 May 1991 and claiming 50,000 members by November of that year. The initiative came from Karel Hyneš, the former official who led the unsuccessful attempt to retain some continuity with the old unions until his defeat at the congress in March 1990. The political profile of the body was clear from the start as it launched strong attacks on the ČSKOS for abandoning powers enjoyed by trade unions before November 1989. Despite its name, its membership was largely restricted to the Czech republic.

The only other significant unions are an independent grouping that represents some managerial and professional employees and a number of small unions that organize very specific occupations. Examples include train drivers whose specific position has meant that they believe they can fend for themselves rather than coordinating with other employees. These latter unions tend to be well organized, disciplined and in a position to take highly disruptive action.

Towards the Tripartite

The key to success in uniting the great bulk of unions must have been the perception, at least among their leading activists and officials, that the ČSKOS strategy had merit. The core of this, in line with ILO practice, was the creation and defence of tripartite structures. These were seen as a vehicle through which the unions could influence government policy in exchange for acceptance of an end to the secure employment conditions of the past and of some discomfort during the transition to a market system. It was made very clear from the start that there was no desire to defend the alleged gains of socialism. 'Those were not gains', responded the first ČSKOS Chairman Igor Pleskot, 'they were inventions to bamboozle the people'.[12]

There is, however, a major ambiguity over the possible role for unions – and this will apply particularly clearly in a society experiencing a major transformation – that can be derived from ILO documents. Recommendation No.113, issued in 1960 and concerning consultation at the industry and national level, refers to the desirability of 'the public authorities' seeking 'the views, advice and assistance . . . of employers' and workers' organizations' both on employment related matters and on 'the elaboration and implementation of plans of economic and social development'. The former of these areas was regarded by the ČSKOS as the core of its activities, and it even threatened a general strike in April 1990 when it seemed that it might not be consulted at all. Unions were undoubtedly in too disorganized a state to have carried out their threat, and the government anyway had no objection to consultations once the shape of their potential partner had been clarified.

It was, however, a different story with the wider area of economic development in general. Unions played no role in the major debate on the strategy for economic transformation which culminated in a vote in the federal parliament in September 1990.[13] They were not explicitly consulted nor, it can be added, were they able to formulate any ideas that amounted to a substantial contribution. In effect, they were settling, at best, into a narrower interpretation of their role in the evolving political structure.

Their peripheral role in this major debate may have helped to jog leading officials into realizing that they were in danger of being ignored even during the discussion of important issues of social legislation.[14] Criticisms mounted within the ČSKOS that the leadership had failed to formulate a programme, failed to overcome internal organizational weaknesses and was degenerating into empty threats and wild rhetoric. A major target was the outspoken Igor Pleskot, who was accusing the government of an anti-union bias when, it seemed to others, he could have been seeking the means to exploit scope for a constructive dialogue. The urgency of the situation seems to have been appreciated on all sides and the different unions were finally able to bury their differences, and their hesitancy, and to agree on a programmatic statement entitled *A Market Society Yes, but a Social Market Society*.[15] Pleskot was then replaced by the more mild-mannered Roman Kováč.

The basic argument in the new programme was that the difficult period ahead would generate problems best settled by negotiation and agreement without 'grandiose gestures and empty phrases'. That meant creating a tripartite 'council of mutual agreement' which would sign 'general agreements'. These would include acceptance of the rights of trade union activity and of the right to strike. The government was to agree to solve problems of unemployment, and associated regional and sectoral issues. There was to be automatic indexation of pensions and of wages and an agreement was to be reached on how this should be done for 1991.

Some in the federal government, such as the free market enthusiast and Finance Minister Václav Klaus, were initially sceptical of the value of such an approach. He certainly had no interest in the kind of interventionist economic policies that could be implied by the unions' programme. The dominant position, however, had always been compatible with the unions' approach. That was certainly the view of Prime Minister Marian Čalfa and Minister of Labour Petr Miller, a former active dissident who later joined the Social Democrats. Moreover, this position was fully consistent with the Civic Forum's initial policy statements on the need for social justice and an acceptable guaranteed minimum for all. It was also consistent with the aim of creating a modern society fit to join the 'mainstream' of European life, and even with IMF advice that placed considerable emphasis on the maintenance of social peace. Moreover, union leaders were showing no will to oppose government policies. They echoed the fears of Klaus and others that 'social demagogues' would try to use employee discontent to delay economic reform. The solution, they argued, was to find an agreed legal framework as the best way to limit the scope of likely social conflicts.

The Council of Economic and Social Accord was formed on 30 October 1990 with a union side represented by six from the ČSKOS and one from KUK. There were seven federal government representatives and seven from the employers' side, although their presence was little more than a token gesture as a powerful employers' organization had yet to emerge. Similar tripartite bodies were formed at the Czech and Slovak levels.

The first task was to settle the issues of trade union recognition and powers. As with many other topics that came before tripartite bodies, the road to agreement was not easy, but did prove to be possible after some compromises from both government and unions. The controversy centred on three issues over which unions were consulted, but their views were challenged either by the government, or during debates in parliament. These concerned laws on collective bargaining and on the right to strike and a number of changes to the Labour Code – originally approved in 1965 and not fundamentally amended in the ensuing years – the most important of which concerned the right to participate in management.

The government's initial draft for a new law on strikes was opposed by union leaders in private discussions.[16] In June 1990 they went public, with Pleskot describing clauses ruling out 'political strikes' as 'bizarre and ridiculous'. As he enthusiastically pointed out, 'the current governments emerged out of a general strike with a clearly political character'.[17] Union opposition was strong enough to persuade parliament not to pass the law and the legal position in relation to strikes remains to be clarified.

The issue of participation centred around formal powers from the past including the right to veto dismissals. These powers had not been used when most needed, for example to defend opposition activists against political victimisation, because union organizations had been subservient to the existing power structure. Their indefinite continuation, however, was hardly compatible with a market economy. Nevertheless, the union view was that strong safeguards were required at least for a transitional period. Controversy was to focus on a clause in the general preamble to the Labour Code which gave 'workers' the right and duty 'to participate in the development, management and control of activities' of the employing organization. The organization was in turn obliged to 'create and improve the conditions to facilitate a continual broadening of that participation'.

Klaus persuaded the government to insist on the deletion of this clause – which he condemned as a 'Bolshevik practice' – at a government meeting on 1 November, with union representatives in attendance. The ČSKOS called on Parliamentary deputies to stick to an earlier government version which had allowed some participation in management, and expressed the determination to demonstrate 'the power of the unions'.[18] A strike alert was declared on 27 November, meaning that preparations were under way for a general strike. A compromise was finally reached, and the amendments to the Labour Code passed on 5 December gave employees the right of access to information about 'basic questions of the organization's development' and about its 'economic results and perspective'. They were also given some control over dismissals as they had to be consulted first and this helped allay their fears that the need for redundancies could be used by management to remove quietly those people they found troublesome.

Some on the union side believed they had suffered a defeat while others, recognizing that their nominal powers from the past could not be maintained, saw the outcome as their 'greatest victory'.[19] They were probably right to be satisfied as they had succeeded in influencing parliamentary deputies, despite a lack of previous experience of political involvement, and the threat of a general strike had not been completely dismissed. Above all, they could be satisfied with the emerging legal framework. Far from reflecting a neo-liberal or monetarist agenda, the changes were fully consistent with a firm commitment to the kind of 'social market economy' that Klaus frequently claimed to abhor.[20] The key points in ensuring this were the law on collective bargaining, passed on 4 December 1990, the continuation with often only minimal revisions of most existing labour law – as confirmed by the acceptance of much of the existing Labour Code – and a Charter of Human Rights approved by the federal parliament on 8 February 1991.

The new law on collective bargaining removed any specification of what was to be included, and the two sides were no longer obliged to reach an agreement. There were, however, general limits specified including both the minimum wages for particular jobs and some maxima in relation to conditions and benefits for employees. In practice, collective agreements have frequently contained substantial repetitions of existing laws, with only minor points of clarification that relate to specific local conditions. Generally, the impression is that any changes have not meant a serious weakening of protection enjoyed by employees.

Indeed, some protections have been increased by an important paragraph in the Charter of Human Rights which states that conventions of international organizations approved by the Czechoslovak government take automatic precedence over all existing Czechoslovak law. Thus, for example, ILO conventions guaranteeing the right to strike within constraints set by the law could be used by unions to insist that all strikes were legal unless ruled out specifically by law.[21]

Moreover, a number of ILO conventions that had been accepted but not even published by previous Czechoslovak governments now had the force of law. These included conventions on collective bargaining, on outlawing discrimination on grounds of sex, religion or political conviction, and on forced labour, which was found to be in conflict slightly with existing labour law. Some new laws were introduced during 1991 and 1992, with the guiding philosophy still the notion of an employee protected by ILO conventions and active trade unions.

Revisions to existing laws often did no more than take account of institutional changes, while still continuing with much of the strong protection for employees of the past. Thus there were still clear limits on the length of the working day and week, set at 8 and 43 hours respectively. The terms for overtime, work during public holidays and over abnormal shift patterns had to be negotiated with the appropriate trade union. The same applied to the procedure for redundancy, which was essentially similar to a law introduced as long ago as 1970.[22] The requirement to reach an agreement with a trade union might have been meaningless in the past when unions enjoyed less genuine independence, but after 1989 it could become a real constraint on management. Moreover, it meant that any attempts to impose certain kinds of flexibility, most noteably short-time working, were completely ruled out where unions did not exist. Thus the legal framework is in place for a structure of legally binding agreements giving unions considerable power over conditions of employment.

Tensions in the Tripartite

The 'General Agreement' was signed on 28 January 1991:[23] it was seen as the first great success of the new Council for Economic and Social Accord. Last minute compromises enabled all sides – governments, unions and employers' organisations – to sign a binding agreement for

1991. There was recognition of the need for an 'active' employment policy and for index-linked unemployment benefit starting at 65 per cent, falling to 60 per cent of the former wage.

A minimum wage was set at a level equivalent to 60 per cent of the average industrial wage, with almost 100 per cent indexation, as part of a recognition that the weakest in society should not be asked to bear an impossible burden. Redundancy money was to be paid equivalent to twice the former monthly wage, a figure unlikely to deter many managements from necessary reorganization. A complex indexation system was worked out to prevent the drop in real wages from exceeding 12 per cent in the first quarter. In no subsequent quarter were they to fall more than 10 per cent behind the December 1990 level.

In one respect the General Agreement and tripartite system represented a clear gain for the unions, as they were consulted in regular meetings over issues directly related both to employment relations and, with a few exceptions, to the position of the weakest in society. There was, however, a continual tension within the tripartite system. The union side regarded it as the peak of their activity, took all the negotiations very seriously and hoped the agreements reached would be binding on all participants. The government, it quickly became clear, could not regard the General Agreement as sacrosanct. To them it was a general statement of political intent rather than a binding document. They were under the most obvious pressure to break the letter of the General Agreement when it conflicted with other objectives of economic policy, but the sheer weight of legislative work also led to delays over new laws requested from the trade union side.

The first area of serious dispute was the indexation of minimum wages. A higher rate of inflation at the start of 1991 and a larger drop in living standards than expected meant that strict adherence to the letter of the General Agreement would have increased coverage from 13 per cent of the labour force in February to 20 per cent at the end of March. This, the government estimated, would have led to a continuation of inflationary pressures. It therefore exercised its right to reopen discussions. In July 1991, when it was clear that no agreement could be reached, it unilaterally abandoned the clause on minimum wage indexation. The unions then withdrew in protest from federal level talks, but were soon back trying to press their views on other issues of concern.

A second area of dispute, pinpointed by the ČSKOS in summing up the results of the first six months of the General Agreement, related to the absence of a promised employment policy with defined aims, and of promised sectoral policies for energy, fuel, steel, transport and communications.[24] Surveying the position in a way that could put pressure on the government by highlighting areas of discontent, the ČSKOS suggested that they had made concessions on living standards, had failed to persuade the government to deliver a more interventionist industrial policy and had had to fight to be consulted even on laws that affected them most directly. At this stage, however, there was little sign of an upsurge of militancy.

A third and potentially the most serious source of conflict related to a fall in real wages substantially beyond that foreseen in the indexation agreement. Money wages grew by only 16.4 per cent in 1991, against a 53.6 per cent increase in retail prices. Some sectors did reasonably well, with finance and insurance showing money wage increases of 58 and 37 per cent respectively, but several branches of industry failed even to record a ten per cent growth in money wages. This, then, was an issue that directly affected the majority of employees.

Strictly speaking, the government had not broken its word as it had only agreed to the rules for a wage control system that set maximum pay increases. State enterprises had in most cases been unable to pay anything like that level owing to severe financial difficulties. Nevertheless, the unions could argue that many enterprises had signed collective agreements guaranteeing payment of the increases specified in the General Agreement.

The precise legalistic arguments were not important. The real point was that by the autumn of 1991 criticism of the government could be backed up with a threat of mass action coming from the metal workers' union. A one-hour warning strike was organized in central Slovakia on 25 November 1991, with claims of full participation from practically all organizations of that union, plus displays of solidarity from other sectors.

This action was not motivated purely by discontent over the government's failure to honour its agreements. It was part of a more general 'cry for help' from a group of employees. Press reports at the time leave little doubt that participants were concerned in very general terms with declining living standards and at the loss of past job security. As one researcher put it, the strikes were understood by some as an attempt to strengthen the unions' hand within the tripartite system, but many others saw their action as 'a means of self-defence against worsening living conditions'. In this sense, they could be seen as 'the first sign of the formation of a specific employee interest'.[25] Union demands within the tripartite were thus a means to give an ordered focus to a more general working class discontent. To a certain extent they could be judged to have failed, since – as the later development of Slovak politics was to demonstrate – much of the discontent was focused onto distrust towards the federal authorities, and onto political support for Vladimír Mečiar's Movement for a Democratic Slovakia.

This was hardly surprising, as militancy was geographically very limited. Strike action was restricted to a particular region in which discontent had been bubbling for some time. Central Slovakia, with a heavy dependence on the rapidly declining armaments and engineering industries, had no prospects of major new job creation. The metal workers' leadership in the Czech republic could not have expected such solid backing even for a short strike and therefore contented itself with 'different methods' of pressing its worries on the government.

Nevertheless, the government was impressed enough to accede to union pressure, at least to the extent of making an apology for not having kept to all aspects of the General Agreement. Statements by leading ministers also suggested a recognition that the decline in living standards had to be halted. The government was, however, not impressed enough to make major concessions to union demands when negotiating the 1992 General Agreement. As with the 1991 agreement, this embodied an acceptance from the union side that transition to a market economy requires sacrifices alongside a commitment from the government to modernize employment law, with clear steps towards the incorporation of elements of the European Social Charter.

The main dispute during negotiations concerned the government's insistence on the continued need for a wage control policy. Opposition to this was one of the few economic policy issues around which all unions could unite. Although not many employees stood to gain very much, no group felt threatened by the prospect of an end to wage controls. Unions backed up their case by arguing that living standards had fallen enough already, that controlling wages conflicted with the logic of the market, that there was no real threat of a relaxation leading to higher inflation, and that the cuts in living standards had themselves been a major factor contributing to economic depression.

Their arguments had considerable merit and the employers broadly supported the union position. Nevertheless, they merely succeeded in causing a considerable delay with the agreement at federal level signed only on 30 April. Moreover, the final document was much vaguer than the 1991 agreement, with the only real government commitment in general economic policy being a firm reiteration of the need for an active employment policy. This time the government wisely avoided any more precise commitments and it was free to work out a wage control policy on its own.

Union leaders were complaining again at the end of 1992 that the government had failed to keep to its side of the agreement. Promised legal changes had been delayed in the legislative rush to achieve the destruction of the federation. There was, however, no repeat of the open conflicts of late 1991. Thus the tripartite system lasted out the federation and continued into the successor republics. The next section aims to place that in the context of the developing industrial relations and political situations, thereby setting the scene for a discussion of the trade unions' attempts to formulate more general programmatic principles.

The Industrial Relations Context

Employee protests in the period prior to the break-up of the federation can be grouped into four main categories. The first were essentially political protests associated with destroying the communist power structure. The last significant example was a ten-minute strike on 11 April 1990, organized on the initiative of the Civic Forum group in a Prague factory around the demand for the confiscation of the Communist Party's property. These protests had significance for the development of trade unions primarily in so far as they confirmed that unions could never aspire to become the leading force in the velvet revolution. Moreover, they helped reinforce the pressures dissuading union leaders from taking any stand that embodied even a hint of opposition to the general direction of political and economic changes.

The second category of protests comprises 'cries for help' from manufacturing enterprises facing financial catastrophe. A small number of strikes have taken place from mid-1990 onwards in large Czech and Slovak engineering enterprises, generally around the demand for govern-ment assistance to prevent immediate financial catastrophe. In these cases, the conflict is clearly not between employees and management. Indeed, the latter made very similar protests, albeit using different methods. Generally speaking, and despite the government's rhetoric about the need for toughness, means have been found to delay bank-ruptcies and factory closures.

These conflicts can be seen to some extent as a continuation of the bargaining for resources from the centre that characterized the plan formulation process before November 1989. They have served to confirm that the principal means for unions to protect their members involve pressure on government bodies rather than negotiations with employers. They might have led into attempts to work out an alternative economic programme, with a strong emphasis on an active industrial policy. That course would have brought unions closer to the Social Democrats and other opposition parties. It has, however, not been pursued, not least because, as is shown in the next section, discontent in workplaces has not been powerful enough to give such a strategy a guarantee of strong support among union members.

The third category of conflicts relates to public transport, which has been hit by a reduction in subsidies – once accounting for 10 per cent of costs – rising cost of fuels and a general reduction in use due to the economic difficulties accompanying the government's transition strategy. Prices, however, have still been controlled by a government frightened of allowing a higher rate of inflation. Financial difficulties, pointing to the need for sudden and dramatic reductions in services, led to a one-day strike by 15,000 Czech rural bus drivers on 10 February 1992, the biggest case of strike action in the Czech republic prior to the break-up of the federation. The federal government conceded that it had made mistakes and agreed to 'look into' the demand for a coherent transport policy. The threat of a one-day strike by all transport workers was withdrawn, but the problems faced by the sector have not been resolved. Tension continued into 1993, especially between railway workers and both the Czech and Slovak governments.

This conflict, then, like those in enterprises facing financial catastrophe, is not between employees and managers. It is between all those who work in the sector, with management often privately supporting the unions' stand, and the government. That, however, has not necessarily strengthened the unions' position. The ČSKOS, the Social Democrats and the Communists supported the bus drivers' strike, but government ministers and political parties of the right and centre were extremely hostile. There was talk of legal sanctions although, for reasons already explained, a court could have accepted that the strike was within the law.

Opinion polls showed a clear majority willing to accept that the strike had been a means of drawing attention to unresolved problems in the transport sector. Roughly half of those with an opinion, however, saw the strike as an ill-considered act causing substantial harm. Nearly a third saw it as a politically-motivated act behind which stood the 'old structures', meaning former Communist officials. Thus the lesson of the bus drivers strike was that pressing political demands through industrial action carried the clear danger of political isolation. Trade union leaders, particularly in sectors not directly related to transport, could reasonably have feared that they were jeopardizing the gains achievable by consensus in the tripartite structures.

The fourth category of employee protest, which could be seen as a genuinely 'new' form of industrial dispute, has occurred in those few enterprises that have the resources to pay higher wages, or in those cases where employees feel their bargaining position to be genuinely strong. These, then, are not acts of desperation or despair. They are cases of a genuine trial of strength between management and employees. They typically do focus on collective agreements. The most obvious cases have occurred in the Škoda car factory, now merged into the Volkswagen group and producing cars at far lower costs than would be possible in Western Europe. Wages are among the highest for Czech manual workers, but unions complain of an intransigent management that is unwilling to satisfy their aspiration for Western European rates of pay.[26] Another, slightly different, example is the Prague underground, where employees' awareness of a serious labour shortage in the capital has strengthened their efforts to secure higher wages.

Generally, however, industrial relations *within* enterprises have been as peaceful as before November 1989. The continuity in labour law has been matched by a very gradual evolution in the wage structure within enterprises, which contrasts markedly with attempts at a rapid transition to a market system in the areas of price liberalization and privatization. The old wage structure was based on the classification of jobs into a series of categories depending in theory on the 'quantity' and 'quality' of work required. The rules had been evolved over the years through modification within enterprises and through government decrees. The effect of this had been to create a pattern of wage differentials that ensured balance between supply and demand for particular occupations and broad harmony between groups that worked beside each other.

New rules were finally introduced on 1 January 1992. As many as 292 laws and directives relating to enterprises were swept aside, only to be replaced by centrally-determined pay scales – amounting largely to a simplification and systematization of what had applied in the past – specifying 12 broad categories.[27] These, however, set minimum wage levels only. Higher figures could be negotiated in collective agreements. Yet it is fairly clear that wage negotiations have amounted to no more than discussions of across-the-board percentage increases. The existing pattern of differentials within an enterprise has largely been maintained.

Three points can be made on this evolving system of industrial relations. The first is that the focus has not yet shifted to relations between employees and the immediate employer. The second is that open conflicts, remarkably few of which have led to significant strike action, relate to the very specific situation of an economy and society in transition. This is not yet a full market system in any meaningful sense. Indeed, there are still strong similarities with the bargaining over subsidies and special treatment that characterized central planning. The major difference is that they have now come into the open and that unions have been able to play a role as an independent force.

The third point relates to the extent to which industrial relations depended on the political situation. Unions' efforts were geared towards influencing government rather than individual employers and that met a willing response from the Civic Forum during its early development. There were, however, potential pressures for change once Civic Forum broke up. During 1991 the initiative shifted steadily into the hands of a confident right wing, centring on Václav Klaus's Civic Democratic Party. Its stated aim was the elimination of socialism 'in all its forms'.

Nevertheless, there was no strong pressure for a firmly 'anti-union' approach in policy-making. A more vigorous approach might have been consistent with the neo-liberal thinking of the Czech right wing, which ought to abhor any regulation of the labour market. It was, however, constrained by the need to maintain a coalition with partners that prided themselves in taking a less 'dogmatic' position. Moreover, Klaus's conception of economic transition was based on the assumption that privatization had to precede any changes within enterprises. It was therefore perfectly consistent to postpone any other policy measures that might encourage opposition during the transition. Moreover, as the next section will demonstrate, there was very little reason for Klaus to regard unions as a major obstacle to his immediate objectives. They faced enormous difficulties in formulating coherent programmatic principles, but they were not in general opponents of his strategy for economic reform and they were not firm allies of a left-wing opposition. That was, at least for the time being, too weak and lacking in self-confidence to provide them with an adequate channel for influencing political developments.

Towards a Programme

On 30 October 1991 the ČSKOS accepted a new programmatic document which contained both long-term objectives and a list of targets for the period up to the June 1992 elections. Ultimate objectives included a 40-hour week, entitlement to five weeks holiday, and full employment. The great ambiguity, of course, was over whether this meant opposition to, or support for the government's reform strategy. There was a careful reference to 'a socially and ecologically orientated market economy', but that could even be compatible with Klaus's view that the market was the best basis for solving social and ecological problems. It could certainly mean creating the market part first and then seeing to the 'social' element later. Indeed, there was a recognition of the need for 'sacrifices', albeit with the usual caveat that they should not be borne 'only' by 'those strata that are dependent on wage labour'.

There were three vaguely identifiable trends within the ČSKOS leadership over what this programme might mean. These can be identified in terms of the 'schizophrenia' referred to in the quote from Richard Falbr at the start of the article. Each was a different solution to the dilemma of representing the desire to support changes in the economic system, while simultaneously maintaining some distance from its social effects.

Vladimír Petrus, chairman of the union federation for the Czech republic, clearly believed that the government's reform strategy was the key to the prosperity that could make the unions' long-term objectives realizable. It was only conceivable, he believed, 'where a conservative and liberal government is in power', adding that 'in view of the state of the Czech economy, I know of no left road which would be able to lead out of the marasmus'.[28] To him, then, the 'social' element could be no more than a cautious supplement to vigorous, market-oriented reform. After the 1992 elections he even expressed strong support for the new Czech government's commitment to further accelerate reform, suggesting that that was the best basis for overcoming social problems.[29]

Although this was probably not the dominant view among top union officials, it had considerable backing at lower levels. A unique survey of activists in the Czech textile industry in early 1992[30] showed only nine per cent seeing themselves as standing politically on the left. Although 77 per cent were 'dissatisfied' with political developments, 84 per cent expressed the conviction that radical economic reform was essential. Indeed, nearly 40 per cent of those intending to vote supported Václav Klaus's Civic Democratic Party, which was clearly identified with the view that reform should be accelerated without too much concern for immediate social consequences.[31]

These attitudes were reflected at grass roots level with a quite remarkable willingness to accept the need for restructuring and redundancies. It can be added that one of the arguments used against wage control was that it 'conserves over-employment'.[32] The pattern of activity from union organizations suggests no strong feeling for protests against managements that seemed to be trying to find a viable future for their enterprises. Thus, to take one example from many, a union leader in the hard-hit textile industry could warn; 'we must see it objectively, the structure of industry cannot remain as we have inherited it'. Unions therefore sought alleviation of social problems, for example with early retirement but, as one leading activist announced in an obvious allusion to farmers' more vigorous methods of protest,[33] 'women will not be blocking Wenceslas Square with sewing machines'.[34]

This compliant attitude was not universal, but it was probably typical throughout the Czech republic. Job losses in many enterprises were relatively painless for much of the Czech population as foreigners, pensioners and other peripheral groups suffered first. In the bigger cities alternative jobs were frequently available and there were clear signs of recovery in 1992, fuelled by a massive boom in tourism, with unemployment barely above two per cent for the whole republic by the end of the year. Prague actually suffered from a labour shortage. In Slovakia the level of unemployment was around ten per cent.

Alongside a widespread acceptance that the government's reform strategy had to be accepted, there were even cases of unions or of some activists clearly siding with the government against ČSKOS positions, when that seemed best to serve their sectional interests. Thus some whole unions and some other basic organizations – such as health workers and the Prague underground, whose employees were very vociferous in pressing their sectional demands – complained that the legal obligation to pay a minimum wage was draining resources that could go to stabilizing the more skilled sections of the labour force.[35]

The second, and clearly opposing trend can be represented by Stanislav Hošek from the miners' union who was for a time a Vice President of the ČSKOS and stood as a Social Democrat candidate in North Moravia in the 1992 elections. He accused the government of treating social policy 'as a mere supplement to economic reform', while he thought there should be a clear unity 'between the economic and the social'.[36] He later explanded this into a broad critique of the whole ČSKOS strategy.[37] It had, he claimed, been a mistake from the start to declare the unions to be non-political. It had also been a mistake never to agree on 'limits' to the transformation, in the sense of its costs in terms of inflation, unemployment and the like. That had limited their ability to offer new ideas and left the leadership able only to respond to what members were suggesting. The alternative, he argued, was for a more actively political role. That would not have meant an exclusive link with any one party, but Hošek made it clear that the policies of the clearly right-wing Civic Democratic Party should be opposed while unions should try to influence politics through the parties of the left and the centre. He therefore wanted to resolve Falbr's dilemma by following the leading economists associated with the Social Democrats in searching for an alternative economic strategy that would avoid the unpleasant social costs.

This approach, however, did not command unanimous support even among miners. Although they appeared to be the most militant section of the workforce, they have been aggressive only in pressing their own sectional demands. Discontent throughout 1990, initially vaguely directed at high pay for members of parliament, uncertainties in the energy sector and other general issues, was gradually focused onto some very specific points. In particular, miners wanted the government to cover the costs of earlier retirement and compensation for poor health.

By November 1990 there was a strike alert in the country's biggest coal field and the possibility of a national miners' strike could not have been completely dismissed. This was an important factor strengthening the hand of unions generally during negotiations at the time over trade union powers.

In late 1992 the central issue was a plan for transition to market conditions and rationalization of the industry worked out by Thyl Gheyselinck, the Belgian adviser to the Czech Minister for Economic Development. A national demonstration in Prague on 11 November, with participation from leading miners' representatives from four Western European countries, led to some softening of the government's stance. The Czech miners, it must be added, had never doubted that 'unprofitable' mines would have to close. Their claim was that this should be supplemented with help for the creation of alternative employment, which they believed to be the usual practice in Western Europe.

At the same time, many miners helped the Civic Democratic Party to win 40 per cent of the votes in the 1992 elections in North Moravia where Klaus headed the list of candidates. Miners had, in fact, done relatively well in economic terms with wages in 1992 still 33 per cent above the industrial average – compared with 47 per cent in 1989 – and little fall in employment instead of the redundancies feared and predicted. Militancy has therefore largely been restricted to sectional demands amounting to corrections to the government's reform strategy, rather than the formulation of a complete alternative.

Towards the end of 1991, when unions were trying to put the greatest pressure on the government, a number of other leading figures went at least some way towards distancing themselves from the government's reform strategy. Not surprisingly, the metal workers were particularly articulate. Chairman Alojz Engliš presented a critique of government policy that had much in common with the position of the Social Democrats and of other opposition parties.[38] The crucial point was his identification of the drop in real wages as itself the cause of economic depression, and therefore in turn of a further downward spiral in living standards. That opened the possibility of proposing an alternative reform strategy which did not require such heavy sacrifices from the population. The details of the economic arguments are not essential here.[39] The point is that, even if other trade union leaders held a similar position, they lacked the power to mobilize their members around a confrontation that could force such a major change in government thinking.

The third and dominant trend was therefore always more conciliatory. Roman Kováč, the Slovak gynaecologist who led the ČSKOS for 18 months, contented himself with extraordinarily general statements, suggesting 'some reservations' over government policies. He was, however, adamantly opposed to unions adopting a specific political orientation, as his key immediate objective was to convince the government and employers of the benefits of the tripartite system as a means to reach consensus and preserve social peace. His term of office ended in March 1992 and he toyed with standing for the federal parliament for the Christian Democratic Movement, the main force in the Slovak government at the time. He finally decided to stand under the banner of Vladimír Mečiar's Movement for a Democratic Slovakia, believing that its great political breadth would provide a good environment for developing a trade union perspective.[40] After the break-up of the federation he narrowly missed election by the Slovak parliament to the presidency of the new republic. Instead, he remained a Deputy Prime Minister.

His successor in the union post was Richard Falbr, a lawyer and member of the Social Democratic Party who led the union for public service employees. He too insisted that 'unions must remain above parties'[41] and warned frequently of the great difficulties in holding the different unions together. During his time in office there were some possible attempts to adopt a more active stand on major political issues, but they were followed by hasty retreats into the accepted 'non-political' stance.

Indeed, even the metal workers union, which seemed at times to be edging towards a critique of government policies, at other times beat the familiar retreat into acceptance of the general course of development. Jan Uhlíř at one point warned against unrealistic hopes aroused by promises that privatization 'would solve everything at once'.[42] Particularly the untried and innovative voucher method, which had been greeted with considerable scepticism by many professional economists during the debate on the strategy for economic reform in the summer of 1990, was viewed with suspicion. The ground was being set, Uhlíř argued, for 'a further great disappointment'· as 'the period of the greatest social uncertainty will set in precisely after privatization'.

As it became clear that voucher privatization,[43] contrary to some initial expectations, was extremely popular, these highly plausible doubts began to fade. Union complaints were limited to a vague and uncoordinated discontent that consultation on individual enterprise privatization plans had often proved meaningless. As Uhlíř, a Civic Movement member, acknowledged 'I am not an opponent . . . I have bought a voucher book'.[44] Indeed, it was more usual throughout 1992 and 1993 to hear complaints that privatization was proceeding too slowly.

In mid-1992 an assessment was produced of the economic results of the first half year which cast doubts on government claims that recovery was already under way.[45] This could have been the prelude to an attempt to formulate a serious critique of government strategy, but there followed hasty reassurances that this was no more than a general document reflecting the attempted 'professionalization' of unions. A report was produced in July outlining the possible effects of the break-up of the federation which warned of serious dangers for both successor republics.[46] The union leadership hesitated over even discussing the document, presumably fearing that they would be accused of siding with opposition parties, but a copy was leaked to the press. An attempt was then even made to survey opinion among union members, with the obvious possibility that public opinion could have been mobilized to support the federation.

No such effort was made. Survey returns showed 60 per cent of union members in the Czech Republic and 48 per cent in Slovakia resigned to separation and Falbr indicated that there was not a strong enough feeling to persuade the union leadership to do anything.[47] The union representing the agricultural and food industry workers in the Czech republic had even threatened to pull out of the ČSKOS if its leading officials 'meddled in politics'. Strictly speaking, its affiliation was already questionable, as it had failed to pay the necessary contribution.[48]

Nevertheless, Petrus gave a firm reassurance that unions would try neither to accelerate nor to prevent the break-up, as either of those courses would amount to 'a denial of the results of the elections'. That would not have been strictly true, as the election results gave no mandate for the destruction of the federation and opinion polls consistently showed a majority in both republics preferring a continuation of some form of common state. It is remarkable that the most vocal concern in the trade-union movement at the time of the break-up of the Czechoslovak federation was that they should not take any stand at all.

After Separation

The break-up of the federation was largely the consequence of a divergence in political developments in the two republics. This has become even clearer during 1993, with Czech politics dominated more definitely than ever by a confident right wing. The implications for trade unions are that they can expect to move steadily towards a role and position in society more in line with Western European practice. The open question is whether the Czech government will succeed in imposing a 'British' system, as Petrus has several times claimed is its objective, or whether employees will continue to enjoy protections associated with

ILO conventions, the European Social Charter, and considerable continuity from the communist past.

Changes in the Civic Democratic Party's approach have been the result partly of its liberation from the need to compromise with other political forces that essentially agreed with the unions' notion of a social market economy. Thus it has proposed revisions to the Labour Code which would reduce the extent of the unions' guaranteed role in protecting employees: private employers will be allowed to make more decisions without consultation and without agreement from unions and will therefore have less need to recognize unions at all. There have also been ideas for downgrading the tripartite meetings with the assumption that government can step aside leaving just unions and employers to negotiate with each other. Several on the union side have always rather naively assumed that this would eventually happen, once independent employers had emerged and once the job of minimizing the social costs of transformation had somehow been completed. The implication now, however, would be to eliminate the unions' automatic channel for pressing demands on at least some aspects of social and economic policy.

Economic developments that fit with this trend include the ending of wage control at the start of 1993,[49] shifting the focus of wage determination more clearly into collective agreements, and the progress of privatization. Although this is taking considerably longer than Klaus and his political allies originally assumed, the time will come when large numbers of privately-owned firms can bargain seriously with unions. Some may decide to take a more active role in changing work practices, wage differentials and payment systems. That could then encourage a further clarification of the party structure, with the Civic Democratic Party becoming associated with such aggressive managements, and pressing for the kind of changes in labour law that they would appreciate. The Social Democrats could be expected to emerge as the obvious ally of unions seeking to retain strong powers to protect employee interests. That, however, would only be the unions' choice if they were so firmly shunned by parties on the right that they could see no other option to committing themselves in a way that would risk a loss of support from among their own members.

The main political difference in Slovakia is that there is no right-wing force with a natural hostility to unions and labour market regulation. The economic changes, however, are fairly similar, with the difference that the problems facing the government are considerably more severe. Unions have therefore been actively protesting against falling living standards and worsening conditions for employees as a whole. The combined effect of these two factors is likely to slow the transformation of trade unions towards more familiar 'Western European' practices. Indeed, in view of the potential instability within the ruling Movement for a Democratic Slovakia, it is even conceivable that unions might at some point play a still more actively political role. In the absence of such a clearly defined party structure as in the Czech Republic, they may still have an important part to play in deciding who is able to govern the country and hence in shaping the party structure of the future.

NOTES

1. It is, of course, also far from clear how far the workforce was involved in the process of negotiating these agreements. Perhaps of even greater significance, when there was a chance of active participation, they may often have had little operational meaning. 'Difficult' issues were often deliberately omitted from formal agreements, so that union representatives could concede a worsening of conditions at a later date when control 'from below' was less of a worry. The issue is covered in Bohuslav Kahle, 'Kolektivní smlouvy v roce 1990', *Práce a mzda*, Vol.38, No.1 (1990), pp.1–2.
2. Martin Myant, *Transforming Socialist Economies: The Case of Poland and Czecho- slovakia* (Cheltenham: Edward Elgar, 1993), pp.19–20.
3. This was no small prize. Union assets were valued in March 1990 at around Kčs 5.5 billion (Dana Zárubová and Jana Kašparová, 'Co se stalo s majetkem ROH', *Sondy odborových svazů*, 1993, No.17, p.4). Kčs 3 billion was held in savings while the rest was mostly in buildings, equivalent in value to roughly 0.05 per cent of the federation's total building stock. By maintaining this continuity, the new union structure could inherit a ready-made publishing house, with a daily newspaper. Buildings in prime locations have been rented out to foreign hotel companies, providing a steady income for the support of the new union centre's activities. Office space has also been made available at zero rent in many towns for social security and employment offices, thereby helping to confirm the unions' close links with the development of new social services. The political implications of this wealth are difficult to assess, but it may have encouraged the trend towards a 'non-political' role for unions partly by laying the basis for a con- tinuation of the unions' traditional welfare role and partly as a means to minimise the possible risk that union property might be confiscated. This had seemed to be a pos- sibility in the light of an early version of the law confiscating Communist Party property.
4. Igor Pleskot, '17. listopad', *Sondy odborových svazů*, 1992, No.47, p.4.
5. Karel Gemrot and Marcela Lišková, *Model hospodaření odborové organizace* (Prague: Práce, 1992), Ch.3.
6. *Hospodářské noviny*, 15 June 1993. It should be added that trade union officials consistently presented a different picture, claiming that their primary role was in representing employees against employers who were otherwise very reluctant to concede anything. Evidence on the development of industrial relations in workplaces, discussed later in this article, does not suggest that so complete a transformation into a 'normal' role for unions has as yet taken place.
7. Dagmar Rejlková, 'Odbory pod lupou průzkumu', *Sondy odborových svazů*, 1991, No.40, p.10.
8. *Sondy odborových svazů*, 1992, No.14, p.3.
9. L. Jurina, *Hospodářské noviny*, 18 Feb. 1992, and Rudolf Bednárik, 'Vyjednávanie medzi podnikateľmi a zamestnancami v malých súkromých firmách', *Práce a mzda*, Vol.40, No.1 (1992), pp.4–5.
10. Jaroslav Jakubka, *Práce*, 14 April 1993.
11. *Práce*, 5 May 1993.
12. *Rudé právo*, 23 July 1990.

13. Myant, Ch.8.
14. Igor Pleskot, *Práce*, 21 Sept. 1990.
15. *Práce*, 27 Sept. 1990.
16. Strikes were, of course, effectively outlawed after 1948. In legal terms they could be treated as violations of labour discipline. In 1976 the right to strike was accepted as part of a general law giving verbal recognition to a number of human rights issues following the Helsinki declaration. This, however, was never translated into a more precise law on the right to strike and therefore remained a meaningless declaration.
17. *Práce*, 21 Sept. 1990.
18. Vladimír Žižka, *Rudé právo*, 29 Nov. 1990.
19. Richard Falbr, *Rudé právo*, 12 Dec. 1990.
20. Myant, pp.171–2.
21. The only mention of strikes in Czechoslovak law was incorporated into the law on collective bargaining and ruled out strike action over a collective agreement that had been signed, was being negotiated, or was subject to arbitration. On a number of occasions employers and the Czech government tried to use the absence of any other stipulations to suggest that strikes unrelated to a collective agreement were illegal. No such case has been brought before a court and the unions have been ready to argue that ILO conventions assert the legality of such strikes in the absence of any other relevant laws.
22. The terms at that time included an obligation on the employer to give advanced warning – a later amendment specified three months – with clear reasons for redundancy, to discuss possible means of redeployment and to select only those with the least family commitments and with the greatest chance of finding alternative employment. The employer was then obliged to try to find alternative employment, with an obligation to make up any loss in pay for a specified period. Where this was impossible, local government bodies were required to pay unemployment benefit. An amendment in December 1989 broadened the right to claim benefit even to those who had never been employed. Changes in a law passed on 31 May 1991 required employers to pay on redundancy the equivalent of twice the average monthly wage, with scope for negotiating up to a maximum of three times monthly pay. The complex system for making up wages of employees redeployed to other firms was dropped as it was becoming too complex to administer in a situation where redundancy was becoming a common phenomenon.
23. Myant, pp.194–5.
24. *Sondy odborových svazů*, 1991, No.38, pp.14–15.
25. Monika Čambáliková, *Hospodářské noviny*, 9 Sept. 1992.
26. The signs of bad feeling in this case are something of an exception in relations with the larger foreign-owned firms. In general, unions have praised multi-national companies as an example that other employers could do well to follow in their competent approach both towards management in general and towards labour relations in particular.
27. Remarkably, simultaneous changes in the non-commercial sector were aimed at a centralization of all wage determination so that the same pay could be awarded for similar categories of work in such diverse areas as the armed force, education and public administration. It has, however, been recognized that the transition must be slow and will require increases in public sector pay.
28. *Hospodářské noviny*, 13 May 1992.
29. *Hospodářské noviny*, 16 July 1992.
30. *Práce*, 26 March 1992.
31. A general indication of leading union figures' political involvement is given by their participation in the June 1992 elections. 16 were given publicity by the Czech union centre. Six were standing on the Social Democrats' platform, two for the Civic Movement, one for the Civic Democratic Party, one for the Civic Democratic Alliance, two for the Peoples' Party, and the rest for smaller groupings that had little chance of influencing government policy. None were elected.
32. Vladimír Petrus, *Mladá fronta dnes*, 14 April 1992.

84   PARTIES . . . AND SOCIETY IN EAST-CENTRAL EUROPE

33. Myant, pp.208–215.
34. M. Mostl, *Sondy odborových svazů*, 1991, No.45.
35. B. Svatoš, and J. Schlanger, *Práce*, 23 Sept. 1991.
36. *Rudé právo*, 2 June 1992.
37. *Rudé právo*, 19 Oct. 1992.
38. *Práce*, 22 Nov. 1991.
39. Klaus had tried to argue that the fall in living standards was largely the result of a fall in exports to the Soviet Union and other former CMEA countries. Detailed studies do suggest that the main factor was the deliberate depression of domestic demand through the government's wage control strategy (Myant, 1993, pp.200–201).
40. *Rudé právo*, 1 April 1992.
41. *Hospodářské noviny*, 13 May 1992.
42. Jan Uhlíř, 'Odborový svaz KOVO a ekonomická transformace', *Ekonom*, 1992, No.1, p.30.
43. For an explanation, see Myant, Ch.11.
44. *Sondy odborových svazů*, 1992, No.25–6, p.1.
45. *Rudé právo*, 9 Sept. 1992.
46. *Hospodářské noviny*, 30 July 1992.
47. *Hospodářské noviny*, 7 Sept. 1992.
48. Richard Falbr, *Hospodářské noviny*, 12 Aug. 1992.
49. A form of wage control was reintroduced in the Czech Republic on 1 July 1993, involving penalties for enterprises that allowed wage increases more than five percentage points above the rate of inflation. The trade union leadership responded with complaints that they had not been consulted and that, in this and in various other government decisions, the General Agreement had been broken. They threatened to change their 'style', but it quickly became clear that they had no intention of trying to mobilize mass opposition to the government.

Great Expectations – Fading Hopes: Trade Unions and System-Change in Hungary

ANDRÁS TÓTH

The transition to democracy in Hungary did not bring a radical revolt against the 'mass organization' trade unions of the communist period. During the communist period, however, the role of the trade unions had to some extent evolved. Thwarted in their striving for an independent expression of their interests in the aftermath of 1956, individual workers bettered themselves through labour mobility and the growing second economy, whilst the trade unions became part of the management structure of the enterprise. This interplay of management intrusion and worker indifference resulted in the persistence of enterprise union sections and the scattered nature of attempts to organize to combat that management role. The changes since 1989 could result in enterprise sections cutting their ties to management, but the financial and personal dependence of the unions, the strength of old traditions and customs, and personal relations have so far conspired to outweigh countervailing forces.

Earlier periods of acute political crisis in communist regimes such as occurred in Hungary in 1956, Czechoslovakia in 1968, or Poland during the 1980s, triggered the collapse of official trade union structures and heralded a large-scale grassroots revitalization of the trade union movement.[1] The development of Hungary towards a pluralist political system and market economy has rapidly accelerated since 1988. By midsummer 1989, 'velvet negotiations' between the newly founded political parties and the Hungarian Socialist Workers' Party, resulted in a peaceful transition to a democratic political system. The first free election was held in May of 1990 and the political obstacles to the 'great transformation' from a command economy to a market economy ceased to exist. With the end of the socialist regime in Hungary one could expect the collapse of official unions and the revitalization of the grassroots Hungarian trade union movement. This study seeks to explain why this did not happen and why there has been no large-scale revolt against the established union structures.

In the wake of the system-change there were substantial changes in the

András Tóth is a Research Fellow of the Institute of Political Science of the Hungarian Academy of Sciences in Budapest. The study is based on research funded by the Hungarian Otka Foundation.

Hungarian trade union movement. First, a free 'independent-of-the-past', grassroots trade union emerged at the beginning of 1988, and this was followed by the emergence of numerous other workplace level organizations. Two important new confederations were formed: the League of Independent Trade Unions in 1988, and then a year later the Workers' Council Movement. In 1990 the influence of these new organizations, and the number of member organizations, rapidly increased. Secondly, the former party-controlled monopolistic National Council of Trade Unions (SZOT) fragmented. Since the beginning of 1990 SZOT under the new umbrella title of National Association of Hungarian Trade Unions – MSz OSz) has split into four confederations and its 19 industrial branch unions into several occupational unions. Several trade-union sections withdrew from the SZOT and its branch unions and proclaimed themselves independent. The organizational transformation of the former union structure was accompanied by a substantial fall in membership.

This led to two types of pluralism emerging. First, a competitive pluralism came into being, both on national and workplace level, between the newly founded grassroots unions and the old unions.

At the national level there was a clear distinction between the old and the new confederations regarding their connection to the socialist past, their attitudes towards the transition, and their relationships towards political parties and economic problems such as privatization. This rivalry was strengthened and envenomed from late 1990 by the growing debate over the SZOT's assets. Meanwhile, at the workplace level, almost all the new unions were established as counter-unions against the existing old ones; their aim was to pursue different policies and different forms and content of interest representation.

This was accompanied, secondly, by a complementary pluralism between the four successor confederations of the SZOT. SZOT's former 19 branch unions grouped themselves into four confederations: one for public service employees, one for the civil service employees, one for manufacturing and transport employees and one for chemical employees. The four confederations have distinct spheres of activity. In addition they have preserved their monopolistic industrial structure in their respective organizational areas.

In 1989–90 the new confederations played an active political role and enjoyed a substantial political influence. The old unions were thrust into the background and were afflicted by a severe crisis of legitimacy owing to the burden of their past.

As differentiation within the union movement began to unfold, a series of public opinion surveys from 1988 to 1990 indicated that there would be a major re-arrangement in the union movement in favour of the new grassroots unions.[2] From the beginning of 1991, however, the tide turned. It became clear that the new grassroots movements would be unable to achieve a breakthrough in their organizational drive. In most workplaces the workers, even though they withdrew from the old union, did not necessarily form a new one. The membership of the new confederations remained low, and their member organizations remained scattered, weakening the overall structure. The organizational drive that they mounted around 1991 began to slow down. The legal regulation of the new Labour Code Act 1992 concerning trade union rights had the effect of preventing several existing new unions from exercising their rights and of hindering the future growth of the new confederations. At the same time the new confederations were sliding towards the political margin. The old unions' presence in the workplace has largely persisted and stabilized. The legal regulation concerning trade-union rights contained in the new Labour Code Act of 1992 was to secure the old unions' monopoly in the workplace. The fragmentation of their structure stopped. On the political level, as the economic crisis deepened, it could be seen that a political revival of the old unions was taking place.

As the shape of post-communist industrial relations unfolds, it becomes more and more obvious that a grassroots revitalization of the trade union movement has been removed from the social agenda and that the trade unions of the past have successfully survived the system change and retained their organizational dominance. It is this author's assumption that one of the causes of the durability of old unions structures lies in their past.

The focus of this contribution is to analyse the changing role of trade unions under the socialist decades and describe the changing relationship of these unions with management and workers. An analysis of the socialist trade unions' will enable us to establish why the old unions have persisted.

In the first part of this study I describe the unions and their transmission belt roles in the Stalinist period. In the second part I deal with the development from transmission belt unionism to enterprise unionism and analyse the changing relationship between employees and their unions.

Transmission Belt Unionism

The communist party took over political power in Hungary in 1948 and began an enforced re-shaping of the trade-union movement in three main spheres: organization and structure, personnel, and function.

The organizational re-shaping of the basically craft-based and locally organized trade union movement was formally decided at the twenty-fifth congress of the trade unions in 1949. The congress proclaimed that there was a single interest in society and that the party had the authority to designate and guide trade union policy and practice. It required, secondly, that the affiliated unions amalgamate and reorganize themselves on monopolistic industrial lines in 19 branch unions. Thirdly, the locally organized union sections were required to reorganize into enterprise sections, whilst the company-level multi-union system had to reorganize itself into a one-company one-union system. The enterprise union section had, moreover, to unite all employees regardless of their professional divisions and without distinction between the rank-and-file and managerial personnel, even up to and including the director of the company. Finally, the internal organizational principle was to be democratic centralism. This meant that once a decision had been passed it was obligatory to implement it without expressing opposing opinions.

From early 1948 numerous campaigns sought to expel, first, the allegedly right-wing social-democrats, then centrist social democrats, and finally left-wing social democrats. The goal was to terrify the cadres and anybody else who showed any courage. Over and above the purge campaigns the communist party gained control over both nomination and dismissal processes at every level of the union hierarchy.

A new set of functions was determined for the re-shaped and now subordinated trade unions. These were, first, to organize the workers for the over-fulfilment of the production plans, to organize the various socialist emulation campaigns – such as the Stakhanov campaign – and to combat shirkers and norm defrauders. A second of their functions was to take part in distributing the state and enterprise welfare benefits and to organize communal entertainments and cultural programmes. In this role the unions functioned as a quasi-governmental department at the national level and as a welfare department of the firm. Thirdly, the unions provided a career for future cadres.

The unions thus became a subordinate organization of the oppressive political dictatorship. They were directly guided and controlled by the communist party at every level of their activity. The unions were the 'transmission belt' conveying central economic policy. The centralization of economic management and the direct and tight government control over production and wage rates terminated any scope for bargaining over performance or wages.[3] The unions were detached from their original social functions: from the integration of workers into professionally based organizations, from achieving autonomy, fair wages and conditions for their members through the control of a given segment of the labour market and the work process, and through collective bargaining. The new function of the unions became, through fulfilment of the transmission-belt role, to restrain worker demands. As the official workers' interest-representing organization became a part of the political-economic management, the function of such a union was to prevent a particular worker's interest from being raised and to render impossible formalized action to safeguard terms and conditions. Although almost every worker was obliged to become a trade-union member, the members could not control the organization. The organization controlled the members.

The interests of trade unions and of workers diverged. Since that time we have to contend with a double history: on the one hand the history of the official trade-union hierarchy, how it pursued and changed its policies; and on the other the history of how the workers attempted to defend their own interests outside the trade unions. Because of severe political suppression, this separation of the interests of workers and trade unions could only become manifest in the 1956 revolution.

During the revolution of that year the workers began to set up workers' councils and the trade unions effectively ceased to exist at the workplace level. In the last days of the revolution, the workers' councils began to form regional and national-level bodies. Although the Soviet troops shattered the revolution on 4 November the workers' councils none the less continued to function and to represent the resistance. In January 1957, the new government led by János Kádár extinguished the workers' council movement by intimidation, beatings, imprisonment and execution.

Development Towards Enterprise Unionism

After the revolution of 1956 the earlier trade-union structure was restored though with strict party control. After the consolidation, the Kádár regime strove to avoid the extreme hard-line Stalinist policies and committed itself to raising the standard of living. From the mid-1960s, a slow reform began leading towards a more enlightened political regime and a mixed economy. This was accompanied by a loosening of the tightly centralized economic management. After the introduction of the New Economic Mechanism in 1968, the independence of enterprises from central government grew substantially. Each company could build up its own internal production methods, management style, labour policy, internal labour market and welfare policy. As the political and economic environment of the unions changed, the viability of a transmission role for the unions decreased. The expectation that trade-union organization could be tightly controlled, and dominated by the centre ceased to exist. Trade unions were able to adopt a double function. The transmission belt role was retained, but they could take up the representation of workers' interests.[4] The SZOT policy of top-down determination of lower union affairs eased. As the strict control of wage-rates was relaxed, the industrial trade-union headquarters lost their puppet-like negotiation roles.

The facade of the monolithic-industrial structure of the trade union movement however, remained untouched. The centralized structure survived and maintained an independent policy-making role in the upper layers of the trade-union hierarchy. But this upper level gradually lost control over the enterprise union sections. A covert enterprise unionism began to develop behind the unaltered facade of the monolithic union structure. The enterprise union sections began to coordinate their activity with the interests of their enterprise. Through this development, these sections became the partners of their company management rather than transmission belts at the disposal of the upper union headquarters. The interest representation of the workers therefore came to mean greater interest representation of a given company in its struggle for more resources from redistribution agencies at government level.[5]

The development towards enterprise unionism was legitimated finally by the amendment of the Labour Code in 1968. The new Labour Code outlawed multi-employer collective bargaining, and preserved an arbitration right for the upper level of the union hierarchy only in cases of disagreement at the company level between management and the enterprise's trade-union section. The Code had decentralized all trade-union rights to the enterprise level making collective bargaining at the company level between employers and the respective trade union section obligatory. Besides bringing regulation of employment down to the company level, the new Code designated a new role for the enterprise sections. These were given the power to exercise participation rights as the representative of all employees in the given enterprise. The expanded rights of the company union sections paved the way for them to become part of the leadership of a given enterprise.

Through its structure, its staffing practice, the manner in which it exercised its role and its functions, the union section was deeply embedded within the power structure and the political-economical management of the enterprise. In the next part I describe the characteristics of these four areas. The examples that I use are drawn from one company where I conducted research. This company is a traditional manufacturing (tool-making) factory in Budapest, employing around 700 workers.

The Structure of the Company Union Section

Each enterprise had only one union section. Virtually all employees were members of this section, including the top management of the company.

The union section's organizational structure followed that of the enterprise. Each level of the company hierarchy had a corresponding union activist partner: a shop steward corresponded to a foreman, a senior shop steward corresponded to a supervisor and a secretary corresponded to the director respectively. Alongside the vertical structure there were trade-union committees corresponding to the functional departments of the management: the social and welfare committee corresponded to the welfare department, whilst the economic committee corresponded to the financial department. The executive committee was the top board of the section. It consisted of senior shop stewards and the presidents of the functional committees. Democratic centralism remained the internal organizational principle. The company's party organization exercised control over the staffing and policy of the union section.

Staffing

One of the main characteristics of the staffing practice of the enterprise unions was the intrusion of managerial personnel into union leadership positions.

Occupation of union leadership positions was usually by middle and lower management. Several research results show that in the majority of cases, the shop steward and senior shop steward positions were occupied by foremen, head of sections or deputy supervisors.[6] For example, in the toolmaking factory most of the senior shop stewards were foremen or deputy supervisors. The president of the executive committee was a deputy supervisor, who was also the senior shop steward at his shop. The supervisor of the maintenance shop was the chair of the economic committee of the trade-union section – although a foreman was the senior shop steward at this maintenance shop.

The highest position in a union section was secretary of the executive committee. This was a full-time position, given a certain number of employees. As several investigations show, the full-time trade-union secretary's income and fringe benefits were determined and covered by the company, in general, on a deputy-director level. Their career path also was determined mainly by the enterprise. For example, in the tool-making factory the secretary at the time of the research began his career as an apprentice. Later positions included skilled worker, shop steward, foreman, Young Communist League secretary inside the company, head of the welfare department of the company, and then finally trade-union secretary.

In several companies, where there was no possibility to pay a full-time secretary, the lay secretary was a managerial person such as the personnel director of the company, the head of the company's social policy department, or even in some cases the deputy director.

Besides this doubling of roles, the relationship between management and unions was also determined by personal relationships. For example, in the toolmaking company the trade-union secretary began his apprenticeship in the early 1950s in the same shop as the director, and their friendship determined the relationship between union and management.

Co-operative Collaboration

'Co-operative collaboration' connotes the way in which an enterprise union acted and practised its rights. The relationship was characterized by mutual trust between the management and the union rather than antagonism and confrontation. As the director of the toolmaker company said: 'The relationship of the union and the management could not be described as peaceful coexistence, because coexistence presupposes a different viewpoint. We act together in peaceful co-operation'.

As an example of 'co-operative collaboration' I describe the negotiation process of the collective agreement in the toolmaking company in three steps.

In the first step, the director of the company and the secretary of the company trade-union section send a jointly-signed letter to every supervisor and to the corresponding senior shop steward. This letter states that the existing agreement is about to expire and calls upon them to evaluate the implementation of the agreement and make their proposals to amend it.

In the second step, every shop-floor local section of the union holds a meeting with its shop steward and with the respective foreman, with the former in the chair. At these meetings, the workers voice their problems concerning the agreement and propose amendments to it. The participating foreman responds verbally to problems that are raised or promises to solve them. At the meeting, they decide together which questions should lead to amendment of the agreement. After the meeting, the shop steward and the foreman write a record of the meeting, which contains the proposals. In the event of disagreement between the foreman and the union members, the different opinions of the parties are also recorded. In the round of negotiations in 1985 and 1990 there were no disagreements.

In the third step shop stewards hold a meeting at senior shop steward supervisor level, where they summarize the amendments. The corresponding supervisor also participates in that meeting. They make a common decision, which leads to cases being taken to enterprise level. They compose a joint record which contains the proposals and, in the case of disagreement between the supervisor and shop stewards, a record of the differing opinions. In the round of negotiations in 1985 and 1990, there was disagreement in only one shop. In that case the strong feeling for co-operation resulted in the director and the secretary of the union section accepting that the case represented a serious conflict and talking with their representatives to resolve the differences.

In the fourth step, the executive committee of the section, with the participation of the director, makes proposals to amend the company collective agreement.

In the fifth and final step the trade-union executive committee negotiates with top management to sign the agreement.

Trade Union Rights

The main functions of a union section in an enterprise were to participate in the decision-making process so as to determine company strategy and policy; secondly, to regulate employment through collective bargaining; thirdly, to fulfil welfare services; and finally to represent the interest of their members.

In the enterprises the most important forum of decision-making was the 'company-quartet'. The quartet consisted of the director of the company, and the secretaries of the party, the Young Communist League, and the trade union. The quartet had a weekly meeting, and on its agenda were all important questions relating to the company. The quartet guaranteed that the union could take part in the running of the company. Whilst trade-union secretaries had a weaker say than other members of the quartet, they could access all the important information and express their opinion about all important questions.

Beside this participation in the quartet, the Labour Code stipulated that in every question that might affect employment the management had to ask the opinion, or gain the assent of the union section before the decision was made. Although, in questions of great importance, the executive committee had to give its formal approval, the decision had already been negotiated and decided on by the company party organization.

Collective bargaining was the main tool available to unions for regulating employment in conjunction with the management. Although bargaining was compulsory, the regulatory scope of these agreements was fairly restricted. The terms and conditions of employment were set by legal regulation. Collective agreements were only a complementary measure, so as to accord with clauses of the Labour Code and various other laws and departmental orders.

The trade union section played a substantial role in the distribution of social and other welfare benefits, organizing cultural entertainments, commemorations and holiday activities, usually at the expense of the company's welfare budget.

As was mentioned above, the interest representation of the workers was tantamount to the interest representation of the given company in its struggle for more resources from redistribution at governmental level.

Within the company, the occupation of union leadership positions by managerial personnel opened the way to an 'embryo-bargaining' role for the unions. On the one hand the overlap of roles meant a subordinate position for the union, with puppet negotiations taking place to legitimate the various decisions of the management and assure the supremacy of staff personnel over workers. On the other hand, the different factions of middle management tried to legitimate their position and achieve more resources from top management through the union. For them this doubling of positions secured a new bargaining space where their claims took on not only a strictly economical, but also a political colouring. These clashes of factions within the union emerged as an 'embryo-bargaining', except that those engaged in the bargaining in the union were from management, and not members.

It could in principle have happened that groups of workers might use the union to bargain for their own interests. But the relevant sociological literature suggests that the workers' struggle to safeguard their customs and practice, or to achieve better terms and conditions, was fought through informal groups and never emerged into the formal world of unions. In these cases of overt clashes, the unions always placed themselves on the side of management and turned against the workers.[7]

Because of the tendency for management to hold union leadership positions the workers could not depend on the union to defend them against management arbitrariness and represent their interest against the management. However, in several cases the union, although it accepted the decision of management, tried to help the affected members individually, by exploring new solutions. For example, in 1988 the tool-making company made redundant all the women who were returning from their maternity leave. The decision, although it was illegal, was not opposed by the union. But the trade-union activists tried to help their colleagues by asking their friends and colleagues in other companies, if there were any vacancies, to fill them with the victims of the company's decision.

The workers, however, were able to develop individual strategies to compensate for the missing union roles, the unions themselves becoming indifferent to the workers' viewpoint. In the course of the reforms some concessions were made to the workers which related to workshop relations. In the evolving social-political atmosphere the continual search for internal enemies ceased, yet nothing more than neutrality was allowed. The breach of the Labour Code Act and employment contract ceased to be a criminal act. The strict wage tariffs were diluted. Central control was made to operate on the total wage outflow of each company and not on the wage of an individual worker. This company-related average wage system gave each company the possibility of building up its own internal labour market and paying workers on the basis of their value to the company's interest.[8] Almost until the end of the socialist regime there was a labour shortage. From the beginning of the 1960s a second economy emerged. In the early 1980s two-thirds of the workers were engaged in the second economy. Most of the employees could make up for their disadvantaged positions in their employment through the second economy. The second economy gave workers the possibility of reshaping their expectations towards the enterprise. They could work out a balance between internal labour-market positions and second economy activities.

The coincidence of a labour shortage and this second economy allowed the workers to accept the goal of the management to create an internal labour market. In response, the workers developed different labour market strategies.[9] Because the trade unions were expropriated by the management and there was a ban on grassroots associations, the workers through turnover, absenteeism or going slow covertly and informally tried to safeguard their individual interests and informal bargaining. It was possible to break the contract and easily find other work, because of the labour shortage. Through overmanning it was possible to occupy a relatively low-grade job in exchange for relatively loose management control and relatively low expectations of efficiency, and work in the second economy.

Although each worker was a trade-union member, they could live the life of a 'trade-union-free' worker. The trade union did not control individual bargaining with the supervisors. Individually, one could do a good deal by working disproportionately high overtime or by receiving extra bonuses and benefits. The union did not fight for equal terms and conditions for an equal job and did not look out for breaches of the Labour Code. The union did not bring work to a stop because of health and safety danger.

This individualization was mirrored also in the grievance procedure. In the case of a grievance, a worker could launch the judicial procedure for an individual legal redress. The first stage of the judicial procedure was a lay jury at a given company. The company lay jury consisted of three members. One of the members was the legal expert of the company and the two other members were trade union nominees. In this procedure every call for redress remained an individual case subject to an individual award. In the judicial process the union did not intercede on behalf of its member but did provide the lay jury, which acted impartially, as a judicial forum. The union not only would not represent the interest of its member against management in the case, but at the same time it lost the possibility of evaluating the merits of the case and using it as a bargaining tool. The employer was always faced with an impartial and individual judicial process, where the lay jury would make its judgement on the facts of the individual case and never have to face the possibility of the expansion of the issue into a collective dispute.

Conclusion

My conclusion is that in the 1950s the trade unions were the transmission belt of the communist party and played an active role in suppressing the workers. The interests of workers and unions diverged. With the failure of the revolution of 1956 the workers were thwarted in their quest for an organized way of having their interests represented. From the early 1960s there was a transition to an enterprise union model. The company union sections became part of the political-economic management of a given enterprise and were deeply embedded within the power structure of the enterprise. At the same time unions became indifferent to the workers' point of view. The workers could secure their interests individually through labour market turnover, second economy activity and individual bargaining. There was no need for an organization that controlled individual bargaining and work-relations. This meant, however, that it was only possible for the workers to hide or run away, but not to alter relations in the workplace.

After 1988 the interplay of management intrusion and worker indifference resulted in the persistence of enterprise union sections and the scattered nature of attempts to organize against that management role. A counter-union was formed where the traditional system of individual bargaining was exhausted or was not sufficient to safeguard the workers' interests. There were three main causes that led to the formation of a new union. First, professionally homogeneous workers would set up a sectional union in order to establish an organization that was controlled by them and not by the management. The aim of such an organization was to reshape work relations through collective action and defend the members from management arbitrariness. Secondly, an unresolved dispute might trigger the idea of establishing a real union, which acted on behalf of the workers. Unions that flourished as a result of a dispute, remained in most cases sectionally organized. Thirdly, the restructuring, privatization or bankruptcy of a company, which endangered the workers, could lead to the formation of a counter-union aimed at acquiring information about the future, having a say in management, or even altering its plans. In this case, the organizers sometimes enjoyed the backing of a faction of the management, or this faction might even be behind the creation of the organization.

However, in the wake of the system-change, substantial changes at workplace level have taken place both on the side of the company unions and of the management. In autumn 1989 the party organization was expelled from the workplace. The unions could begin to exercise their rights without any external political control. The union remained the only social-based organization within the boundaries of an enterprise. As the economic crisis deepened, the position of union members worsened substantially – a change that could distance the trade unions from the management. The collapse of the socialist system brought an end to the political duty of the management to incorporate the unions into the decision-making process. The company quartet and some other old forms of meeting ceased to exist. The management began to develop a new management legitimacy, based on a knowledge of market and management, on political impartiality and on the modernization of production. These changes mean that the management might now see the unions as a constraint on the path towards 'efficient management'. The changes could result in the enterprise union sections cutting off their ties with the management. However, it is my experience that the financial and personal dependence of the unions, the strength of old traditions and customs, and personal relationships, have up to now far outweighed countervailing forces. Although the enterprise union sections have retained their formal autonomy it is still an open question whether they will be able to transform themselves into an organization capable of acting on behalf of their members, or whether they will remain organizations controlled by management, and whose main function will again be to prevent the expression of the voice of the workers.

NOTES

1. Thomas Lowitt, 'The Working Class and Union Structures in Eastern Europe', *British Journal of Industrial Relations*, No.1 (1982), p.61.
2. *Magyarország Politikai Évkönyve 1988* (Budapest, 1989), pp.462 and 471; and *Magyaroszág Politikai Évkönyve 1990* (Budapest, 1991), pp.440 and 446.
3. Dávid János, 'Is Industrial Society a Community?' *Hungary under the Reform* (research review), No.3, 1989, p.59.
4. Héthy Lajos and Imre V. Csuhaj, *Labour Relations in Hungary* (Budapest, 1990), p.17.
5. Tölgyessy Péter, *Gazdasági érdekképviseletek Magyarországon* (Budapest, 1989), p.15.
6. Laky Térez, *Szakszervezeti tisztségviselök vizsgálata* (Budapest, 1979); Lowitt, 'The Working Class', Nigel Swain, *Hungary: The Rise and Fall of Feasible Socialism* (London; New York: Verso, 1992).
7. Héthy Lajos and Makó Csaba, *Munkások, érdekek, érdekegyeztetés*, Budapest, 1987; Kemény István, *Közelröl és távolról* (Budapest, 1991).
8. Dávid, 'Is Industrial Society a Community?', p.61.
9. Kemény, *Közelröl és távolról*; Kertesi Gábor and Sziráczky György, 'Munkásmagatartások a munkaeröpiacon', *Gazdaságszociológiai tanulmáyok* (Budapest, 1989).

Trade Unions, Political Parties and Governments in Bulgaria, 1989–92

JOHN THIRKELL, BOYKO ATANASOV and GRIGOR GRADEV

In the unstable conditions of political change in Bulgaria there has been space for the trade-union confederations – both that stemming from the communist period and those created since 1989 – to operate in the political arena as driving forces for economic and political change. The most important institutional mechanism for this has been tripartite negotiations involving government, the employer organizations and the trade unions. The development of tripartism in Bulgaria has not, however, been unilinear, but has expanded and contracted with changes in governments. The scope for tripartism has been greatest when there has been either a coalition or a non-party government – and such circumstances have been the outcome of failures by political parties to establish stable and enduring governments.

The development of new forms of organization operating in the political arena and the emerging pattern of relations between them is a central feature of the process of regime change in central and eastern Europe. Under the previous regimes organizational power formally flowed from the single centre of the party and its structures and was transmitted downwards to all other public organizations and institutions. The process of political change has produced a plurality of organizational power centres. Some of these centres derive from the emergence and creation of new independent movements and organizations outside the previous structures but others are based on the previously existing organizations which, in most cases, have undergone a process of transformation. For the latter this has meant externally a process of separation from the formerly ruling party and their constitution as legally independent organizations, and internally the abandonment of the previously funda-mental organizing principle of democratic centralism, as well as other

John Thirkell is Director of the Centre for Russian and East European Management and Labour Relations and Senior Lecturer in Industrial Relations at the University of Kent at Canterbury. Boyko Atanasov conducts research in the Unit for Relations with Political Parties and Mass Organization of the CITUB in Sofia. Grigor Gradev is Research Officer in the Institute for Trade Union and Social Research, Sofia. This research has been facilitated by the contacts deriving from the ESRC East–West Initiative project 'Labour Relations in Transition'.

changes in structures and internal mechanisms. In Bulgaria one of the two main parliamentary parties (in fact a coalition), the Union of Democratic Forces (UDF), and one of the main trade union centres, Podkrepa, are new organizations deriving from a social movement. The other main political party, the Bulgarian Socialist Party (BSP), and the other trade union centre, the Confederation of Independent Trade Unions in Bulgaria (CITUB) derive from existing organizations that have undergone a process of transformation – the Bugarian Communist Party and the trade unions of the communist period.

A major feature of the process of creating and transforming organizations in eastern Europe has been the fluidity of organizational boundaries as their functions have varied over time and shifted in response to prevailing conditions.[1] It will be shown that in Bulgaria the fluidity of organizational boundaries has been a particular characteristic of both the new and the transformed trade union centres. This fluidity is partly a product of the specific conditions in Bulgaria but in the case of the latter it is partly due to the development of the Bulgarian trade unions in the 1980s. Relations between communist parties and the trade unions were traditionally very close and the leading role claimed by parties meant that, like other public organizations and institutions, the trade unions were formally dependent upon party approval. In practice, however, there were limitations on the party's monopoly of power and there were elements of autonomy.[2] In the case of the trade unions by the 1980s the traditional 'transmission belt' function had been modified significantly in some countries as labour relations became recognized as an important field of policy. Thus in Bulgaria during the 1980s, when the national strategy for labour relations became a key policy area, the Central Council of the Bulgarian trade unions and its research institute functioned as the major agency in the formulation of national labour relations strategy, although they remained officially subordinate to the party.[3] This tradition of autonomous activity facilitated the role of the Bulgarian trade unions in strategy formulation and organizational transformation in the post revolutionary period. Similarly in the process of political and institutional separation which developed in Hungary during the 1980s as an aspect of economic reform it was significant that although not independent of the party the Central Council of the Hungarian trade unions claimed in discussions with an ILO mission that in practice they enjoyed a significant measure of 'autonomy'.[14]

For the analysis of the post-communist political processes in eastern and central Europe Stadler has drawn attention to the effects that political and economic dependence on the external international environment has on the internal political processes in countries like Poland,

Hungary and Bulgaria which have a high level of foreign debt. He has suggested the bargaining triangle as a way of conceptualizing this dependence with the 'international environment' 'government' and 'internal interest groups' as the actors (see the diagram in Michael Waller's contribution to this collection). Stadler argues that 'we can speak of dependence of the government on the international environment when socio-economic interest groups are either excluded from the triangle or are included to such a limited extent that the government's policies are mainly shaped by the international environment' and applies this approach to an analysis of the Polish case.[5] As will be shown below the relations of Bulgarian governments to the International Monetary Fund and the World Bank have been a significant influence on the process of economic reform and of the political processes in Bulgaria, but at the same time the trade-union confederations have been included in the discussions with these international organizations.

The concepts of 'dependence' and 'interdependence' have been particularly used by political scientists for the analysis of external relations between countries and of the balance of power between them.[6] However these concepts can also be applied to the relations between organizations operating in the internal political arena of a country. Thus, in the formation of governments, parties may depend on the support of other parties when the construction of coalitions is necessary. Similarly where there are interest groups such as trade unions which are organized in such a way that they can mobilize significant power in the political arena, then political parties and governments may become dependent upon them in relation to particular policy areas and to specific events. Thus Przeworski has argued that in the process of transition from authoritarian rule the role of trade unions in the process of reform is critical. He sees the success of reforms, and therefore of governments, as dependent on the willingness and organizational capacity of the trade unions to contain the potential for wage pressures exerted by the workers they organize.[7] Dependence does not, of course, operate only in a single direction, so that trade unions may be dependent upon parties and governments to legislate on matters that concern them. Consequently the relations between governments and trade unions are likely to be characterized by exchange and inter-dependence as well as dependence.

This study aims to describe and analyse the development of trade-union centres in Bulgaria since the political changes in November 1989, together with the dynamics of their changing relationships with political parties and governments, and to assess their role in post-revolutionary politics. The role of trade unions in the sphere of labour relations at industry and enterprise level is not discussed except in relation to the prevalence of industrial conflicts which have actual or potential significance in the political arena. In particular this study seeks to explore the nature of the relations of dependence and interdependence between the trade unions, the political parties and successive governments – that is, of the relative balance of power and influence between these organizations in the political process. Specifically it will be argued that in the particular conditions of Bulgaria during this period the relationship of political parties to the trade union centres was to a significant extent one of dependence and that, in the exercise of power in the political arena, parties and governments needed the consent of the trade union centres.

A mainly historical approach, which focuses on events and the action processes of the different agencies operating in the political arena, is adopted for three main reasons. First, the nature of the relationships between the trade unions and the political parties has varied significantly between periods in response to changes in conditions; secondly, the organizational boundaries of trade unions also varied between periods; and thirdly, although the main focus is only on what was actually done a historical approach facilitates consideration of instances of the counter-factual – that is, of what did not happen but might conceivably have happened or possibilities that were considered but not pursued. The presentation is divided into three periods corresponding to the main changes in politics and governments and it focuses on the interactions and relations between the different power centres and interest groups. The first period is from November 1989 to December 1990, in which there were three Communist (or Socialist after the renaming of the party) governments. The second runs from January to September 1991, when the Popov coalition government was in power. The third begins with the election of the opposition Union of Democractic Forces to form the government with the support of the ethnic-based (Turkish) Movement for Rights and Freedom in October 1991 and ends with the replacement of the Dimitrov government in December 1992 by the Berov government of 'experts'. These periods mark significant stages in the politics and development of economic reform and policy.

Communist and Socialist Goverments, November 1989 to December 1990

In contrast to the relatively peaceful transitions in, for example, Hungary and Czechoslovakia, an immediate consequence of the political change in November 1989 in Bulgaria was widespread industrial and ethnic conflict.[8] These conditions exercised a strong influence on the organizational development and political roles of what were to become the two main trade-union confederations – the Confederation of Independent Trade

Unions in Bulgaria (CITUB) and the Podkrepa Confederation of Labour, and also on the pattern of party formation.

Podkrepa 'support' had been founded as a clandestine trade union in February 1989 by a small group from the intelligentsia. Activities began in September and were initially confined to contacts with the Western mass media. After the political change of 10 November it came into the open and took advantage of the strike wave to advise and assist the workers involved and to recruit them as members. At this stage, however, despite its being involved in industrial relations and having created a membership base it defined its primary goal as the political one of dismantling or changing the system and overthrowing the Communist Party as the necessary condition for systemic change. The philosophy was that there could be no real change while the party retained power, and it thus transcended the normal functions and boundary of a trade union. The formation of Podkrepa as a trade union was technically legal in the period before the political changes in November when alternative parties were not legal, and it played a very active role in the foundation, on 10 December, of the Union of Democratic Forces and in its subsequent development as the principal umbrella organization for the various groups and formations that opposed the Communist Party.

Podkrepa duly became a constituent member of the UDF, which was established as an alliance of autonomous political parties, organizations and movements headed by a National Coordination Council on which each member had one vote, irrespective of the size of its membership. A significant illustration of the role of Podkrepa as a political rather than conventional trade union organization was its activity on behalf of the Turkish minority. The issue of the Turkish minority and its rights had been the subject of a campaign by the Zhivkov government from 1985, which evoked strong nationalist sentiments among Slav Bulgarians. From its early days Podkrepa declared its support for the rights of the Turkish minority and publicized it as a human rights issue. This led to many Turks joining Podkrepa as an organization for political protection, and in return membership of Podkrepa was encouraged by the Turkish-based political organization – the Movement for Rights and Freedoms.

As noted, the Bulgarian Trade Unions were closely linked through their Central Council to the Communist Party and the state. There was, however, a rapid process of separation from both. On 25 November the Central Council decided that to regain the support of workers the defence of workers' interests must have priority and this required independence from the party, the state and from the employers. For the leadership, the organizational process of transformation and of separation from the party and the state was facilitated by the depth of the industrial relations crisis and by the rapid emergence of Podkrepa as an alternative and competing trade union centre. These conditions made it easier for the provisional leadership to justify the processes of separation from the party and of internal transformation. The latter involved the abandonment of democratic centralism as an organizing principle and the adoption at the Extraordinary Congress in February of a confederal structure.

The context of extreme fluidity of organizational functions and boundaries at this time is illustrated by the referendum held in January 1990 of the members of what was to become the CITUB. At a general political level the referendum functioned as a mechanism for securing the legitimation of the organization in the changed political conditions. The explicit purpose of the referendum was to secure endorsement of the leadership's strategy of securing a General Agreement with the government as the fundamental condition for economic, industrial and political stability. However, members were also asked whether they would support the idea of the trade union's participation, with its own programme and candidates, when the election was held. This position was supported by two-thirds of the 1.8 million respondents. The inclusion of this question was a response to the growing pressures on the trade union from different sides. These pressures included, first, the growing tensions between the party and the trade unions as the latter began to assert their independence; secondly, attempts to exclude the trade unions from the national round-table set up to promote political progress; and thirdly, Podkrepa's aim to play a major role in the political arena. The example of Solidarity as a trade union moving directly into the political arena in the Polish election in the summer of 1989 provided a model for such action.

In the early months of 1990 the CITUB exercised a pivotal role in the process of political change in Bulgaria. By 22 January its claim to participate in the national round-table had been conceded and it was a major political force in the successful demands for the resignation of the Communist government of Atanasov at the end of January. This was followed by the Socialist government of Lukanov (the party having abandoned democratic centralism at its January congress and changed its name, after a referendum of its members, in April 1990).

The issue of Communist Party organizations in enterprises and in institutions emerged very rapidly. The workplace organizations were one of the main bases on which the party's power was built and consequently the continuation or dissolution of these organizations became a major political issue. In the January trade-union referendum respondents had been asked whether they agreed with the establishment and operation of political parties in workplaces, and two-thirds had said they were opposed to them. In April the workplace organizations of the party were dissolved. However, the relationship between political activity and trade union activity in the workplace remained an important political issue. If there were to be no party organizations at the workplace, was it permissible for trade unions to engage in political activity there? Legally this issue was resolved by the Law on Political Parties passed 10 April and subsequently by the Constitution of July 1991 (Appendix 1). These placed restrictions on the involvement of trade unions in political activity and in relation to political parties and appeared to separate trade unions (and, by implication, social movements) from the political process. Thus the party's abandonment of the workplace to the trade unions was balanced by the attempt to exclude trade unions from political activity. Such a legal balance, which was not attempted, for example, in Hungary or the Czech Republic, can be seen as a clear recognition of the perception of the trade unions' potential influence in the electoral and political processes.

In the first part of 1990 Podkrepa's primary objective of changing the political system meant that it aimed to secure the fall of the Lukanov government and was reluctant to participate in measures that might ease that government's situation. It is a plausible example of the counter-factual that if the CITUB had chosen to side with Podkrepa at this time of political and industrial turbulence the Lukanov government would have been brought down. The CITUB leadership, however, judged that at this stage such action would not have been in the interests of national economic, social and political development and might, moreover, have fostered divisions in its membership. At its constituent congress in February 1990 the role of the Confederation at the political level had been defined as one of political independence and of 'constructive opposition'. This meant that in a period of deepening economic crisis, when the necessity for radical changes was widely recognized, the Confederation judged that it was not in the national interest to promote unrealizable and populist demands which would destroy institutions and ultimately retard economic and political development. Consequently the major features of CITUB strategy centred on the establishment of industrial relations structures and mechanisms which it regarded as essential for peaceful transition.

The CITUB used its inherited right under the Labour Code to initiate the legislation for the Law on Collective Labour Disputes adopted by the National Assembly on 6 March 1990. This helped to reduce the number of strikes and improved social stability. In exchange it secured the mechanism of a General Agreement, which had been one of its main demands since January. This was signed on 15 March and covered a wide range of industrial relations issues including employment, wages (particularly increases in the minimum wage and pensions) social development (holidays and social funds) and health and safety. The Agreement was seen as requiring the creation of a national tripartite forum which became the National Commission for the Coordination of Interests. The CITUB also played an active role in encouraging the creation of the national organization of employers as the third party in the tripartite structure.

The general election of June 1990 posed the issue for the trade union confederations of whether or how they should participate. In May the CITUB, the employers' organization and the government signed a joint declaration that organized political activity in the workplace, including pre-election action, was inadmissable. In exchange the government agreed that there should be no job losses until after the election. The leadership of CITUB decided that its position as an agency of 'constructive opposition' was incompatible with direct participation. However, it held discussions with the main political parties on their policies and issued an appeal to its members to vote for those candidates whose positions on economic and social issues were closest to those of the Confederation. Although Podkrepa had joined the National Commission in May, it refused to accept the CITUB strategy of abstention from political activity in the general election when, to the surprise of many, the Lukanov government was returned to power. Arguably, if the CITUB had adopted Podkrepa's position the chances of Lukanov's re-election would have been lower.

Subsequently, the CITUB and Podkrepa co-operated in tripartite negotiations for an Agreement on Social Peace during the summer of 1990, but towards the end of the year Podkrepa supported a series of strikes. These were later endorsed by the CITUB, and these strikes were instrumental in bringing about the fall of the Lukanov government in December 1990, a clear demonstration of its dependence on the trade union confederations. At about the same time it was announced in *Duma*, the Socialist Party's newspaper, that the Peoples' Trade Union 'Edinstvo' (Unity) had been set up. Although formal links with the Socialist Party were denied, there was an impression that its creation had been inspired by members of the BSP who were critical of the political role played by the CITUB. The fact of its creation at this time and its putative link with the BSP is a further indication of the importance of trade unions in the political arena.

The Popov Coalition Government, December 1990 to September 1991

The context for the creation of a coalition of the BSP with the UDF was that of macroeconomic stabilization as the first stage of economic reform. This was a time of great external dependence because the financial assistance sought from the International Monetary Fund was conditional on the adoption of the IMF's policies, including price liberalization. This was both the key step for stabilization and the one with the greatest risk for social unrest. Given the part played by the confederations in the fall of Lukanov's government and the need to ensure as far as possible the prospects for maintaining popular consent the IMF insisted on a binding agreement on social peace which would have all organizations with power to press their interests, including the trade unions, as parties to it. Representatives of the IMF therefore met the leaders of both confederations to secure assurances about their policies. Subsequently there have been further meetings, though not on a regular basis, and also with the World Bank.

In exchange for their agreement, the confederations secured the institutional development of the tripartite structures and an extension of the coverage of tripartism. The Agreement on Social Peace of January 1991 provided a fixed ratio between the minimum wage and the 'social minimum' and a revised mechanism for indexation. The National Commission became a standing body which met almost weekly and had seven subcommissions, including one to deal with privatization. Under the Lukanov government the tripartite relations had formally been consultative, with the responsibility for the implementation of agreements resting with the government. Under the coalition government the relationship became one of joint decision-making, and in March it was agreed that the Commission's decisions would be binding on state organizations at the lower levels.[9] Thus the trade union confederations achieved centrality in the formulation of national economic strategy.

In the preparations for the election in the autumn of 1991 both confederations were active in relation to aspects of the electoral and political process, though in different ways. As in 1990 the CITUB had discussions on its policies with the main parties and was very conscious of the increasing need for a voice in the national assembly. At one stage it was hoped that a social-democratic political formation might emerge, corresponding to the broadly centrist political stance of the CITUB. There were therefore detailed discussions with those centre parties of the UDF whose political orientation could broadly be characterized as social-democratic – including the Bulgarian Social-Democratic Party itself – as well as with other parties. However, before the election there was a split in the centre grouping of the UDF and as a result the 20 representatives of the CITUB were included in the electoral lists of parties which failed to pass the four per cent threshold. Podkrepa as a constituent organization of the UDF played a more direct role in the election. Of all the organizations within the UDF it had the best established structures in the different localities. Podkrepa formed special citizens' committees as a legally legitimate mechanism for circumventing the constitutional prohibition on the participation of trade unions in political activities. These committees nominated candidates on the UDF list and operated as the UDF's principal campaign agency in different parts of the country. Without this organizational support from Podkrepa the UDF would have been weaker and its success in the election can be seen as the product of its dependency on Podkrepa.

The Dimitrov UDF Government, October 1991 to December 1992

The election results showed the depth of political polarization. The UDF was only narrowly ahead of the BSP and was dependent on the support of the Turkish-based Movement for Rights and Freedoms to form a government, while parties supported by 20 per cent of the voters failed to pass the four per cent threshold necessary to secure parliamentary representation.[10] After the election Podkrepa announced that with the election of a non-socialist government its main political goal had been achieved, and it formally withdrew as a constituent of the UDF, declaring its intention to concentrate on industrial relations functions. However a significant group of deputies (between a quarter and a third of the UDF group in the assembly) and some ministers were, and remained, members or supporters of Podkrepa. They formed therefore a potentially significant grouping in the assembly.

Dimitrov's government was committed to a liberal free market economic policy following monetarist policies for the control of inflation and the budget deficit. Dimitrov soon made clear that the government wished to reduce the influence of tripartism in the formulation of national economic, employment and social policy, which was declared 'ineffective' and was held to be creating obstacles for the government. In this period Dimitrov spoke in positive terms of Podkrepa but ignored the CITUB. Towards the end of 1991 the government initiated legislation for the confiscation of the property of the former Communist Party and associated institutions, such as the Fatherland Front which it had formerly sponsored. With the support of Podkrepa, a group of UDF deputies added the CITUB to the list of organizations whose property was to be confiscated. This became a major political issue in Bulgaria and led to the involvement of the ILO and international trade union organizations. It was finally resolved when Podkrepa and the CITUB signed an agreement on the redistribution of property in October 1992.

Podkrepa found that the dominance of monetarism in government economic policy created trade-union problems which gradually pressured it into alliance with the CITUB. At the end of 1991 a split in the leadership of Podkrepa led to the formation of the National Trade Union Podkrepa. The leaders of the new organization said they were leaving Podkrepa because its involvement in politics was too great and the leadership style was undemocratic. Differences between the government and Podkrepa at one time led to its leader, Konstantin Trenchev, being barred from leaving the country. The distancing of Podkrepa from the government was followed by the development of closer relations between the government and the other unions which had separated from Podkrepa illustrating the interdependence of trade unions and parties in Bulgarian conditions.

In May 1992 the economic crisis and the convergence of the CITUB and Podkrepa on policy issues – they issued joint memoranda to the government in April and again in May with the support of the employers – led to a government reshuffle and the formal revival of tripartism through the formation of a National Council of Social Partnership. However the trade union confederations judged that the government had failed to implement decisions agreed in the National Council. There were a number of strikes during the summer, and disagreements about the rate of indexation of wages and the payment of wages in the health and education sectors. The Council lapsed as an institution in September.

During the autumn of 1992 the Dimitrov government was in continuing crisis and it fell when the Movement for Rights and Freedoms withdrew its support. The crisis was eventually resolved by the creation of what was termed a 'government of experts' – that is, a non-party one – under Berov at the end of December. Once again the key external task for the government was to secure a fresh agreement with the IMF. Internally the key change was the restoration of tripartism as the central mechanism for the formulation of national economic strategy. For the first time the institutions of tripartism were given full legal status in the revised Labour Code of January 1993, so that Podkrepa and CITUB were once again at the centre of the process of strategy formulation on economic and social policy. In addition there were provisions for the establishment of tripartite councils at the lower organizational levels of industry, in the regions and in the municipalities. In 1991 the CITUB had already, in fact, initiated some tripartite commissions at local level with the regional and municipal trade unions, the local employers and the local council, which led to some local tripartite agreements. The prospect of the further development of this process is potentially of great importance for bringing the trade unions formally into a relationship with local government and hence with local parties and politics.

The Organizational Characteristics of Bulgarian Political Parties and Trade Unions

Among the common features of trade unions and political parties as organizations are institutional structures, memberships and policies, with institutional structures susceptible of being local and regional as well as national. At the national level the membership size of trade union confederations is a major basis for their claims to participate in the formulation of national strategy. Political parties on the other hand derive their power from elections, and the size of their memberships are not necessarily correlated with election results. In Bulgaria the only political party with substantial membership and developed local and regional structures (inherited from the Communist Party) is the Socialist Party. Its structure makes for relatively coherent strategy formulation at the national level, while its local structures have been especially effective in rural areas. Membership remains substantial (probably 300–400,000 in 1993), although it is drawn disproportionately from the older sections of the population. Apart from the BSP there are the parties affiliated to the UDF and a multiplicity of other parties with small or local memberships. In the 1991 election 37 registered parties received votes, though only three surmounted the 4 per cent threshold required for parliamentary representation.[11]

Although the UDF secured the most votes its organizational structures were much weaker at both the local level and in terms of strategy formulation at the national level. The analysis of the UDF as a political institution by Dr Konstantin Trenchev, the President of Podkrepa, was a critical one: 'The inherent mistake of the UDF was its failure to institutionalize itself. In actual fact it represented formations with small organizations and with no solid structures within the country'.[12] Podkrepa was active in seeking to promote solutions to these weaknesses at both the local and the national level. At the local level it offered to provide the UDF with institutional structures based on its local union structures. At the national level it supported UDF attempts to move from a federal to a more centralized model of strategy formulation and one in which local organizations were expected to endorse national policies. The rejection of these proposals stemmed from opposition to the concept of transforming the UDF from a coalition to a more centralized organization and to concern about the power that Podkrepa would derive from its role in the creation of local UDF organizations. This episode is important as a further illustration of a trade-union confederation acting as the principal agent in the attempted transformation of a political organization.

The situation of the trade-union confederations, with their structures at national, industry, regional and municipal levels, has been rather different. The data on trade-union membership at different dates show that despite a fall in numbers they remain organizations with mass memberships (Appendix 2). The unions are able to claim to represent the interests not only of the employed but also pensioners (about 25 per cent of the population) and the growing numbers of the unemployed and in specific cases also of ethnic groups (Podkrepa's role in representing the interests of the ethnic Turkish minority has been described above; the gypsies in one district of northern Bulgaria are affiliated to the CITUB). Survey data at the beginning of 1993 showed that the voting intentions of CITUB members were distributed across the political spectrum. Organizationally, therefore, the trade unions could claim to articulate and aggregate the interests of a high proportion of the population, thus performing a representational function for their members which is only partially undertaken by those political parties with small memberships.

Conclusions

The dynamics of Bulgarian politics have been shaped by a particular configuration of external and internal dependencies. The high foreign debt and the need to attract external investment for technological innovation have created conditions of continuing dependence on international agencies for successive governments. Thus the establishment of the Popov coalition at the end of 1990 and of the Berov government at the end of 1992 were closely connected with periods of negotiations with the International Monetary Fund. This dependence has been asymmetrical and not a relationship of interdependence in the sense discussed by Keohane and Nye.[13] The external dependence has influenced the pattern of internal dependencies. Thus industrial conflict has been a major element in Bulgarian politics at particular periods, while governments have had only limited benefits to offer the majority of the electorate. Consequently the necessity to secure political consent, or at least to maintain a situation of 'social peace', has made them highly dependent on the main trade union confederations. Trade-union opposition or the loss of trade-union support led to the fall of two governments in 1990, while the attempt by the Dimitrov government to exclude trade unions from effective tripartism contributed to its weakening and eventual fall. Dependence on trade-union support and the balance of power between governments, parties and trade unions as organizations necessarily shifts in response to changes in conditions and to events. Thus in periods of industrial crisis and in negotiations with the IMF governments have been highly dependent on trade union consent. Equally there has been a similar dependence by parties at the time of the elections held in 1990 and 1991. Thus, despite the apparently strong legal separation of the trade unions from political parties and exclusion from political activity the trade union confederations have been leading agencies in the political arena.

Outstanding features of the post-revolutionary Bulgarian political arena have been its instability – six governments and two elections in three years – and the polarization of party politics between the BSP and the UDF. At the level of party politics it is arguable that it is the survival of the BSP that has been the main force shaping the pattern of Bulgarian party politics. Despite some defections, for example by the Alternative Socialist Party, the BSP has survived as a major integrated, relatively cohesive and stable political institution, albeit with several internal groupings. In contrast, the federal structure of the UDF, with each affiliated party having a vote on the National Coordinating Council, has made it a relatively fissiparous organization in which the determination of policy and the securing of cohesiveness is more difficult. In practice its integration has been to a considerable extent dependent on the existence of the cohesive opposition from the BSP and it has not so far achieved the full organizational integration as an anti-socialist party favoured by some of its constituents. The institutional consequence of the polarization between the BSP and the UDF is that so far it has inhibited the growth of political groupings more in the centre of the political spectrum, of the type associated in western Europe with the concept of social democracy.

The relations between the parties and the different confederations and national trade union organizations have been a continuing theme in post-revolutionary politics. The history of the development of trade unions and political parties in western and northern Europe provides examples both of trade unions creating or facilitating the establishment of political parties especially in the context of developing labour movements and of political parties creating trade unions. Post-revolutionary Bulgarian history also provides examples of both, though it is not appropriate to speak of the emergence of a labour movement there. Podkrepa as a union played a major role in facilitating the development of the UDF as a new political formation, while the BSP was associated with the emergence of Edinstvo. However it is significant that in 1992 the BSP report on 'Trade Union Policy' made no mention of Edinstvo. The report noted that BSP members were to be found in a range of different trade unions and, though it urged them to participate actively in union affairs, it did not attempt to specify the form participation should take.[14] When the Podkrepa leadership became distanced from the power groups in the UDF in 1992 the unions that broke away from Podkrepa became associated with these groups.

The uneasy balance between the political and industrial roles of trade unions has been a recurring issue for confederation leaderships. Podkrepa's foundation as an anti-communist organization meant that the dominant theme of its constitutent congress in 1990 was that of opposition to the Communist Party and membership of Podkrepa and the Party were clearly incompatible. At its second congress in 1992 the issue of whether BSP members could be members of Podkrepa was hotly debated. The congress decided that BSP members could join Podkrepa, but that they could not hold executive positions.

Although the formal withdrawal of Podkrepa from the UDF did not take place until after the election of the UDF government in October 1991, the question of the relationship between its political and industrial roles had been earlier recognized as a strategic issue. Thus in July 1990 Dr Trenchev's view, as President of Podkrepa, was that it was necessary for Podkrepa to avoid the mistake made by Solidarity, which had begun as a revolutionary trade union but had lost membership when it became a party as well as a trade union.[15]

In the turbulent conditions of January 1990 the possibility of CITUB fielding candidates in an election was a question posed in its referendum. Subsequently its centrist political position, and the absence of a significant party political centre, has kept it from direct alliance with any political party. Although at one stage the leadership of the CITUB identified the feasibility of facilitating the emergence of a social-democratic political formation as a strategic issue it was soon recognized that the pattern of political polarization between the BSP and the UDF foreclosed on the emergence of any significant centrist 'social-democratic' grouping. These conditions have created a duality in the political position of the CITUB. On the one hand it has lacked a party political voice of the kind enjoyed by Podkrepa through its relation with the UDF. On the other hand the cross-party nature of its membership and its independence have given it the opportunity to articulate the economic and social interests of a substantial segment of the Bulgarian population.

In the unstable political conditions in Bulgaria there has been space for the trade-union confederations to operate in the political arena as leading agencies in the 'bargaining triangle' and indeed to operate as driving forces for political, economic and social change. The trade unions have been in a position to articulate policies intended to protect as far as possible both the immediate and the longer-term interests of their members. The most important institutional mechanism for this has been tripartite negotiations at national level through the National Commission. Tripartism has become widely established in eastern and central Europe since the creation of the Hungarian prototype in 1988, and there is evidence that international agencies have encouraged its development as a means of securing social stability. This study has shown that in Bulgaria tripartism derived at first from the initiative of the CITUB in early 1990. However, in contrast to some other countries, the development of tripartism in Bulgaria has not been a linear one and its scope has expanded and contracted with changes in governments. The general conclusion is that in Bulgarian conditions the scope for tripartism has been greatest when there has been either a coalition or a non-party government. Such circumstances were of course the outcome of failures by political parties to establish stable and enduring governments.

NOTES

1. See Michael Waller's contribution to this collection.
2. Michael Waller, 'Groups, Interests and Political Aggregation in East Central Europe', *Journal of Communist Studies*, Vol.8, No.1 (1992), pp.136–7.
3. K. Petkov and J.E.M. Thirkell, *Labour Relations in Eastern Europe: Organisational Design and Dynamics* (London and New York: Routledge, 1991), p.43.
4. Report of an ILO Mission: *The Trade Union Situation and Industrial Relations in Hungary* (Geneva: International Labour Office, 1984), p.19.
5. Andreas Stadler, 'Problems of Dependent Modernization in Eastern Europe', in Michael Waller, Bruno Coppieters and Kris Deschouwer (eds.), *Social Democracy in a Post-Communist Europe* (London: Frank Cass, 1994).
6. Robert O. Keohane and Joseph S. Nye, *Power and Interdependence: World Politics in Transition* (Boston, MA: Little, Brown, 1977), pp.8–11.
7. Adam Przeworski, *Democracy and the Market Political and Economic Reforms in Eastern Europe and Latin America* (Cambridge: Cambridge University Press, 1991), p.181.
8. J.E.M. Thirkell and E.A. Tseneva, 'Bulgarian Labour Relations in Transition: Tripartism and Collective Bargaining', *International Labour Review*, Vol.131, No.3 (1992), p.356.
9. Ibid., p.360.
10. Dobrinka Kostova, 'Parliamentary Elections in Bulgaria, October 1991', *Journal of Communist Studies*, Vol.8, No.1 (1992), pp.199–201.
11. Kostova, ibid.
12. *Trud*, 23 Jan. 1993.
13. Keohane and Nye, p.9.
14. 'Za Sindikalna Politika na BSP na Savremenniya Etap', Doklad za Plenum na VC BCP. 27 June 1992.
15. Petkov and Thirkell, p.222.

APPENDIX 1

The Law on Political Parties of April 1990 (excerpts)

Art.13 (1) A public organization that is not registered as a political party cannot conduct the activity of a political party.

(2) A trade union or other public organization that is not registered as a political party cannot conduct organized political activity in enterprises, institutions or organizations.

(3) By organized political activity is meant holding mass rallies, demonstrations, meetings or other forms of campaigning in favour of, or to the prejudice of, political parties, as well as of candidates for election.

(4) When a trade union or other public organization conducts political activity as defined in the preceding section the district prosecutor requires it to stop this activity or to register it as a political party within one month.

(5) If an organization does not cease political activity or register as a political party within one month as required by the prosecutor it is dissolved under Article 22.

Electoral Law for the National and District Assemblies and for Mayors (excerpts)

Art.41 (4) Organizations or movements that are not registered as political parties cannot participate in electoral alliances or nominate candidates for [Assembly] deputy, for district councillor or for mayor.

Art.54 (4) Provisional executive committees, provisional managements, other state institutions and trade unions cannot distribute election campaign materials or conduct other campaigning activity.

Bulgarian Constitution of July 1991

Article relating to trade unions and politics:

Art.12 (2) Associations of citizens, including trade unions, cannot advance political goals and carry out political activity which is appropriate to political parties.

APPENDIX 2

Membership of Trade Union Confederations

At the end of 1990 and in early 1991 the memberships claimed by the three largest centres were:

CITUB	3 million
Podkrepa	350–400,000
Edinstvo	230,000

(from 'The Revival of Trade Unions in Bulgaria', CITUB 1991, p.3).

At the end of 1991 the memberships claimed by the centres were:

CITUB	2.5 million
Podkrepa	600–700,000
Edinstvo	250,000

The total workforce was about 3.8 million
(Thirkell and Tseneva, p.358 – see note 8)

At the beginning of 1993 a survey of local CITUB organizations covering 52 per cent of total employees was carried out for the CITUB. Extrapolation on the basis of this survey suggests the following:

CITUB	68.6 per cent	1,640,000
Podkrepa	9.2 per cent	225,000
Other Trade Unions	0.7 per cent	17,000
Non-members	21.5 per cent	520,000

Note: Podkrepa claimed a membership of 700,000 towards the end of 1992.
    A poll carried out by the National Centre for the Investigation of Public Opinion for all

citizens over 18 gave the following percentage data on trade union membership (46 per cent of the sample said they were in employment):

CITUB	17.4
Podkrepa	6.5
NTU Podkrepa	0.1
Other Trade Unions	0.8

The Feud Within Solidarity's Offspring

RADZISŁAWA GORTAT

Solidarity as an organization never fully recovered from the impact of the imposition of martial law in December 1981, though it retained its mythic status. The round-table talks in 1989 were negotiations between elites; society no longer believed in the efficacy of pressurizing government from below. Since then Solidarity has suffered a profound identity crisis. The Union was disoriented after 1989 by the rivalries between political forces that stemmed originally from it, and particularly by the 'war at the top' between Wałęsa the president on the one hand and the Mazowiecki government on the other. Solidarity was led to extend a 'protective umbrella' over the early reforming governments, but this was withdrawn as the consequences of those governments' policies began to bite. Divided internally, the Union did enter the electoral contest, gaining representation in the Sejm as a result of the 1991 elections, only to fail to surmount the hurdle for representation with the 1993 elections.

The main problem in the formation of Poland's democratic system is best expressed if 'parties and trade unions' is rephrased as 'parties versus trade unions'. Poland was the only country where the transformation to political pluralism and a new economic system was rooted in a ten-million-member social movement that in 1980–81 took the form of a trade union – that is, Solidarity. This fact constitutes the reason why Poland's contemporary history is following a different path from that of countries where opposition to the communist regime was weaker and was originally organized in civic movements or national fronts.

The declaration of martial law in December 1981 enabled the communist authorities to postpone the inevitable changes. But it did more: it broke the continuity of Solidarity as an organization, and effectively destroyed its political influence. Solidarity was never to regain its original form. It survived as an active but numerically reduced clandestine structure of democratic opposition and as a myth of a great movement. Outside the trade union itself, which was outlawed, a number of politically and ideologically differentiated underground circles began to grow in importance. The balance between working members on the one hand and members of a political and advisory nature on the other tilted towards the

Radzisława Gortat conducts research in the Institute of Political Science in Warsaw University.

latter. The 1988 strikes were able to do nothing to change this state of affairs. They were strong enough to force the establishment to make certain concession on behalf of the opposition, but they lacked the substance needed to restore the movement to its previous state. Unlike in 1980, when the initiative was in the hands of strike leaders, in 1988 it belonged to an alternative democratic elite derived from the opposition of the 1970s and 1980s and hardened by the years of martial law.

A key turning-point in Poland's transformation was to come, not with the compromise between the government and the striking workers, but during the ensuing round-table talks. The re-establishment of the Solidarity Trade Union was only one part of a wider agreement between elites. For a variety of reasons society, unlike some years earlier, no longer believed in the efficacy of pressurizing the government from below. The Solidarity movement never managed to regain its original size, retaining in 1993 only a sixth of the members it had in 1981 (1.7 million as against over 10 million). The union element in the movement of social opposition was drastically weakened during the summer of 1989. The need to mobilize social support for independent candidates that took part in the semi-democratic elections of 4 June 1989, and the electoral victory of the Mazowiecki government – a victory that set in motion the process of the transfer of power – were wholly responsible for the new circumstances.

Moreover, new pro-democracy organizations came into being along-side the reactivated trade union. A very important role was played here by the Citizens' Committee formed by the Solidarity leader, Lech Wałęsa. A number of local electoral committees were formed that were subordinated to this Committee. It was at this point that a legalized free press and the first political parties were established. Most important of all, however, was the fact that a great part of the Solidarity leadership found their way into parliament (and thus into the Civic Parliamentary Club) and later into the government. Sudden access to power made them feel like an emanation of the nation rather than the representatives of particular social groups.

The Solidarity Trade Union as a Promoter of System Reform

These shifting circumstances did not result in a swift reduction of the Solidarity trade union to the level of the many other organizations that sprang into existence in the public arena. On the contrary, Solidarity still bore a message and was also a symbolic vector of the new reality. Indeed, the Solidarity trade union, with its potential membership of many millions, and with its charismatic leader, was still for many months to come the country's primary, and perhaps the only, guarantee that the political changes were irreversible. This was extremely important for the democratic elites which operated in a reality that was still to a great extent controlled by the old forces.

Solidarity's political importance was also determined by the fact that many influential leaders, and in particular Lech Wałęsa himself, did not develop ties with either the parliament or the government. Very often these people played the role of arbiter on the political scene. This can be clearly observed in the case of the provincial Citizens' Committee which were dissolved so that they could not compete with the Union.[1] Duality was thus avoided. However, one of the key characteristics of the political breakthrough in 1989–90 was the visible tension that had arisen between Lech Wałęsa's Solidarity headquarters in Gdańsk and the Mazowiecki government in Warsaw.

In this power struggle the initiative was definitely on the side of the government. Having an economic team led by Leszek Balcerowicz, an independent economist with few ties to Solidarity, made it possible to turn away from the policies agreed upon at the round-table talks and from promises made during Solidarity's election campaign.[2] Lack of expert advisers and a blind faith in its power soon caused the Union to find itself on the defensive. This was in part the effect of the attitude of Wałęsa himself, who felt, not without reason, that he was the leader more of the nation than of the Union. He declared openly that reforms towards a free market economy would be impossible to implement if the representation of labour was too strong.[3]

The new non-communist government used its vast social support to introduce a radical economic policy of 'shock therapy', which involved grave social consequences but on which the Union was not consulted. The Union opened a 'protective umbrella' over the government as it struggled to put into effect the difficult reform programme. Union activists who were dedicated to the historic cause of rejecting communism did their best to halt revisionist tendencies inside their Union. Conflicts were settled through compromise, which was found thanks to the Solidarity ethos, fear of a restoration of the *ancien regime*, and the hope of better things to come in the future.[4]

As Jacek Kuroń correctly predicted, the shock therapy programme had one major advantage: it fired the public imagination and offered hope, which made the burdens imposed by the reform bearable.[5] Many Union activists sincerely believed that the reforms would bring about an improvement in the standard of living soon. They awaited with impatience the arrival of the new private owners from whom they could demand substantial pay rises.

But these sweet illusions were not the only reason for the Union's help-lessness. Equally important was the fact that on both sides of the negotiating table were supporters of the same traditions for whom the path that the system transformation was taking was more important than the interests of particular groups. As the new political leadership was taking over, a new process got under way whereby union activists joined the govern-ment and the administrative apparatus. It very often happened that union leaders walked away from negotiating tables as directors or even ministers. The new apparatus needed all the professionals it could get, and often found itself offering government posts to influential union leaders.[7]

Social disappointment with the reforms came relatively soon and brought about major changes in the political arena. It also altered the behaviour of those who supported the new leadership. Discontent arose and grew within the Union, giving rise to voices urging that the 'protective umbrella' held by the Union over the government be withdrawn. Adding to the general sense of vexation was political unrest. On one side was the weakening Gdańsk circle gathered around Lech Wałęsa and the National Committee of Solidarity, on the other stood some democratic opposition activists whose ambitions were not satisfied by the new political order created after the round-table talks, nor by Mazowiecki's government.[8]

The Trade Union as an Unintentional Promoter of Party Diversification

Social and political tensions that had been set in motion by the pain caused by the system transformation surfaced most evidently during the presidential campaign of 1990, which was later to be termed the 'war at the top'. With the communist bloc dissolving and Poland's communist party no longer in existence, Solidarity could for the first time show signs of its internal diversity. These concerned such matters as the tempo and direction of the reforms, and the scale of reprisals to be taken against communists, who were adapting to the new circumstances very well. The 'war at the top' was initiated by ambitious politicians. Some of them were aware that social discontent was building up and that it could be defused by creating an atmosphere of new hope, which would enable them to postpone taking responsibility for unfulfilled promises. Others – lower level activists and members of Solidarity – truly believed that their Union's leader's candidacy meant a drastic change in the direction of the reforms: a lesser burden shared by all, but a larger one for the former 'owners of the Polish People's Republic'.[9]

The Unionists were quick to adopt a skilfully formulated political rhetoric, which became the motor driving the reshaping of the Polish political structure. Their efforts not only made Wałęsa president, but also created a deep rift in the hitherto monolithic democratic camp, dividing it into two warring factions. The crystallization of the factors that were to shape the formation of political parties was a side effect of this situation.[10]

Again this was not without consequences for the Union. Clashes between both Solidarity candidates for the presidency pushed the Union to the verge of disarray. The acute nature of the conflicts can be illustrated by the case of Zbigniew Bujak, a legendary underground activist and leader of the strongest regional organization of Solidarity, who was expelled from the Union's ranks when he declared his support for Mazowiecki.[11] Another portion of the Union's activists were lured away from it by Lech Wałęsa and his political camp. But even worse was the fact that the pro-Wałęsa group was not a true ally of Solidarity. Although extensive political possibilities were open to it, no attempt was made to correct the government's social and economic policies. Instead of the promised 'government of change' and of a 'new beginning' the liberal Bielecki government was formed. It continued the neo-liberal policies of its predecessor.

Revulsion from the Mazowiecki camp, which organized itself into the Democratic Union directly after the presidential elections, and a general disillusionment with most political organizations to which the Wałęsa faction became prone – especially the Centre Alliance and the Liberal-Democratic Congress – was transformed into an anti-party phobia. Under the new leader Marian Krzaklewski the unionists suddenly discovered that no party supported employee interests on the political scene.[12] A further explanation for this attitude was the Union's desire to eliminate parties that were infiltrating its structures. Solidarity was still the best organized and most widely recognized institution in the public arena.

The Union as an Independent Political Force

After the setback that it had suffered as a result of its involvement in Lech Wałęsa's presidential campaign, the Union determined to seek new ways of influencing the country's political scene. During Solidarity's third National Convention in February 1991 it was finally decided that the 'protective umbrella' which had been extended to the Solidarity governments should be done away with.[13] In addition the Convention came to the conclusion that the Union needed its own, completely independent and direct method of influencing the legislature and the government, and it decided that this purpose would be best served by presenting its own candidates in the upcoming national elections, and thus being in a position to create its own parliamentary group. Nevertheless the issue caused controversy for several months. Political contacts made during the presidential campaign were not fully exploited in all constituencies. This enabled more or less formal alliances to be made between local Solidarity branches and parties derived from Wałęsa's political circles – in particular with the Centre Alliance and, in two regions, the Christian National Union.[14] There was a general, and dominant, distrust towards parties and their activists. Establishing an electoral alliance at the national level was impossible. Moreover, the very idea of taking part in the elections was controversial, although it was a decision that had been formally taken. One of the major arguments against participation was an apprehension that the Union might win too great a victory, which could lead to its having to form a government and thus taking full responsibility for the country's future. What, in that case, would become of its role as a trade union?[15] These and other fears led to four regional Solidarity organizations refraining from entering the electoral contest.

The electorate dispersed these optimistic fears by giving Solidarity Trade Union candidates only 5.5 per cent of its votes. In place of an enormous success came a prodigious failure. The result made possible the formation of a 27-member parliamentary group which, instead of contributing to the cause of Solidarity, became a source of problems and conflicts. In the politically diverse Sejm the Union group found itself being heavily courted. This situation led to its being drawn into taking responsibility for the nation and for the reforms, which meant putting the Union back onto a course that it had abandoned a year earlier.[16] Its internal divisions deepened further when its parliamentary group participated in the formation of a government of the centre-right, which embarked upon a policy inimical to labour and to the trade unions. Active support for the Suchocka government in particular produced clashes between the Union leadership and its parliamentary representation. Although all the Solidarity deputies signed a declaration of loyalty to the Union, some of them refused to respect the Trade Union Council's decision to reject the government's project for the state budget. The Union's parliamentary group found itself on the verge of a split.[17]

Those conflicts were only the tip of the iceberg. The whole Union was affected by a deep identity crisis as it proved incapable of defending its members against growing unemployment and a permanent fall in the standard of living.[18] Frustrated shop-floor activists went on illegal strikes more and more frequently. This was also stimulated by rivalry with more radical trade unions (that is, Solidarity '80 or some branch organizations of the OPZZ), whose popularity was growing.

At the end of 1992 the Suchocka cabinet started negotiations with all the trade unions on an *Enterprise Pact* in an attempt to control mounting strike pressure. The Pact was to provide a comprehensive regulation of industrial restructuring and give employees some influence over the privatization process.

Before the *Enterprise Pact* could be passed by the Sejm another wave of strikes swept the country in April and May 1993, involving public sector workers who until then had showed reluctance to take such forms of protest. The tough government line towards striking teachers and health service workers made the Solidarity Trade Union position more and more radical.[19] Its radicalization was also brought about by an onslaught on trade union rights by conservative politicians close to the ruling coalition.[20] At the same time the Union structure was increasingly infiltrated by the internal pro-Wałęsa group 'Network' and by right-wing opposition parties.[21] This presented the Solidarity Union with the threat of disintegration.

In these circumstances its leaders decided to take radical steps. Under their pressure the Union deputies proposed a vote of no-confidence which brought down the Suchocka government and led to the proclamation of new elections. Several Solidarity deputies, however, refused to support the no-confidence vote. They later joined the ranks of the Democratic Union and ran on its lists in the September elections.

The Great Loser

This time, too, notwithstanding the protests on the part of its activists and deputies mentioned above, the Solidarity Trade Union decided to present candidates independently.[22] The key slogan of the election campaign approved by the fifth Union congress in June 1993 was 'To complete the Solidarity revolution'. That campaign was conducted under overtly anti-party banners: *'Partii trzysta – przyszłość mglista'* – ('Parties galore, future obscure' – literally 'Three hundred parties – future unclear'), 'Let's choose from Solidarity only', 'Solidarity forever'. The Union's weekly paper tried to convince the public that 'whereas political parties lack social backing, Solidarity, not being a political party, is the only example in this parliament of a *normal party* with a real social backing, and most importantly, responsible to its social base'.[23] The attacks on trade union leader Marian Krzaklewski were interpreted as chagrin on the part of other parties because they proved to be incapable of getting a firm footing with the unionist electorate.[24] In another interview he said: 'We have to choose the trade union option rather than supporting parties, because trade union rights are bound to be reduced, or trade unions may even be eliminated altogether.'[25]

In the elections of September 1993 Solidarity received 4.9 per cent of the total vote. It was short by 14,000 votes of the number required for it to cross the five per cent threshold, and it was thus left outside the parliament. The measure of failure is even more evident if it is taken into account that only one in four Solidarity unionists voted for its list and only 15 per cent of those who voted for Solidarity Union in 1991 elections did so in 1993. The majority of them decided to support the post-communist parties – the PSL and the SLD – or the Union of Labour.

The September elections marked the end of the Solidarity era in Polish politics.[26] The future of the Union has since then been an open question. Its leaders tried to head the process of crystallization of an anti-communist opposition outside parliament.[27] That is the role in which they feel most comfortable.[28] Typically unionist functions still absorbed much less of their attention. The majority of the Union rank-and-file, however, seemed to have the opposite expectations. Both sides awaited the clarification of the policy of the new government constituted by the post-communist parties.

NOTES

1. *Rok 1989. Bronislaw Geremek opolwiada, Jacek Żukowski pyta* (Warsaw: Plejada, 1990).
2. Tadeusz Kowalik, 'Zmiana ustroju – wielka operacja czy proces społeczny?', in Radzisława Gortat (ed.), *Społeczeństwo uczestniczące – gospodarka rynkowa – sprawiedliwość społeczna* (Warsaw: Uniwersytet Warszawski. ISP PAN, 1991); Leszek Balcerowicz, *800 dni. Skok kontrolowany. Zapisał Jerzy Baczynski* (Warsaw: Polska Oficyna Wydawnicza 'BGW', 1992).
3. Lech Wałęsa has stressed that the most urgent goal for Solidarity and for himself is to implement political and economic reforms and only later will the time come for more intensive involvement in trade union activity. The problem lies not only in the sequence of tasks, but in contradictory goals. 'We shall never catch up with Europe if we build a strong union which strongly opposes reform. Solidarity has started these reforms and must help to reconstruct the economy' (Paweł Lawiński, 'Ile wytrzamacie?', *Tygodnik Solidarność*, 1989, No.18).
4. Andrzej Urbański and Józef Orzeł, 'Co Solidarność powinna, czego jej nie wolno', *Tygodnik Solidarność*, 1991, No.8; Wodzimierz Pańków, 'Pod parasolem NSZZ Solidarność', *Tygodnik Solidarność*, 1993, No.23.
5. Jacek Kuroń, 'Podziały w Solidarności. Dlaczego?', *Życie Gospodarcze*, 1991, No.23.
6. 'It is much better for the Union to negotiate with private owners than with a poor state', said Bogdan Borusewicz: 'W roli parasola', *Tygodnik Solidarność* (interview), 1991, No.7.
7. Andrzej Gelberg, 'Zmiana biegu', *Tygodnik Solidarność*, 1992, No.5.
8. Jacek Kuroń, *Spoko, czyli kwadratura koła* (Warsaw: Polska Oficyna Wydawnicza 'BGW', 1992).
9. Jacek Kurski, *Wódz* (Warsaw: Pomost, 1991).
10. The promoters of party diversification were Lech Wałęsa's supporters, who were the first to break up the unity of the Solidarity camp. It was done under the banner of the battle for pluralism as a necessary element of democracy (Lech Kaczynski, 'Ucieczka do przodu', *Tygoknik Solidarność* (interview), 1991, No.5.
11. Janusz Rolicki, *Zbigniew Bujak: Przepraszam za 'Solidarność'* (Warsaw: Polska Oficyna Wydawnicza 'BGW', 1991).

12. Jacek Kurski, 'Maraton spraw', *Tygodnik Solidarność*, 1991, No.17; 'Od fallstartu do wygranej', *Tygodnik Solidarność*, 1991, No.20.

13. 'III Krajowy Zjazd Delegatów NSZZ Solidarność. Podstawowe dokumenty' (Gdańsk: mimeo, 1991); Maciej Jankowski, 'Nie mamy partnera, mamy wroga', *Tygodnik Solidarność* (interview), 1991, No.8; Jacek Kurski, 'Deparasolizacja, czyli szansa dla rządu', *Tygodnik Solidarność*, 1991, No.22.

14. See, for example, the position taken by the leader of the Łódź regional union structure, Andrzej Słowik: 'Partyjny gigant i związkowy karzeł', *Tygodnik Solidarność* (interview), 1991, No.6.

15. 'Scheda po Lechu', *Tygodnik Solidarność*, 1991, No.9.

16. Bogdan Borusewicz, 'Fakty i pakty', *Tygodnik Solidarność* (interview), 1991, No. 39.

17. 'Gdańsk – Warszawa, wspólna sprawa', *Tygodnik Solidarność*, 1993, No.44; 'Jedyna rosądna droga', *Tygodnik Solidarność*, 1991, No.45.

18. Piotr Marciniak, 'Can they Find a Way Out?', *Telos*, No.92 (1992); 'Koniec epoki Solidarności', *Przegląd Społeczny*, 1992, No.5; Kazimierz Kloc, 'Inny Sierpień', *Przegląd Społeczny*.

19. Zygmunt Wrzodak, 'Checmy wzmocnić Solidarność', *Tygodnik Solidarność* (interview), 1993, No.21.

20. Kazimierz Michał Ujazdowski and Rafal Matyja, *Równi i równiejsi (Rzecz o związkach zawodowych w Polsce)* (Warsaw: Oficyna Wydawnicza Rytm, 1993).

21. Jerzy Baczynski, 'Wędka z Sieci', *Polityka*, 1993, No.15.

22. 'Solidarni raz jesnoma', *Tygodnik Solidarność*, 1993, No.27; Jagtenka Wilczak, 'Ostatni wielcy odeszli', *Polityka*, 1993, No.27.

23. Tadeusz St. Piotrowski, 'Czy Solidarność silą proreformatorską', *Tygodnik Solidarność*, 1993, No.31.

24. Marian Krzaklewski, 'Atak ze wszystkich stron', *Tygodnik Solidarność* (interview), 1993, No.27.

25. Marian Krzaklewski, 'Nie damy się nabrać', *Tygodnik Solidarność* (interview), 1993, No.24.

26. Wojciech Arkuszewski, 'Koniec drugiego kanawału', *Życie Warszawy*, No.233, 1993.

27. The Solidarity leader declared that he was willing to co-operate with centre-right and right-wing parties in order to change the configuration of forces that emerged after the elections. (Marian Krzaklewski, 'Poczekajmy dwa tygodnie', *Tygodnik Solidarność* (interview), 1993, No.42. The trouble is that those parties are hostile to labour and the trade unions. This dilemma is difficult to resolve as the debate between potential allies showed ('Dyskusja liderów opozycyjnej prawicy', *Tygodnik Solidarność*, 1993, No.43).

28. Marian Krzaklewski stated that 'among the groupings that were left outside parliament the Union found itself in the best position, since electoral defeat did not mean losing any of its previous means of action' ('Poczkajmy dwa tygodnie').

Trade Unions and Economic Transformation in Poland

KAZIMIERZ KLOC

Trade unions in Poland are split into three main groupings. The first, Solidarity was initially close to the government whilst the second, the OPZZ, was widely regarded as a collaborator with the old power structure. 'Independent' unions boast of having no political affiliations. All unions have been influenced by shifting employee attitudes as support for government economic policies has declined. Disputes initiated by Solidarity have been directed towards continuing economic transformation. Spontaneous protest actions have reduced the credibility of trade unions. Uncompromising attitudes on any side are inappropriate and could carry serious political dangers.

Trade Unions in Poland after 1989

Three major trade union organizations emerged in Poland after 1989. These were Solidarity, the independent trade union formed after the Gdańsk strikes of 1980, trade unions associated with the All-Polish Alliance of Trade Unions (OPZZ for short in Polish[1]), and unions established after 1989 which were independent of both main groupings.

Solidarity performed a historically crucial role in 1980–81 when this trade union, or rather social movement, was the main force opposing the communist system. At that time, its membership was approximately ten million. Following its restoration after eight years of outlawed activity, Solidarity contributed decisively to the ultimate collapse of communist rule in Poland. In June 1989 it won the partially free elections by taking all the seats for which it was allowed to compete. Since then, however, it has been searching for its place in the new political and social configuration and trying to define its role. Put very generally, it has evolved over the past four years from a social movement with clear political ambitions into a reform-minded trade union.

As an instigator of the political transformation, Solidarity provided an 'umbrella' protecting the initial changes in society. As noted in the previous contribution to this collection, it generally supported the reforms associated with the so-called Balcerowicz programme, even though they

Kazimierz Kloc teaches and conducts research at the Warsaw School of Economics.

amounted to a departure from its own economic concept of the 'self-governing republic' as formulated back in 1981. The union abandoned its idea of employee-controlled management of state-owned economic entities and switched to supporting radical market solutions involving a profound transformation of ownership relations. Although Solidarity reestablished its trade union structures after 1989, it has not been able to regain its previous size. Its membership is currently around 1.7 million.[2]

The unions forming the All-Poland Trade Union Alliance (OPZZ) are the second important part of the union scene in Poland. This trade union organization, formed in the later stages of martial law and holding its first national assembly in November 1984, claimed to organize over 60 per cent of the labour force during the latter part of the 1980s. It entered the transformation period with a 'communist collaborator' label. It then defined itself as a pure trade union. It has tried to avoid a high profile involvement in politics while stressing its role as a defender of the interests of employees. It therefore adopted a form of neutrality towards the economic transformation. Although it does not reject market-type reforms, it has concentrated on outspoken criticism of the economic policies of successive governments and on emphasizing their negative impact on working people. According to OPZZ data, its membership exceeds four million.

The third part of the trade union movement is made up of a considerable number of diverse organizations. They initially came into being as a result of divisions in the two major organizations described above. These developments gave rise, for example, to the Solidarity 80 trade union. This organization, which originated from the Solidarity mainstream, opposed the strategy of compromise with the communist administration, reflected in the round-table negotiations in the spring of 1989. Later, Solidarity 80 took a critical stance towards the whole package of economic reforms implemented by Solidarity-dominated governments. In its official declarations, it concentrates on typical trade union activities aimed at protecting employee interests, above all in the state-run sector of the economy. Solidarity 80 claims almost 500,000 members.

The Mineworkers' Union Federation is an example of a trade union which formerly operated within the OPZZ structures and then became independent. Its secession stemmed from disillusionment with what it saw as the excessive willingness of the OPZZ to compromise in face of the changes occurring in the coal industry. Like some other unions, including the Polish Teachers' Association, the miners' union was also keen to break away from the organization that was still regarded as a 'collaborator' under the former regime. It claims a membership of 250,000.

Apart from unions that have emerged out of splits from the OPZZ, a number of new representative bodies have been established from scratch. In many cases, these are small organizations of employees performing specific jobs in one enterprise or sector. Examples include the Union of Railway Locomotive Drivers in Poland, the Union of Employees of Plants Operating on a Continuous Basis and the Union of Air Traffic Controllers. Most union organizations of this type have adopted a militant, demand-oriented posture. They place great stress on their independence and on their origins. They boast of zero involvement with the Solidarity ethos or with the legacy of the OPZZ. They claim that this gives them an advantage, making it easier to attract new members and to win employee support. Activists of the leading unions of this kind have been planning to set up a third country-wide trade union organization.

The trade union scene in Poland, as presented above, has also been characterized by shifts in the overall positions of particular unions within socio-economic life.[3] In 1990 and 1991, a major role was played by Solidarity as the protective umbrella. Gradually, however, the social consequences of economic changes, leading in the first place to a decline in real incomes and to growing unemployment, have widened the gap between the union's policies and its members' expectations.

Employee disappointment was first noticed by Solidarity organizations in workplaces. That led them to adopt a more radical attitude which was then picked up by sector-level union structures. This occurred especially in the areas worst affected by the recession which were experiencing the most rapid rises in the level of unemployment. Factory, regional and sectoral level Solidarity structures began pressing more and more for a removal of the 'protective umbrella' held by the union's Home Commission over the economic policies of successive governments.

The OPZZ however, still suffering from its origin as a former regime union, did no more than complain verbally about the consequences of government policies. Nevertheless, growing employee discontent encouraged the OPZZ to take more radical steps. It thereby gradually moved out of the social and political isolation it had experienced in the first two years of economic transformation. Nevertheless, relations with Solidarity were characterized by a mutual reluctance to engage in any forms of co-operation. This refers primarily to Solidarity, which even forbade its factory commissions from setting up joint strike committees with other unions during enterprise-level disputes.

This left other unions, such as Solidarity 80 and some of the larger unions that had left the OPZZ or that were established as completely new organizations, in a favourable position from which to develop their activities. Thus the role and scope of these activities increased in

1992. Assuming that the general line of the two largest union groupings remained unchanged, this trend could be expected to continue in the coming years.

Employees and Trade Unions

In Poland in 1992 approximately nine million people were employed outside agriculture. The above data on trade union membership, based on information from the organizations themselves, points to a unionization ratio of around 70 per cent. This is undoubtedly an exaggeration. It is moreover clear that employees do not place a great deal of faith in trade union activity.

One piece of sociological research indicates that only one third of employees hope for any improvement in their living standards or for protection of their interests as a result of trade union activity. Fifteen per cent of employees put their faith in Solidarity, ten per cent in Solidarity 80 and nine per cent in the OPZZ. In the opinion of approximately 30 per cent of employees, the only option is to rely on oneself, as no organization can protect employee interests effectively. The remaining third could express no opinion.[4]

A number of sociological studies have pointed to employee disappointment with trade union activity during the economic transformation. Criticisms relate not only to the traditional trade union role of representing and protecting employee interests, but also to the unions' broader impact as a social movement. In particular, employees have criticized the reform process, methods of privatization, the authorities' attitude to state-owned enterprises and the distribution of the costs of the transformation. As the impact of economic changes became more pronounced, so employee discontent has centred on the threat of unemployment and the difficulties with satisfying basic needs in life.

Over the first three years of an economic transformation programme based on neo-liberal economic concepts, employee attitudes have been subject to a gradual process of changes. In the first stage, covering 1989 and the first months of 1990, a large part of society was convinced of the necessity of a radical economic transformation aimed at the creation of a market economy. This was reflected in support for the government's economic policies and in a willingness to accept the need for temporary sacrifices in the interests of stifling inflation. Thus price liberalization, coupled with firm wage restraint, led to a substantial fall in consumption. The operation has been judged by its supporters to be a success, as they can claim that society swallowed the bitter pill of deteriorated living standards.

The second stage of changing employee attitudes towards the transformation of the economic system started in the second half of 1990 and lasted until the end of 1991. It was characterized by a growing disenchantment with the high costs of the economic transformation and by an increasingly visible social disintegration. At that time, employee fears centred on the rapidly growing level of unemployment. From a recorded level of zero under central planning, it rose to 6.1 per cent of employees at the end of 1991 and 11.4 per cent at the end of 1992. There were wide regional variations, with 4.2 per cent unemployment in Warsaw at the end of 1992 against figures of over 20 per cent in some more isolated small towns and rural areas. Nevertheless, the majority of employees working in state-owned enterprises and in sectors financed directly from the central budget felt threatened. They therefore demanded job security rather than wage rises.

This growing sense of social disenchantment led to increasing disappointment with the two main trade union bodies, creating scope for the development of new trade unions. Eventually, both Solidarity and the OPZZ became more militant. In 1991, and especially 1992, both trade union organizations staged, without coordinating their actions, a number of country-wide protest actions and strikes.

Unions and Strikes

There was a general tendency for the number of strikes to increase as support for government policies declined. In 1990 official statistics recorded 250 strikes with 115,687 participants leading to the loss of 159,016 working days. In 1991 there were 305 strikes, involving 221,547 participants and with the loss of 423,106 working days. Generally speaking, strike activity was most pronounced in areas of highest unemployment.

There were national protest actions in 1991 and 1992 which generally took the form of token, or 'warning' strikes. Most of them were staged over price rises, for example to protest against increases in the price of energy which was still subject to state control. In other cases they were expressions of the unions' dissatisfaction over the absence of negotiations with government representatives prior to decisions leading to further declines in living standards.

Trade union organizations also gave backing to several regional actions protesting against the government's failure to decide on policies for regional regeneration in areas threatened with high levels of unemployment. The first major focus of this kind of action was the Łódź region, hit hard by the fall in consumer demand for its traditional textile products. The rate of unemployment at the end of 1992 stood at 15.4 per cent, which was above the national average and exceptionally high for a major conurbation. The aim of this kind of protest was to force the government to negotiate with trade unions and to take decisive action on issues that had been raised repeatedly by the union side.

The most interesting information on the positions of different unions in relation to employee protests comes from an analysis of government figures on disputes and strikes within particular enterprises and sectors during 1991 and 1992.[5] Wage demands were raised in most of the surveyed disputes. This, however, did not always mean that pay was the trade unions' main concern. Equally important in many disputes were demands for the revision of planned lay-offs, for the formulation of enterprise restructuring programmes and for privatization procedures that would provide employee participation. As the recession deepened, so job protection often became a greater concern than unrealistic wage demands.

At the enterprise and sector levels, Solidarity and OPZZ activists differed considerably in their assessments of who was responsible for the difficulties employees were experiencing. OPZZ activists blamed the government and the systemic transformation. Their Solidarity counterparts, generally defending the government they were associated with, attempted to put the blame on managerial staff, especially the so-called 'old *nomenklatura*'. Despite that difference, workplace organizations of the different unions usually co-operated with each other. The mutual distrust between the union centres was less pronounced at the enterprise level.

Sixty per cent of conflicts and strikes during 1992 were initiated by Solidarity. In 25 per cent of cases the Solidarity factory commission supported demands put forward by another trade union or employee group. Solidarity was the initiator of conflicts particularly in cases in which the ultimate list of demands was not confined to pressing for more pay. Equally important were the demands for enterprise restructuring, privatization, job protection and management change. These demands were consistent with the union's policy of support for the general direction of economic restructuring. Thus enterprise-level activists, acting under strong employee pressure for more pay, were seeking solutions to other problems faced by enterprises.

Trade unions associated with the OPZZ were less likely than Solidarity to initiate industrial disputes. Despite being in Solidarity's shadow, they supported the demands put by Solidarity organizations in roughly 50 per cent of cases, leading to frequent co-operation during disputes. This was especially important when disputes escalated into strikes. The OPZZ organization claimed to be the instigator in 25 per cent of disputes surveyed. In some cases both unions acted independently, competing with each other. Indeed, 80 per cent of employees in enterprises experiencing disputes and conflicts had a negative impression of co-operation between unions.

Other unions were involved in only one conflict out of three. In most cases they just supported demands put forward by someone else. In 25 per cent of cases they defined themselves as a dispute instigator. These were either conflicts in which all unions were involved or conflicts instigated solely by a trade union other than Solidarity or the OPZZ. It should be pointed out that in this latter case, the remaining two trade unions stayed aside or even opposed the conflict, dismissing the third union's demands either as excessive or as concerning a small group of employees only.

The fact that a union declares itself to be the instigator of a dispute need not be particularly significant. In 15 per cent of disputes surveyed the actual instigators were all employees of an enterprise or employee groups and their demands were taken up by a union organization which then claimed to be the initiator. In some of these cases employees lost confidence in their trade union representatives and in their ability to act effectively. These were precisely the situations that gave the opportunity for new trade unions, with their populist ideology, to gain credibility by taking up employees' demands.

The Dangers Ahead

During 1992 several representatives of the centre-right parties in the government coalition began complaining that growing trade union radicalism and strength could lead to a union-dominated state and, consequently, to a deceleration in the economic transformation process.[6] At the same time, activists at various levels of different union organizations accused the government of torpedoing negotiations. They complained of protracted talks that were bringing no concrete results, while the position in some sectors and regions was steadily deteriorating. Union activists complained that, even when agreements were reached, the government would not stick to them.

The experience of union activity during the economic transformation demonstrates the dangers of inflexible attitudes. Had Solidarity continued with its consistent and unlimited support for neo-liberal methods of economic transformation, the result would probably have been the union's self-destruction. On the other hand, the approach of avoiding political commitments by a restriction into pure trade union activity would not have contributed to solving the problems of the economic transformation and would have risked blocking further changes. Unfortunately, past governments seem not to have understood the social consequences of changes taking place in the Polish economy at a time when extreme attitudes on both sides could lead to escalating social conflict.

The negoiation and signing of the 'Pact on the State-Owned Enterprise in the Process of Transition', or Enterprise Pact, in early 1993 showed a willingness on both sides to seek new solutions. Unfortunately, the Solidarity union finally and definitively withdrew its protective umbrella precipitating the fall of the Suchocka government before the relevant legislation could be passed through parliament. After the elections of September 1993 a new government was formed made up from the 'post-communist' parties. It remains to be seen whether it will maintain its current intention to ensure the acceptance of the relevant laws. It does however seem likely that, irrespective of changes of government, the start that has finally been made to tripartite negotiations – involving the state, trade unions and employers' organizations – will be continued in the future.

NOTES

1. *Ogólnopolskie Prozumienie Zdwiązków Zawodowych* (All-Polish Alliance of Trade Unions).
2. 'Z pozycji kibica' (Interview with Marian Krzaklewski), *Rzeczpospolita*, 1993, No.146.
3. Kazimierz Kloc, 'Polish Labor in Transition (1990–1992)', *Telos*, 92 (1992).
4. See, for example, Julian Gardawski and Tomasz Żukowski, *Polityka i gospodarka w oczach pracowników* (Warsaw: Ministerstwo Pracy i Polityki Socjalnej, Fundacja im. Friedricha Eberta, 1992), and *NSZZ Solidarność wczoraj i dziś. Uczestnictwo związków zawodowych w życiu publicznym* (Warsaw: Centrum Badania Opinii Społecznej, 1993).
5. Kazimierz Kloc and Władysław Rychłowski, 'Konflikty w okresie przełomu ustrojowego', unpublished report of empirical research results, 1992.
6. Kazimierz Michał Ujadowski and Rafał Matyja, *Równi i równiejsi (Rzecz o związkach zawodowych w Polsce)* (Warsaw: Oficyna Wydawnicza Rytm, 1993).

Trade Unions, Industrial Relations and Politics in Russia

SIMON CLARKE

Unions under socialism had little involvement in industrial relations. They were primarily concerned with supporting communist power through a welfare function. Independent workers' organizations emerged under Gorbachev, but they were very small compared with the official unions. The transition to a market has led to a reconsolidation of paternalistic corporatism. Social tension has been defused as the official and new unions have jostled for position, all failing to become a channel for employee grievances. The official unions' frequently militant rhetoric belies passivity, the roots of which are grounded in the continuation of past practices. The workers' movement has had little influence on Russian political development, although the current situation cannot be stable.

Trade unions in the Soviet bloc were primarily political organizations, charged with overseeing the implementation of party policy in the social sphere. With the collapse of the Soviet system and the abolition of the Communist Party the trade unions have to find themselves a new role. At the same time, with the transition to a market economy and the mass privatization of the system of production, workers have to find some means of representing and defending their sectional and collective interests. In this study I explore the extent to which there has been a convergence of these two imperatives in Russia. To what extent have the former state trade unions found themselves a role in the new society, both in the system of industrial relations and in the political sphere? To what extent have workers been able to develop organizational and political forms through which to defend their own interests? In particular, what is

Simon Clarke is a member of the Department of Sociology at the University of Warwick. This study is based on research on trade unions, industrial relations and workers' organizations which has been conducted with Dr Peter Fairbrother, in collaboration with groups of Russian sociologists, since 1991. This has involved extensive fieldwork in six regions of Russia, focusing on the regional and local levels of trade union and workers' organization, with intensive case study research in twelve enterprises, and monitoring of another thirty. Although use has been made of documentary, archival and published sources, the judgements and conclusions are based primarily on our own interview materials. The research has been funded by the University of Warwick Research and Innovations Fund, the East–West Programme of the ESRC (Grant No. Y309253049), and the Nuffield Foundation. The author is very grateful to Peter and to all his Russian friends and collaborators.

the role of tripartite structures in providing a negotiated framework for the transition?

In the first section, the role of trade unions and the form of industrial relations in the Soviet system are briefly examined. In the second section the growth of industrial conflict and the rise of the independent workers' movement between 1987 and 1991 are treated. In the third section I look at the development of industrial relations in the transition to the market economy. In the final sections the political role of the old and the new unions is analysed.[1]

Trade Unions and Industrial Relations in the Soviet System

The Leninist conception of trade unions under socialism defined the unions as the transmission belt between the communist party and the masses, and as a school for communism. The trade unions were accordingly constructed on strictly hierarchical lines, according to the principles of democratic centralism, and subordinated at every level to the communist party – in the Soviet case, the Communist Party of the Soviet Union (CPSU).[2] The trade unions, under the leadership of the communist party, were said to represent the interests of the working class as a whole, against all sectional interests. For this reason the principle of occupational unionism was rejected in favour of the principle of branch unionism, with all those working in a particular branch of production being members of the same union.

Under Stalin the unions were moribund, but they acquired a progressively more important role as the regime sought to provide material and moral incentives to stimulate the growth of productivity, in place of purely repressive forms of control of labour. In theory, the primary role of the trade unions was to encourage the growth of productivity, for example by organizing production conferences and socialist competition. These activities, however, never succeeded in mobilizing more than the core of party and union activists, being regarded with scorn by the majority of workers. In practice, the unions' primary role was the distribution of social and welfare benefits, including the allocation of places in vacation centres and sanatoria, kindergartens and pioneer camps, the allocation of housing, and the administration of the bulk of the state social security system.

In the words of the present Deputy Director of the official Russian trade union federation (*Federatsiya nezavisimykh profsoyuzov Rossii –* FNPR), the unions were 'not trade unions at all, but the social and welfare department of the central committee of the CPSU'. Within the enterprise the trade union was universally identified with the Communist Party and the enterprise administration, performing its welfare and distributive functions to provide a paternalistic reinforcement of their authority.

Soviet trade unions collaborated with the enterprise administration in preparing social development plans, and signed annual collective agreements with the administration, but the role of the trade union was at best an advisory one. It had often merely to rubber stamp proposals drawn up unilaterally by the administration. Trade unions also had a nominal obligation to defend the considerable legal rights of workers in the face of management violation in such areas as health and safety, disciplinary violations, dismissal, illegal overtime working, and underpayment of wages and bonuses. The union had to approve any revision of norms, and no worker could be dismissed without the approval of the union. In practice, however, grievance procedures were rarely used and it was very rare for the union to do anything but endorse management decisions.

Industrial relations were handled not by the trade unions, but through the management structures. Wage rates were determined centrally, and norms determined by the administration. In practice, however, line managers had a great deal of discretion, which they would use to negotiate with workers informally to ensure that their shop or section met its plan targets. This informal negotiation was essentially on a personalized and individual basis.

Conflict at shop level was endemic, and centred on such issues as the calculation of wages and bonuses, the allocation of overtime, work allocation, the provision of supplies of parts and raw materials, disciplinary infractions, and the distribution of social and welfare benefits. However, in the absence of any means of collective expression of workers' grievances, conflicts were handled on an individual and discretionary basis by foremen and line managers, normally at the level of the primary work group: it was very rare for conflicts to be referred beyond the level of the shop. Any attempt on the part of workers to organize independently was ruthlessly suppressed.

Short work stoppages were not uncommon under the old system, but would usually involve only a handful of workers, and would be rigorously hushed up for fear of repercussions from above. Only rarely would a stoppage involve a whole shop, and quite exceptionally a whole factory. In the event of a work stoppage senior managers or party officials, or both, would arrive at once, reassure the workers, and meet their demands immediately, the victimization coming only later. Worker activists might be tolerated if they kept within the limits of the system and retained the confidence of their fellow workers, but could be ruthlessly victimized if they over-stepped the bounds.

The Growth of Industrial Conflict and Independent Workers' Organization

The first independent workers' organizations developed during 1987, in response to Gorbachev's attempt to mobilize shop-floor pressure in support of '*perestroika* from below'. The first organizations developing out of such conflicts were typically led by long-standing activists with primarily political motives. However, the independent workers' movement made only limited progress between 1987 and 1989, and strikes remained sporadic, spontaneous and small-scale.

Independent workers' organization grew more rapidly in response to the political polarization during 1989, as both 'democrats' and 'conservatives' sought to mobilize support among workers. Local democratic groups were formed to contest the elections of 1989 in most cities, and looked to workers for support. The United Workers Front (*Ob"edinennyi front trudyashchikhsya* – OFT), with its roots in the conservative elements of the trade union and party industrial apparatus, was formed to mobilize workers in opposition to the 'democrats'.

The most rapid and dramatic development of the workers' movement was in response to the miners' strikes of July 1989, when workers' committees were set up in many enterprises and, in the coal-mining regions, at city and regional level. Although no mine was on strike for more than a week, the strike swept through all the major coalfields and won huge concessions. The miners had broken through a fundamental barrier, by showing that it was possible for workers to achieve their aims by organizing independently and by taking strike action. The victory of the miners thus gave courage to activists everywhere.

The new generation of workers' leaders were typically young and well-educated, many being workers by choice or as a result of victimization. Many had been active in the CPSU or official unions, often having recently become involved in official structures, in the spirit of *perestroika*. However, their disillusionment with official structures turned to a radical rejection of the whole system as it became clear that reform was impossible without fundamental change. While the 'democrats' fought to create a place for themselves within a reformed system of class rule, the majority of the worker activists wanted to abolish all forms of privilege and exploitation.[3] However, with the discrediting of 'socialism' they lacked a clear ideology within which to express their aspirations.

The two main features of the ideology of the new workers' movement were a radical workerism and a radical democratism, which turned the rhetoric of the system against itself. The ideology and iconography of the

Soviet system was strongly workerist in asserting the priorty of manual over mental labour, and stressing the unproductive character of all labour that did not produce a physical product. Soviet workers were fragmented, disempowered and repressed, but retained a contempt for the system and for the white-collar workers and managers they regarded as its toadies. This was expressed in the workerist ideology provided by the system as the means of dividing mental from manual workers. Similarly, under the impetus of *perestroika*, workers took at face value the ideology of workers' participation and workers' control which was negated by the practice of democratic centralism. These two features were expressed in a number of different ideological forms, from the ultra-liberalism of the Democratic Union (*Demokraticheskii soyuz* – DS), through syndicalism (the miners' movement) and anarcho-syndicalism (KAS, *Spravedlivost', Nezavisimost'*) to the neo-Bolshevism of *Rabochii*, Workers' Unions and the various splinter 'Marxist Workers' Parties'.[4]

The different political groups used widely different rhetorics to express similar aspirations. The Democratic Union denounced Gorbachev's elections as a fraud and backed the demand of the more radical workers' groups that the Communist Party should be expelled from the enterprise: this was at a time when the leading 'democrats' were afraid to antagonize the party, indeed most were still party members. The Confederation of Anarcho-Syndicalists played an active role in helping establish a number of workers' groups, and built up an information network which still exists at the time of writing (1993). The various neo-Bolshevik parties based their programmes around the demand for the dictatorship of the proletariat, which did not mean the neo-Stalinism of the OFT, but the subordination of the intelligentsia to the workers and the transfer of power to the Soviets.

The differences and antagonisms between most of the groups were not differences of principle as much as personal differences between their leaders. It took fiercely individualistic and strong willed people to stand out against the system, and such people were not willing to subordinate themselves to anybody else's programme. However, outside the coal-mining areas the level of worker organization remained very low, with a proliferation of tiny groups struggling to survive with minimal resources. In practice people attached to apparently very different political forces worked closely together on the ground in strike committees and workers' committees, established on the basis of the workplace or the locality. Nikolai Travkin's Democratic Party of Russia was the only party to make a point of recruiting workers and establishing workplace cells. It was also the only party with a significant, though still tiny, working-class membership.

In the coal-mining regions the strike committees remained in being, converted to workers' committees. In Kuzbass a regional workers' committee and a Union of Kuzbass Workers were established. The activists initially adopted the strategy of taking over the official structures, and many strike committee members were elected to positions in the official union at the level of the local mine, and on the Labour Collective Councils of the mines. However, it had become clear by the spring of 1990 that this strategy was having little success. In the autumn of 1990 the miners set up their own Independent Miners' Union (*Nezavisimyi profsoyuz gornyakov* – NPG) although it was virtually indistinguishable from the workers' committees.

Although the independent workers' movement grew in strength between 1989 and 1991 it owed its position more to political patronage than to the development of an organizational base within the working class. In many cities individual worker activists were elected to local councils in the 1990 election, and got some protection from their political position, generally linking with the democratic factions which came together to form Democratic Russia. The NPG and miners' workers' committees had close links with the democratic movement, and with the Interregional Group of People's Deputies, which gave them political and material resources. *Sotsprof*, which had been formed as the Association of Socialist Trade Unions in 1989 and which became well known in the West through its connection with Boris Kagarlitsky, initially enjoyed the tacit protection of official structures. It was regarded with great suspicion by the rest of the workers' movement.

Its first congress in July 1989 was jointly sponsored by the official trade union federation (the *Vsesoyuznyi tsentral'nyi Sovet professional'nykh soyuzov* – VTsSPS), and addressed its resolutions to the Central Committee of the Communist Party. Moreover *Sotsprof*, unlike any of the other independent trade unions, admitted management to membership, and allowed its members to retain membership of the official union. Sotsprof was torn by internal conflicts through 1990, and was unsuccessful in recruiting any significant numbers of workers before the end of 1990. Nevertheless, it achieved its political influence by becoming closely linked to the Social-Democratic Party, with which it signed an agreement. The Confederation of Free Trade Unions (*Konfederatsiya svobodnykh professional'nykh soyuzov* – KSPS), whose leaders came out of the Democratic Union, had even fewer members than Sotsprof, but had financial backing from abroad. A number of other independent trade-union federations were primarily commercial organizations, enjoying the tax advantages accorded to trade unions. Various initiatives sponsored by Moscow intellectuals, such as the Confederation of Labour and the

Union of Labour Collectives, were given a good deal of publicity but came to nothing.

At the level of the enterprise, even in the coal mines, the official union remained dominant, administering the system of 'authoritarian paternalism' through which management maintained the fragmentation and subordination of the workers. Industrial conflict increased steadily with strikes becoming more frequent. Nevertheless, independent workers' organization within the enterprise remained very weak as the administration responded to growing conflict with a dual strategy of immediate concession to workers' economic demands and victimization of independent activists. Independent workers' groups remained very small, usually confined to one or two shops, with only very loose connections with any wider organizations, which were mainly important in providing legal services and political contacts. It was only where activists enjoyed strong support from workers, and the patronage of locally powerful political structures, or support from a faction of the enterprise administration, that they were able to survive.

It was above all the continued strength of the system of authoritarian paternalism in the enterprise that limited the emergence of independent trade unionism in the workplace. It also politicized such independent workers' organization as did exist, and led the independent workers' organizations to look to the liberal democratic movement, with its proclaimed opposition to party rule, for support and direction. The hope of the majority of independent worker activists was that the destruction of the administrative-command system, the transition to the market economy and mass privatization would break the power of the *nomenklatura*, and open up repressed class divisions to create the space for independent workers' organization. Thus even the neo-Bolsheviks voted for Yeltsin in the 1991 presidential election.

Industrial Relations in the Transition to the Market Economy

The hope that the transition to a market economy would destroy the system of authoritarian paternalism has not been realized. In place of a clarification of class relationships, there has been a reconsolidation of paternalistic corporatism. The rhetoric of socialism has simply been replaced by the rhetoric of 'social partnership', with little change in its essential content. The system of industrial relations within the enterprise has changed very little.

The enterprise administration has lost the support of outside political bodies and repressive agencies in preventing the workers from organizing independently, but this has been compensated by the workers' growing fear of unemployment and economic insecurity in the face of high inflation. Although central wage determination has largely ended with the collapse of the administration-command system, pay increases in compensation for inflation are determined unilaterally by the administration. Industrial conflict is still handled primarily through the management structure, although line managers more readily refer disputes 'upstairs' than they used to do in the past.

The focus of the rhetoric of social partnership is the annual collective agreement, and the one major change in labour legislation in the first year of reform was the Law on Collective Agreements passed in March 1992.[5] The significance of this law is that it established the collective agreement as the outcome of a process of collective bargaining in which there were clearly defined distinctions in rights and duties between employers, employees and the state. Although collective agreements in the past had required the signatures of the enterprise director and trade union chair, they had not resulted from partisan bargaining, but had been prepared by a mangement commission and adopted by a meeting of the whole labour collective. In practice, however, there has been little change in the character of collective agreements and the form of their adoption, and the rhetoric of 'social partnership' has been used to express not a conciliation of potentially opposed interests, but the traditional paternalistic structure of representation of corporate interests.[6]

The 1992 Law on Collective Agreements gave equal rights to all properly constituted trade unions. It thereby provided a focus for the activity of the independent trade unions, which were able to propose amendments or even alternative collective agreements in a handful of enterprises. Initially such proposals were greeted with horror by the management, but such independent initiatives were soon absorbed into the traditional system, as independent worker representatives were invited to join the enterprise commission and so were absorbed into the framework of 'social partnership'.

The official trade unions have been largely discredited, and their activity within the enterprise is confined to their welfare and distribution functions. Since the autumn of 1992 there has been a tendency for the enterprise administration to take over many of these functions itself, in order to give greater weight to its paternalistic claims and to back its ideology of 'social partnership'. In many enterprises the trade union chair has been moved with his or her functions into the administration, to be appointed Deputy General Director for Social Questions – in at least one case while illegally retaining the position of trade union chair – a position which also enables him or her to participate in the privatization privileges accorded to senior management. In such cases the trade union is left with no other function than to rubber stamp management decisions. This does entail some risks for management, since the removal of functions from the union does make it more difficult to control. In practice, however, once deprived of its functions, the union generally becomes moribund and is retained by management only for fear that in its absence workers might form their own organizations.

Successive waves of worker activists have uniformly failed in their efforts to reform the trade unions within the enterprise over the past six years. They have either been absorbed into the bureaucracy or have given up in despair or disgust. Since the powers and resources of the trade union, apart from union dues and social insurance funds, derive from the administration, the administration has very close control over the union's activity. It can simply withdraw resources from a recalcitrant union. The distribution of consumer goods through the enterprise has only added to this control. Although we have met plenty of radical union officials, in our research we have been unable to find a single case in which the official trade union has in practice opposed the management of the enterprise on behalf of the workers. Where it does oppose the administration it represents not the workers but an oppositional faction in the administration backed – or more often before August 1991 sponsored – by the party.

Since the 'victory of democracy' at the end of 1991, independent worker activists have come under steadily increasing pressure. Many have been systematically victimized and dismissed – often repeatedly, since they frequently secure reinstatement through the courts. Membership of an independent trade union provides some legal protection, since union officials are protected against victimization, and the union still has to sanction all dismissals. This, rather than any growth in the strength of the workers' movement, is the main reason why independent unions have proliferated since the beginning of 1992, with their first principle being a refusal to sanction the dismissal of any of their members. However, it is one thing to have rights on paper, it is quite another to defend them through expensive and lengthy legal processes, so it is only the larger unions, with good political contacts, which are able effectively to defend their members.

The collapse of the centre meant that enterprise management was no longer subject to political or administrative control. It was able to act with a free hand in containing and eliminating independent workers' organization, where the latter did not enjoy strong support or powerful political backing. Enterprises were increasingly ready to take advantage of Gorbachev's anti-strike law, which had been passed in 1989 in the wake of the miners' strike, but was rarely used before the putsch. Moreover, the growing reliance of workers on the enterprise administration and the official trade unions for access to essential food and consumption goods distributed through the enterprise gave the latter a greatly increased leverage over the workers. All these factors made conditions extremely difficult for independent workers' organization.

Apart from the strikes of medical and education workers in the spring of 1992 to be discussed below, the level of overt conflict was very low following the introduction of shock therapy at the beginning of that year. However, there remained a very high level of latent conflict within enterprises, and social tension mounted through 1992 as wages lagged behind inflation, as workers were put on short-time or sent on 'administrative vacation', and as cash shortages meant that wages often went unpaid for months at a time. Cash shortages eased from the middle of 1992, and many workers benefitted from wage indexation which halted the erosion of real wages, and in some cases enabled them to regain lost ground. However, additional sources of tension appeared in the growth of pay differentials as managers' – official and unofficial – earnings rose rapidly ahead of those of workers, and in the privatization process. This was almost universally seen by workers as a trick which benefitted only their managers, who alone could afford to buy the bulk of the shares, with share allocations often tied to their newly inflated incomes.[7]

Although conflict has remained largely latent, the growth in social tension is potentially extremely dangerous in the absence of any institutionalized channels through which workers can articulate, negotiate and resolve their grievances. At the same time, the enterprise administration has shown itself to be universally unwilling to provide such channels for fear of the demands that would be unleashed. Enterprise managers have therefore sought to maintain the subservience of the official union, and to suppress any attempts at independent workers' organization by all the means at their disposal, and there is not much that Western management consultants can teach Soviet managers about union busting. Meanwhile, they have done their best to avoid confrontation by responding to the grievances of the workers within the limits of the existing system. They have run into debt to meet the wage bill, put workers on short-time or suspended them on basic pay, rather than allowing mass lay-offs. They have pressed for state subsidies to maintain production and employment, sometimes backed by orchestrated strike threats from the official unions. They have used the enterprise's products to barter for food and consumer goods to be provided for the workers at reduced prices and have backed privatization to the labour-collective as the basis for profit-sharing, in line with the ideology of 'social partnership'.

Management has also sought to exploit and intensify existing divisions within the labour force in order to maintain its control. There have been

long-standing latent conflicts between workers and 'ITR' (engineering
and technical staff), between production and auxiliary workers, between
young and old, and between men and women. Management has exploited
these divisions by widening differentials, and also in determining lay-offs,
with the bulk of redundancies hitting female administrative workers and
older auxiliary workers, in addition to those with poor disciplinary
records – mostly for drunkenness and absenteeism – and 'troublemakers'.
Decentralization of enterprises and associations has also proved an
effective means of setting shops against one another, although it also
carries the risk of disintegration as profitable shops try to break away.

On the other hand, divisions have also opened up within the enterprise
administration, often over questions of managerial style (authoritarian
versus paternalist), and strategy (the retention of existing products and
markets versus development of new ones). The most serious division
within the administration is that between the central administration,
increasingly responding to the pressures of the market, and line management, which is taking increasing responsibility for maintaining production
and enforcing labour discipline.

The shop chief in particular is at the focal point of a growing contradiction between two systems of production: the proto-capitalist system of
market relations, which requires that production be subjected to the
dictates of the market, and the Soviet system of production in which plan
targets are achieved on the basis of informal bargaining with workers, the
latter retaining primary responsibility for the conduct of production.
Shop chiefs are being required to increase productivity, to develop
new products and new methods of production, without being given the
financial or material means which will enable them to buy off the workers
in order to achieve those tasks. They are then expected to resolve the
industrial conflicts that arise, and take the blame if strife escalates out of
control. In such circumstances it becomes increasingly likely that shop
chiefs will take up the workers' grievances in the event of open conflict
with the administration, and this tendency can already be observed in a
growing number of enterprises.

Within this common pattern, economic instability has led to some
divergence between enterprises, depending primarily on their economic
situation.[8] Many enterprises in military and heavy industries, which had
previously been the most privileged, have found themselves in a precarious
economic position. Many of these enterprises see a continued flight of skilled
workers, the collapse of labour discipline, a loss of managerial authority,
and high levels of conflict, particularly between workers and engineers
and technical staff. The enterprise administration tends to avoid conflict,
making every effort to maintain wages and avoid lay-offs. Divisions some-

times appear between one faction which seeks conciliation and another which prefers confrontation and a return to the old system of authoritarian and repressive management, enforced by large-scale lay-offs.

Conflict tends to be fragmented and unorganized, but rank and file pressure, often reinforced by an oppositional faction in management, can lead to the radicalization of the official union leadership. However, even in such cases it proves very difficult for reformers to transform the existing structure and functions of the trade union, squeezed between management pressures on the one side and workers' expectations on the other. Although tension built up in these enterprises in the autumn of 1992, a large increase in subsidies, directed particularly to the military-industrial complex under the guise of conversion loans, temporarily relieved the pressure at least until the summer of 1993 when the promised funds failed to materialize.

Enterprises which produced consumer and intermediate goods in relatively high demand were much better placed to maintain production and to provide barter goods and higher wages for their workers. This is especially true of monopolists and of firms that have opportunities to export. These enterprises have tended to develop a strongly paternalistic management style, with a low level of overt conflict, the main forms of which were small-scale and sporadic affairs over the distribution of consumer goods between different groups of workers. The unions in such enterprises retain their traditional role as agents of the administration, preoccupied with their distributional function. The relative prosperity of such enterprises provides some scope for change, but the paternalistic management style tends to preclude confrontation with the workers. There has been very little fundamental restructuring of production, the main emphasis being on developing commercial and financial opportunities and diversifying production. Economic instability also means that such enterprises remain very vulnerable to a deterioration in their economic conditions.

A very few industrial enterprises have moved in a capitalist direction. These tend to be enterprises that broke away from the state sector by transfer to leasehold or co-operative ownership in 1990–91, and that were then privatized during 1991–2, with the majority of shares initially being sold to the labour collective. These enterprises have often made large cuts in the labour force, mainly laying off administrative, auxiliary and unskilled workers, compensated by substantial pay rises for the workers who remain. These enterprises tend to reject paternalistic methods. Instead, they favour a strengthening of managerial authority and a strong emphasis on material incentives, based on the combination of high wages, substantially increased differentials, and profit sharing through employee share ownership. The distribution of consumer goods tends to be downplayed.

Overt conflict tends to be very limited, partly as a result of prosperity, and partly because trouble-makers are systematically selected for dismissal. Nevertheless, workers tend to be highly aggrieved at increased differentials in favour of management, and at their exclusion from decision-making processes. The union remains in place, but is marginalized and has little role to play. The success of these enterprises depends primarily on the intensification of labour, rather than any restructuring of production, and their ability to exploit market opportunities to maintain high profits and high wages. They are therefore vulnerable to a deterioration in their economic position, which can lead to the radicalization of the workers. Many such enterprises owed their success in 1990–91 to the divergence between state and market prices, and were hit very hard by the liberalization of prices in 1992 which removed this advantage. Others owed their success to a monopoly position in the market, which was retained through 1992, but which made such enterprises vulnerable to political pressure. To cover such risks there is a tendency in such enterprises to diversify into financial, commercial and property speculation.

To sum up, the official trade unions at enterprise level have at best retained their traditional structure and functions, and at worst have been marginalized. Independent workers' organizations have proliferated, but remain very small, are subjected to severe management pressure, and do not play any significant role in industrial relations. These continue to be handled through management structures. However, social tension and latent conflict is growing within enterprises, and this is putting pressure on the management structure. It is very unlikely that the official union will provide an effective channel for workers' grievances, while independent unions remain very weak. In these circumstances it is likely that growing unrest on the part of workers will be expressed through conflicts within the management hierarchy, and particularly between line management and the central administration. It will therefore largely be confined within the framework of authoritarian paternalism and the rhetoric of 'social partnership', giving rise to continued demands for state support as the means of averting deepening conflict. In short, there are very few signs that industrial conflict will provide the basis for the development of independent workers' organization, or of a political role for the working class.[9]

The Development of the Trade Unions – From Developed Socialism to Social Partnership

The All-Union Central Council of Trade Unions (VTsSPS) had asserted its 'independence' from party and government as early as 1987, not as a progressive but as a conservative force. The VTsSPS increasingly stood out against government plans to introduce market reforms, insisting on very substantial social guarantees, such as high levels of unemployment pay, as preconditions for any agreement to new legislation. This rearguard action was extremely ineffective, and simply meant that the unions lost what little impact on policy they had once enjoyed. The VTsSPS was replaced by a new General Confederation of Trades Unions (*Vseobshchaya konfederatsiya profsoyuzov* – VKP) in October 1990, although the change had no real, substantive implications until the collapse of the Soviet Union in the autumn of 1991.

In response to the 1991 miners' strikes the VKP coordinated its activity closely with Pavlov's government, stressing the need for a new system of collective bargaining within a corporatist tripartite framework, and reaching a general agreement with the government in April, including a no-strike pledge. The agreement was not worth the paper it was written on, because the programme presupposed the existence of a system that had already disappeared and the authority of a body which was entirely discredited. The unions themselves were disintegrating *pari passu* with the system itself, as union bodies at every level asserted their independence from higher levels. Following the disintegration of the Soviet Union at the end of 1991 the VKP was reduced to an empty shell, although it still had ambitions to create an international trade union federation.

From the spring of 1990 the official branch unions began to set up separate Republican organizations, including the Federation of Independent Trade Unions of Russia (FNPR), and to reconstitute their regional committees. The formation of the FNPR marked the attempt of the branch unions to distance themselves from the party and the Soviet Union's government, and to weaken the grip of the former trade union centre. It was really another expression of the attempt of the enterprises, associations and concerns, with which the official unions identified, to establish their economic independence. The FNPR leadership was soon involved in a behind-the-scenes struggle with the VKP, as a result of which the FNPR allied itself with Yeltsin in his struggle with Gorbachev: they had a common interest in undermining the central powers and establishing Republican sovereignty.

While the VKP backed Gorbachev in resisting the 1991 miners' strike, the FNPR threatened a general strike if Gorbachev did not back down, and later backed Yeltsin in the Russian presidential elections. The FNPR also called a one-hour strike on 26 April 1991, with support from Democratic Russia, to protest against higher prices and worsening living conditions. It claimed that 50 million workers had responded, although very few enterprises actually struck. At best, the 'representatives' of 50 million workers had attended meetings. The split between the VKP and the FNPR meant that the branch unions, the majority of which were affiliated to both, had their options well covered.

The putsch of August 1991 accentuated the division between the VKP and the FNPR. The latter denounced the VKP's failure to distance itself from the plotters, although it had also sat on its hands at the time, and took the opportunity to establish its position as the dominant union body in Russia. Following the coup the FNPR was cautious in its opposition to the Yeltsin government, insisting that it was a non-political organization which had only trade union aims. Its leader, Igor Klochkov, visited Japan and decided to launch an 'autumn offensive' under the well-tried slogan of 'market wages for market prices'. However, its attempted display of strength back-fired when its demonstrations attracted a derisory turn-out. A warning strike called for November was cancelled, supposedly on the grounds that Yeltsin had accepted the FNPR's main demands.

Following its abortive display of militancy the FNPR became more muted in its criticism of the government, just as the government was launching its neo-liberal programme of 'shock therapy'. The FNPR leadership insisted that it supported the general direction of reform, but differed over its details. The difference over the details amount to a comprehensive programme of opposition to the Yeltsin programme, issued in March 1992, involving demands for the full indexation of wages and benefits, the provision of a comprehensive social security safety net, controls on the prices of essential food and consumption goods, subsidies for unprofitable enterprises, and maintenance of health and education budgets in real terms. Although the FNPR continued to make veiled threats through its frequent references to the dangers of rising social tension, its criticism was largely rhetorical, not least because the official unions were anxious to retain their considerable legal privileges, their control over enormous amounts of government money, and their very substantial property holdings.[10]

The official trade unions were in a very vulnerable position. Lacking the confidence and support of their membership, they had always depended on the power of the party-state for their authority and for their prosperity. The unions enjoyed considerable legal rights and protection against both the enterprise administration and their own members. Moreover, the unions were enormously wealthy bodies. In addition to the one per cent of the wage bill checked off by every employer as membership dues, the unions owned large and prestigious office buildings in the centre of every city. They owned the bulk of the tourist and holiday facilities throughout the country, in addition to the sanitoria, sporting and cultural facilities which had been assigned to them. Over the years of *perestroika* the trade unions had also become increasingly involved in 'commercial activity', nominally to provide food and consumer goods for their members, but also augmenting the wealth of the unions and the fortunes of their leaders. Finally, the unions administered the bulk of social security payments, the funds for which had simply been assigned to the unions by the government without any effective monitoring or accounting. They could be used by the unions at their discretion.

The FNPR and branch unions at national level were finding themselves in increasing financial difficulties as unions at enterprise and regional levels reduced their affiliation fees to the centre. The leaders of the FNPR and of the official branch unions were only too aware of their vulnerability. However much they might oppose the reform programme, they knew that they lacked the popular support to mount an effective campaign against it, and they knew that if they overstepped the mark they could be stripped of their resources overnight.

The independent 'alternative' unions meanwhile had backed Yeltsin, and played a leading role in the defence of the White House. After Yeltsin's counter coup the liberal leadership of the independent workers' movement finally achieved its political aims, and its personal ambitions. The leader of the Kuzbass Workers' Committee, Vyecheslav Golikov, moved into Yeltsin's administration. Mikhail Kislyuk, who had been the intellectual leader of the Kuzbass Workers' Committee at the beginning of the movement, and had managed to be alongside Yeltsin in the White House, was appointed as the latter's Chief of Administration in Kuzbass. The entire Sotsprof leadership moved into government as nominees of the Social-Democratic Party, helping to draft new trade union and social legislation.[11]

The leaders of the independent trade union movement saw Yeltsin's victory as their opportunity to challenge the power and prosperity of the official unions in three important ways. First, they pressed for a re-registration of unions to give workers the opportunity to choose which bodies would represent them, in the hope that workers would throw out the official unions in favour of new bodies. Second, they pressed for a redistribution of union property on the basis of membership following re-registration. Third, they pressed for the removal of the administration of social security funds from the hands of the official unions, and their replacement by a system of state or private social insurance. In practice the independent unions did not press too hard for immediate re-registration because they were afraid that the official unions would be able to use their massive organization and resources to prevail in the process, thereby gaining a powerful legitimation.[12] The priority was therefore to weaken the official unions financially and politically before attacking their mass base.

In the event, the leadership of the independent workers' movement found itself with as little room to manoeuvre as did that of the FNPR. Workers looked to their employers for pay rises to compensate for inflation, and where they were organized looked to independent trade unions to represent them. However, the leaders of the independent workers' movement were unwilling to mobilize their membership, seeing their principal role as one of representing their membership through negotiation with the government, while containing worker unrest in order to prevent a populist backlash. Thus the independent workers' movement soon found itself mimicking the traditional role of the official unions, and equally unable to articulate workers' interests and aspirations.

While the new trade unions were unable to mount an effective challenge to the old, the Yeltsin government was well aware of the danger that the official unions could present if they were to provide the focus of an effective campaign of mass opposition to the 'reform' programme. It suited the government much better to allow the official unions to retain the privileges which maintained them in a position of dependence, while encouraging the official and independent unions to fight among themselves. The result was a tacit compromise between the government and the official unions, in which the latter confined themselves to rhetorical attacks on the government, and the government confined itself to rhetorical attacks on the unions.

Despite their sometimes militant rhetoric, the official unions' opposition to the Yeltsin government was in practice equivocal and ineffective. This passivity was a consequence not only of their dependence on government patronage to retain their legal and property rights. The trade union apparatus was still popularly, and in many cases accurately, identified as the rearguard of the former Communist Party apparatus, so that, while polls indicated that its demands had growing popular support, it had little success in mobilizing that support.

With the disintegration of the hierarchical relationships imposed by party control, the central and regional union bodies had lost their authority over lower levels, and that made it impossible for them to back their threats with concerted action. For this reason the FNPR, almost all the regional committees – the exceptions being the Moscow and St Petersburg regional committees – and the branch unions maintained their support for Yeltsin and his reforms through 1992. They backed price liberalization, privatization, and even the curtailment of the legal rights of workers. The republican union bodies had become essentially political organizations, which rhetorically espoused the interests of the working class in the attempt to defend themselves and their property from political or legislative attack, but which in practice represented their members only to the extent that they represented the interests of the production *nomenklatura* on whom the workers depended for their livelihood and their jobs.

Tripartism

The stand-off between the government and the official unions was institutionalized in the 'Tripartite Commission for the Regulation of Social–Labour Relations', established in November 1991. The FNPR was given the bulk of the union seats, but just short of a blocking two-thirds majority. Tripartism threw a lifeline to the official unions. Their representative claims were seriously threatened by conflicts between state, employers and workers, in which the unions, *de facto* representatives of the employers and dependent on the patronage of the state, would have to declare on which side their interests lay.

The Tripartite Commission, which some – including the Sotsprof leadership – had seen as a device to isolate the FNPR, turned out to be an extremely effective instrument for its neutralization. It was implicated in the consensus of rhetorical resistance to the social impact of reform while giving practical support to the process. This position was shared by official unions and employers, and even regularly expressed by Yeltsin himself in his criticisms of his own government. The impotence of the Commission was symbolized in the fate of the General Agreement, which was supposed to embody the principles of tripartite partnership. It was merely a vague statement of intent which was completely ignored. Nevertheless, the FNPR threw itself into the Commission with gusto, concentrating its efforts on lobbying the government rather than attempting to mobilize popular opposition to the reforms.

The principles of tripartism were also adopted in the only significant labour legislation introduced in 1992, the Law on Collective Agreements. In addition to defining the framework for collective agreements at enterprise level, the law also provided a legislative framework for agreements at national, regional and sectoral levels. The precedent for such agreements had already been set by the 'general agreements' regularly reached between the official unions and Gorbachev's governments, in which the government rhetorically promised to provide various social guarantees in exchange for the rhetorical support of the unions. According to the 1992 law, the General Agreement covers the broad areas of social and economic policy, and is reached between national unions, national associations of employers and the state. Similar agreements are drawn up on a tripartite basis at regional level, and tariff agreements are drawn up on a sectoral basis.[13]

Tripartism can hardly be effective when the three parties are not independent of one another, and have no clear mandate to represent anybody. The employers are not independent of the state, which still owns the overwhelming bulk of productive assets and employs the overwhelming majority of the population, but neither are the unions independent of the employers. The result is that it is not at all clear who is supposed to represent whom on such tripartite bodies, and in practice all three sides represent different aspects of the interests of the ruling stratum. The state representatives express the political interests of the ruling stratum, in maintaining social order and political passivity: the employer representatives, who are nominated by the government, represent the interests of the ruling stratum as putative owners: the trade unions represent the interests of the ruling stratum as managers. Not surprisingly, all three sides have a strong interest in fudging their differences and in suppressing conflict, declaring their common goals in a General Agreement which makes no specific commitments and which is never fulfilled.

Tripartism at national, regional and sectoral levels provided an institutional and rhetorical framework within which the identification of the trade unions with the employers developed apace during 1992 under the banner of 'social partnership'. The employers' side of these bodies was dominated by government nominees, which meant that managers of state enterprises had little direct representation. This was in part a reflection of the fact that the disintegration of the administrative-command system and the abolition of the Communist Party had deprived the managerial stratum of the ministerial and party bodies that formerly represented its collective interests. The trade unions filled the gap, taking on the role of representative of the collective interest of management at sectoral, regional and national levels.[14]

Thus the official trade unions turned out in practice to be the grass-roots base of Arkady Volsky's Association of Industrialists and Entrepreneurs, the industrialists and entrepreneurs who supported Volsky proving to be mostly directors of state farms and backwoods enterprises. The official unions could not participate in Volsky's proto-political party, Civic Union (*Grazhdanskii Soyuz* – GS), because of the legal restrictions on the political activity of trade unions and because of the FNPR's firm declaration of political independence.[15] The leader of the FNPR, Klochkov, nevertheless joined the political council of GS. In July the FNPR signed a separate agreement to establish an 'Assembly of Social Alliance' with Volsky's organization. It immediately began to draw up parliamentary bills and to prepare a draft General Agreement for 1993. The two together sponsored one of the main opposition newspapers, *Rabochaya Tribuna*.

Amendments to the trade union legislation in the course of 1992 merely extended the rights accorded to the official unions to any properly constituted union. The official unions lost control of the tourist industry, but otherwise kept their property intact. The administration of social security was modified, so that social security funds remained nominally the property of the state, although still administered by the official unions. This simply implied that in future, at least in principle, the unions would have to account to the government for the use of these funds.

In contrast to the continued patronage enjoyed by the FNPR, the independent unions received virtually nothing from the Yeltsin government which they had helped to put in place, and had to struggle along with minimal resources. Sotsprof received offices from the Moscow City Council, but Gavril Popov, the mayor of Moscow, refused to give offices to the Independent Miners' Union. Like the independent unions of pilots and air traffic controllers, which had broken away from the official union of aviation workers, it worked from offices in the buildings of the appropriate ministry, provided by the employers. The FNPR was assigned nine seats and the chairmanship of the union side of the Tripartite Commission, and Sotsprof, with virtually no members but guaranteed to support the government, was assigned three seats. However, the Independent Pilots' Union and the Independent Miners' Union received one each, and the Air Traffic Controllers none.

It soon became clear to all concerned that the Yeltsin government was using the Tripartite Commission as a means of neutralizing workers' organizations by playing the new unions off against the old, primarily to the advantage of the latter. The initial result of this was to bring the new unions into closer collaboration with one another: the other new unions had formerly kept their distance from Sotsprof on the grounds of its authoritarian leadership, its willingness to admit employers to membership and to allow dual membership with the official unions, its commercial activity, and its lack of trade union activity. However, as the Sotsprof leaders sniffed the way the wind was blowing they showed themselves willing to collaborate with the official unions, leaving the genuinely independent unions increasingly isolated.[16]

The political manoeuvring of the Sotsprof leadership was also arousing the antagonism of its members. Sergei Khramov, the leader of Sotsprof, declared his full support for both the Russian and Moscow governments, without securing any concessions for his members. Over a third of the delegates walked out of the chaotic Sotsprof Congress in February 1992, at which the powers of the central Coordinating Committee were strengthened, and at which Khramov announced the preparation of a moratorium on strikes, except in support of victimized Sotsprof members.

Meanwhile activists in Sotsprof primary groups were showing growing dissatisfaction with the political and commercial preoccupations of the centre, and pursued their own increasingly independent line. In September

1992 Sotsprof tried to compensate for the loss of its popular base by signing an agreement with Konstantin Borovoy's Party of Economic Freedom – a party whose financial resources and foreign contacts more than made up for its lack of members – while moving closer to the official FNPR. The result was to alienate itself from both official and alternative workers' organizations, which united to exclude Sotsprof from membership of the Tripartite Commission in January 1993. Thus the move backfired as the FNPR and its front organizations were assigned all but one of the seats on the union side, the remaining seat going to the independent pilots' union, itself planning to reintegrate with the official branch union.

The reconstitution of the membership of the Tripartite Commission in January 1993 gave the FNPR its anticipated reward for its participation in Volsky's 'loyal opposition'. At the same time pressure was building up within the FNPR for it to take a more militant and active stand in opposition to the government's reform programme. This pressure came primarily from the branch unions and regional structures of the FNPR. These were representing not so much the interests of the majority of the population, which was being pauperized by the reform programme, as the interests of their employers, who sought to increase their influence over the government in pursuit of regional and sectoral interests.

Regional Trade Union Organizations

The pattern of development of the official unions at regional level was very similar to that at the centre, without the complication of independent unions which had very little regional organization. Like the central organization, the regional federations had considerable property at their disposal, and faced financial difficulties with a sharp fall in affiliation fees. They therefore tended to be even more concerned than the FNPR was at national level with consolidating their political position and defending their property. In many regions the local executive bodies remained under the control of the old *nomenklatura*, and worked hand in glove with the official union federation in the attempt to create a regional power base in opposition to the Yeltsin government and Yeltsin's appointed Chiefs of Administration.

In Moscow and St Petersburg, where the local councils were in the hands of the 'democrats', the official union federations pursued a more active oppositional line. They attempted to mobilize popular opposition to the 'reform' programmes of republican and municipal authorities. They tried to link up with other oppositional forces, including the organizers of the Party of Labour, which was eventually established in September

1992 after a series of splits. Mikhail Schmakov, leader of the Moscow Federation, also had more dubious links with various ultra-right groups. The radicalism of the Moscow and St Petersburg Federations achieved only a limited success in securing popular support, but it brought them into opposition with the FNPR leadership in a conflict which first erupted at the FNPR Congress in the spring of 1992.

The most effective attempts by the official unions to mobilize grass roots opposition to the Yeltsin government were the mobilizations of workers in 'budget organizations', primarily teachers and health workers, in the spring of 1992. The pay of these workers had lagged far behind inflation as municipal authorities found themselves faced with a growing fiscal crisis. These mobilizations were most successful in the coal-mining regions, where the enormous pay increases secured by the miners exacerbated local shortages of both cash and goods and pushed local prices up to levels 50 per cent higher than in neighbouring regions. Workers in industry enjoyed equivalent wage increases, which enterprises could cover by raising prices, but workers in budget organizations, which means principally teachers and health service workers, had no compensating pay increases. During 1992 they were earning one tenth or less of the wages of the miners whose children they taught.

The strikes of teachers and health workers over the winter and spring of 1991–92 were localized and sporadic. Their precise form differed from place to place. In many cases they began spontaneously, with the formation of an 'initiative group', and spread from one school or hospital. However, in most cases the conservative branch unions and local union federations took up the cause on a city or a regional basis. They often enjoyed the tacit or active support of medical and educational administrations and local authorities who saw the strikes as a means of extracting increased funding from the central government.

Although the pay of workers in budget organizations continued to lag far behind that of industrial workers, the strike wave of the spring taught Yeltsin to be more attentive to their needs. The government produced a plan for the indexation of the pay of public sector workers, although it did not provide the resources for municipal authorities to pay for the increases. At the same time the government put forward a new hierarchical pay scale for all public sector workers which promised sharply to increase differentials in the hope of exacerbating divisions among public sector workers along occupational lines. Such divisions had already been opening up, as such groups as doctors and teachers and researchers in higher education sought to pursue their own sectional interests. This led to splits within the health and education unions which began to fragment along occupational lines.

The demobilization of the public sector workers deprived the regional trade union federations of an effective mobilizing lever, and on the whole through 1992 they confined themselves to commercial and political activity. Within the FNPR the nucleus of opposition to the leadership provided by the Moscow and St Petersburg federations progressively expanded to embrace most of the federations of the Urals and Volga regions, so that by the autumn of 1992 there was a majority in favour of the official unions pursuing a strategy of more militant opposition to the government.

This underlay the increasingly conservative tone of the rhetoric of FNPR, undermining the conciliatory position of Klochkov. However, at the same time the concentration of the FNPR on political and commercial activity at national and regional levels had largely cut it off from its trade-union base, for which it seemed to have no functions left to perform. These tensions were reflected in the national mobilization in October 1992, as part of the run-up to the December Congress of People's Deputies, which turned out to be uncoordinated. It attracted a derisory turnout, almost entirely confined to apparatchiks, pensioners and peasants, many of whom were bussed in to city centres for the purpose.

The Branch Unions

The branch unions were monolithic and unwieldy bodies. The branch principle of organization was ill-adapted to articulating and expressing the diverse interests of a membership spread across a wide range of occupations and industries, and this was a major reason for the rise of the new independent unions. The most successful of these organized strategically important workers, such as underground miners and transport drivers who, unlike the branch unions, had a strong bargaining position. In response to this challenge there was some tendency towards a reorganization of the official unions along occupational lines. During 1992 some of the largest unions, including those of agricultural, education, and metallurgy workers, began to split up.

The reorganization of the official unions along occupational lines was most advanced in the union of civil aviation workers. This was divided administratively into different sections in 1990, with air traffic controllers, pilots and ground staff organized in sections corresponding to their different professional interests. The independent unions of pilots and air traffic controllers are explicitly sectional unions. They organize workers who compare their conditions with their professional colleagues in other countries, and use their bargaining strength for their own ends, rather than in support of other cabin crew and ground staff. This raises the possibility of the emergence of sectional unions, representing particular categories of skilled workers. There is certainly a tendency in this direction, not only in the division of the branch unions along occupational lines, but also in the development of independent unionism among particular categories of privileged male workers, such as the underground miners, dockers and bus and train drivers.

In practice sectional unionism has not made much headway. The miners found themselves isolated and under growing pressure as a result of their large pay increases in 1992. The air traffic controllers overplayed their hand and were soundly beaten in August 1992, with the full resources of the state mobilized against them. There are a number of reasons to expect that the possibilities of sustaining such sectional unionism are limited. First, such unions have no control over access to their occupations. Second, the skills of the workers in question are by no means in short supply. Third, the relative 'homogenization' of the Soviet working class means that there is not, in general, a secure basis on which to constitute these workers as a privileged 'labour aristocracy'. Fourth, the solidaristic and egalitarian ideology of the Soviet working class still provides a powerful basis of opposition to such sectionalism. For all these reasons, although the independent unions organize privileged groups of predominantly male workers, they are also well aware of the importance of maintaining a degree of solidarity with other workers to avoid the risk of isolation.

A more likely pattern of restructuring is one in which the official unions are restructured along lines which more closely reflect the occupational hierarchies within the sphere of production. This would then open up the possibility of their developing forms of workplace trade unionism. Again, the civil aviation industry shows a possible way forward. In October 1992 the process of reincorporation of the pilots' union into a federation with the official union began, in connection with a restructuring of pay scales. This put the pilots on the top rung, in a move which clearly sought to set them up as a 'labour aristocracy', in both the union and the job hierarchy. Similar patterns of restructuring are emerging in health, education and the civil service in connection with the introduction of new pay scales for public sector workers. However, the significance of such initiatives should not be overemphasized, since union restructuring had more to do with political and personality struggles than with the development of more effective forms of trade unionism.

During 1992 the differential impact of the reform process introduced growing political tensions between the different branch unions within the official trade union movement. While workers in budget organizations found their pay lagging far behind as public authorities lacked the tax revenue to meet their salaries, the pay of workers in other branches of industry was held back by the inability of employers to pay, which many blamed on the crushing burden of taxation. Meanwhile, other groups of workers found their relative economic situation improving in the new conditions of the market economy. The FNPR had based its political strategy in 1992 largely on the plight of the workers in budget organizations, to the relative neglect of the interests of workers in other branches of production. As a result various branch unions began to establish new federations on a sectoral basis, to act essentially as trade associations representing the interests of their sectors of production, leaving open the question of their continued participation in FNPR.

The FNPR strike call in October 1992 brought these divisions to a head, with the official miners' union and the metallurgists withdrawing from the federation as a result. The miners' union, chastened by its humiliation in Kuzbass in the spring, was no doubt looking over its shoulder at the Independent Miners' Union. The metallurgists had only voted narrowly to affiliate to the FNPR in the first place, and had been courted by Yeltsin's close aide Burbulis ever since the autumn of 1991. There was an element of conflict of personal ambition in the withdrawal of the metallurgists, and in many regions the union did not withdraw from FNPR bodies. However, the miners and the metallurgical workers had objective reasons for wanting to distance themselves from the opposition of the FNPR to the Yeltsin government, however rhetorical that opposition might be. Both groups of workers were heavily dependent on the favour of the government as their closely related industries could not survive without massive government support, and their leaders had a realistic appreciation that the government's strategic economic priorities would be determined politically.

The pressures for a more active and effective representation of branch and regional economic interests grew steadily within the FNPR as the economic situation continued to deteriorate and the budget crisis deepened in 1993. Growing popular discontent and the split between president and parliament opened up a political space for more effective opposition. Nevertheless, although it became increasingly critical of the government, the FNPR continued to adopt a cautious policy. It stood apart from the conflict between president and parliament in the first half of 1993, identifying instead with Volsky's centrism. The FNPR formulated a 'Plan of Collective Action', through which it hoped to harness growing popular discontent and to build a political base in case of elections. It also planned more militant action which was supposed to culminate in a wave of political strikes in the autumn. Nevertheless, the FNPR itself did nothing effectively to implement any such 'plan', and tailed behind the strike calls of a growing number of branch unions – including miners, timber workers and defence workers – and regional federations.

Conclusion

The principal conclusion is that the workers' movement in Russia is still extraordinarily weak, and the working class plays little or no direct political role. Nevertheless, the former official trade unions play an extremely important political role not as working-class organizations, but as representatives of the 'production *nomenklatura*' within a quasi-corporatist system of interest representation. They have to some extent replaced the economic apparatus of the Communist Party which had formerly provided the class organization of this stratum.

Although the official trade unions have weathered the immediate transition, keeping their property and their privileges largely intact, this is not a stable situation. At the base it depends on the reproduction of the authoritarian paternalism on which this kind of class conciliation, based on a displacement of class conflict, is built. As the impact of the market economy leads to a differentiation in the fate of enterprises, this system of paternalism comes under increasing pressure. In the most successful enterprises workers seek higher money wages, in place of payment in kind, and managers seek to restructure production and payment systems in order to take advantage of market opportunities. In the least successful enterprises conflict grows, productivity falls, and disintegration is not far behind. At the same time, authoritarian paternalism provides a powerful force for the preservation of stability, at both the enterprise and the societal level, and its impending disintegration mobilizes conservative political forces which seek state intervention to sustain it. The coexistence of authoritarian paternalism with the development of a market economy is not stable, but we cannot confidently predict which of the tendencies will prevail.

NOTES

1. We discuss the character of Soviet trade unions and the development of the independent workers' movement more fully in Simon Clarke, Peter Fairbrother, Michael Burawoy and Pavel Krotov, *What About the Workers?* (London: Verso, 1993), and in Simon Clarke, Peter Fairbrother, and Vadim Borisov, *The Workers' Movement in Russia* (Cheltenham: Edward Elgar, 1994). We discuss workplace industrial relations more fully in Simon Clarke, and Peter Fairbrother, 'Post Communism and the Emergence of Industrial Relations in the Workplace', in Richard Hyman and Anthony Ferner (eds.), *New Frontiers in European Industrial Relations*, (Oxford: Blackwell, forthcoming), and the prospects for trade unionism in Vadim Borisov, Simon Clarke and Peter Fairbrother,

'Does Trade Unionism have a Future in Russia', *Industrial Relations Journal*, forthcoming.
2. The Western literature is polarized between those who regarded Russian unions as representing the interests of the working class in a kind of 'social contract' (Blair Ruble, *Soviet Trade Unions* (Oxford: Oxford University Press, 1981), and those who regarded them as a slightly more benign face of the KGB (Robert Conquest, *Industrial Workers in the USSR*, London: Bodley Head, 1969 and Leonard Schapiro and Joseph Godson, *The Soviet Worker: Illusions and Realities*, London: Macmillan, 1981).
3. In some cases in eastern Europe the 'new workers' movement' seems to have provided a stepping stone to political power for democratic intellectuals. In Russia the radicalism of worker activists prevented the establishment of such a close relationship with the 'democrats'. Activism led more often into 'commercial activity' than into politics.
4. Most of these organizations were very small, with from 50 to a few hundred members. DS and the KAS, each with a predominantly student membership, were the only organizations with anything like a nationwide network. Workers' groups were based on one city, or even one factory, with loose connections with kindred groups. Only in Kuzbass did the Workers' Committee have even a regional structure.
5. It seems that the Sotsprof leadership was most active in drafting and pressing this Law, which conformed to its own conciliatory rhetoric. Other changes to labour legislation were bogged down primarily, it would appear, because of fear that they would provoke conflict, rather than as a direct result of opposition. Thus a law of labour contract was premature when the majority of workers were not yet reconciled to becoming wage labourers; the removal of legal protection of workers' rights might be judged provocative, as would a reduction in the rights of trade unions. Moreover, there was no particular need to change laws which had never in practice been observed, nor to introduce new ones when there was no proper means of enforcing them. The reform of the social security system, which should have been a reformist priority, was vigorously and effectively resisted by FNPR.
6. The sharp divergence between the rhetoric and the reality of trade unionism is a striking feature at all levels from the shop floor to the national stage throughout the former Soviet bloc. In drawing transnational comparisons it is important to compare like with like. There has been very little published research on the reality of trade union activity in the former Soviet bloc, but it seems likely that, despite appearances to the contrary, patterns are very similar. Former official unions have a new leadership and a new political rhetoric, which varies according to time and place from radical opposition to abject submission, but as unions they all work in the old way, and all aspire to re-create their old political role. Where new unions have appeared, there is a strong tendency for them to fit into the mould of the old, performing a conciliatory role as trade unions, with their trade union activity subordinate to the political, or commercial, ambitions of their leaders. At the present stage neither provide an effective framework within which workers are able to express their own interests and aspirations. None of this is surprising, given the common background of state socialist economic and political structures and of a fragmented, demobilized and demoralized working class.
7. On privatization see Simon Clarke, 'Privatization and the Development of Capitalism in Russia', *New Left Review*, 196 (Nov.–Dec. 1992).
8. The following description is based primarily on our own case studies and the observations of our collaborators.
9. Very much the same could be true throughout the former Soviet bloc, with the partial exception of Poland, where independent workers' organization is better established. The former official unions have largely retained their membership throughout eastern Europe. However, this need not indicate their authenticity as workers' organizations, as their apologists would have it, but rather their toothlessness, which makes their survival convenient for both employers and government, provided that they confine their oppositional activity within acceptable limits.
10. Although there were sharp divisions within the leadership of the FNPR, with Klochkov resisting attempts to unite FNPR with the 'conservative' opposition, in my view its

policy was in practice determined primarily by its need to defend its substantial corporate interests.

11. The independent workers' movement owed its strength almost entirely to its political connections, and its financial position almost entirely to its 'commercial' activities. Sotsprof probably had no more than 1,000 members at the time, and even the Independent Miners' Union probably had no more than 5,000. Very few even of this small number paid any dues or held membership cards. As noted above, very few activists in the workers' movement moved into positions of political leadership, but many used their political contacts for commercial benefit.

12. The management of the giant AZLK car factory in Moscow responded to the challenge of an independent workers' organization – nominally affiliated to Sotsprof – with a reregistration in the spring of 1993: workers were invited by their line managers to sign up for the official union before starting work!

13. Tariff agreements, which involve employer representatives, trade unions and the Ministry of Labour, were signed in many sectors, but in most cases they merely embodied existing pay scales and branch labour regulations. Absolute pay levels were not determined by these agreements, but pragmatically by the government in response to various pressures.

14. Just how strong were the pressures to take on such a role is well illustrated by the fate of the largest of the independent unions. Both the miners' and the pilots' unions found themselves thrust into the role of representing their members by lobbying for the sectional interests of their industries in Moscow, partly as a result of their privileged access to government circles, but mainly because the employers were unable to forge a similar unity of interest.

15. This same consideration prevented the official unions from participating in the formation of the Party of Labour (PT) put together by a small group of leftist intellectuals, although they coveted the name and maintained a watching brief over the party.

16. Sotsprof's influence waned through 1992 as it lost access to its political base, the Ministry of Labour, following ministerial changes.

Parties and Trade Unions in Eastern Europe: The Shifting Distribution of Political and Economic Power

MARTIN MYANT and MICHAEL WALLER

Political parties in the competitive systems of the Western world, as Paul Lewis records in his contribution to this collection, act as a channel for citizen demands, aggregating them, giving them coherence and translating them into policy; through the electoral process they provide the governments that will conduct that policy; they regulate elite competition, offering an orderly means of accession to governmental power and playing a crucial role, again through the electoral system, in the alternation of power; and, through these and other aspects of their political action, they educate society and confirm the order of which they constitute so important a part. Providing thus a link between civil society and the state, they live in a house of power. In the normal run of things, the exercise of state power is the goal to which their action tends.

Trade unions, in this pluralist scheme, and in so far as their role extends into the realm of national policy-making, form a part – if a major and qualitatively distinct part – of the lobby. Not seeking to govern, their role has come to be, in an industrial age, to defend the material interests of their members through consultation with, or pressure on, whichever part of the structure of government is most open to their demands. Their relations with political parties are therefore necessarily complex. In cases where they share a similar constituency, the roles of party and trade union can none the less conflict; and yet, on the other hand, a wide discrepancy in their constituencies does not prevent a trade union from co-operating with a governing party.

This contrast in the roles of party and pressure group is a central component of pluralism as the Western world understands that concept, and indeed the concept has been generated by the experience of the societies of that world. As such it forms a part of the model of political organization to which the countries of eastern Europe aspire as they emerge from communist authoritarianism. Their history, however, has reflected very different notions about the relationship between party and trade unions, drawn from experiences of a very different kind, which cannot but influence the process of their democratization.

Some ten years before the Russian revolution, in debates within the

Bolshevik party about the organization of the future socialist society, Lenin's rival Bogdanov recommended that the running of the economy should be handed to the trade unions, that politics should be the realm of the party and should be regulated by the principle of democratic centralism (which at that point had not acquired its Stalinist associations), whilst the organization of cultural life should be in the hands of *proletkul't* – 'proletarian culture' – a concept which did in fact assume organizational form, but which also was to wither on the branch of Stalinism.

Such notions reflected a syndicalism that was strong in the socialist movement at the turn of the century. It was a syndicalism of which – like the anarchism to which it was so frequently wedded – Lenin himself was profoundly suspicious. The notion that the trade unions should organize the economy independently of the party was present in many of the debates of the early years of the Russian revolution, assuming a particular prominence during the civil war years, when Lenin's view of the primacy of the party, as itself representing working class power and as privileged in its exercise of that power, predominated. The issue was determined some time after Lenin's death with the political elimination of the trade union chief Tomsky in 1929. From that point on the trade unions settled into their role as 'transmission belts' linking the masses to the regime, which became a prime characteristic of the Stalinist political system, and was itself transmitted to the communist systems of eastern Europe.

All this is familiar enough to need no elaboration. What does merit attention is the fact that these 'mass organizations' of the communist system were, precisely, extensive and fully articulated organizations enroling virtually every person employed in the economy. Whilst their political autonomy was minimal, their social role was immense, and as the chief channel for the distribution of welfare benefits and holiday facilities, as well as for the provision of cultural amenities, they were a part of the daily life of the average citizen. Moreover, when the communist monopoly of power collapsed, it was the parties that bore the brunt of the opprobrium attaching to communism's dismal record. Adroitly proclaiming their independence, the trade unions of the communist period were able to maintain their presence at the grass-roots of society, outnumbering at the time of writing the other trade union organizations that the new freedom of association spawned, including the Polish Solidarity itself. Meanwhile the political parties that the newly enfranchised electorates have called on to reorganize society and the economy have for the most part very shallow roots in society indeed, or none at all, whilst the communist parties themselves, stripped of their monopolistic role and carrying the blame for communism's failures and for the years of Soviet oppression, have a severe problem of identity which is only partially compensated for by the organizational advantages that they have inherited.

The structures of communism, therefore, have had a particular influence on the configuration of the forces that have been summoned by history to fashion the new polities of eastern Europe. Whilst one of the major conclusions that can be drawn from the material presented in this collection is that the trade unions have consented to acquiesce in policies that have demanded severe sacrifices from the workforce, the massive presence of the formerly official trade unions on the political stage is a very particular feature of the eastern European transition.

The newly formed trade unions, on the other hand, present characteristics that contrast with those of the former 'mass organization' unions of the communist period. One in particular, which they share with the new political parties, is a marked ambiguity about their role. Most prominently in the case of Solidarity, but also in that of the Bulgarian Podkrepa, a leading role in the challenge to communist power has pulled certain of the new trade unions of the transition towards a parliamentary, and indeed at times governmental role. Meanwhile certain of the newer parties are likewise confused about their role, as when business and other interest associations have entered the parliamentary arena as political parties, on the quite reasonable assumption that this new arena offers them swifter and more effective influence on policy-making than does organization in a still poorly structured, and generally less evident lobby.

This concluding chapter sets side by side the experience of the political parties in their search for implantation in society with that of the trade unions, revealing the role that the trade unions, new and old, have played in ensuring stability during a period of political flux and economic hardship that might have been expected to elicit quite other results.

A Comparison of Party Formation

The collapse of communist power had different sequels in the countries of eastern Europe as concerns the process of party formation. The differences depended, in the first instance, on the nature of the transition, the ability of the communist power structure itself to accommodate or even to initiate the beginnings of political change and the nature of the former opposition movements. In the Czechoslovak case the communist system, unable to take serious reform initiatives thanks to the heritage of post-1968 'normalization', allowed relatively little scope for the development of an active opposition, but was swept aside most completely and most quickly.

Power was taken first by a broad democratic movement, the Civic Forum in the Czech Republic and Public Against Violence in Slovakia. It was as if civil society, in the sense of a broad social movement undifferentiated except in its rejection of communist tyranny, was conquering the space usually reserved for parties, but this proved to be no more than a brief interlude, especially in the Czech Republic. Those within Civic Forum who believed that a party system which they perceived as outdated would be replaced by broader, more tolerant, and less partisan movements, have been removed from political power.

Indeed, the Czech Republic is now the nearest in eastern Europe to what could be seen as a 'normal' western European political system. Politics is dominated by a confident and reasonably united neo-liberal wing. This has a reasonably clearly defined support base among those who have gained, or expect to gain, from the political and economic changes. There is also a discernible left, although, as in some parts of western Europe, it is divided between social democrats and communists, both of whom are unsure of themselves and are highly unlikely to have a major infuence on political developments in the near future. They have, however, a clearly defined social base with the Communist Party in particular enjoying very solid backing from those in the older generation whose political thinking was shaped around the time of the Second World War and who see nothing but threats of insecurity in recent political and economic changes.

In both Poland and Hungary, the opposition was far more developed and had to some extent taken organizational form before 1989. In Hungary it had even had the opportunity to clarify its own divisions and there was a strong tendency towards the rapid formation of political parties. These, however, as has been argued by Attila Agh, were not linked to clearly defined constituencies.[1] Their role in interest articulation was diffuse. Those that emerged as the strongest in electoral terms were, instead, predominantly ideology-based, their leaderships being bound by personal ties born of the struggle against communism. The initial proliferation of parties, which sometimes grew out of interest groups or discussion clubs that had been allowed scope to exist shortly beforehand, could be seen as actually halting the development of civil society, which had been such a feature of the period of challenge to communist power.[2] Instead of pressure and interest groups emerging, with the aim of influencing political parties, everyone with an axe to grind saw the objective as personal election to a seat in parliament. This was a relatively short-lived phase. Parliamentary elections in 1990 gave dominance to a small number of political forces which could provide the basis for a manageable parliamentary democracy. But the governing coalition that emerged from that early election lacked the unity, self-confidence and sense of purpose that characterize the right wing in the Czech Republic.

This process of party formation was somewhat more complicated in the Polish case. The relatively early and prolonged transition from communist power kept the diverse opposition groups together for some time, under the Solidarity banner. Differentiation of the party system was postponed in Poland, partly because the first fully free election in October 1991 was preceded by partially free elections in 1989 which left intact the confrontation between the anti-communist forces grouped under the banner of Solidarity and the still ruling Polish United Workers' Party. This, coupled with a lax electoral law, meant that even the elections of 1991 failed to lead to the decisive narrowing of parties that could force a redefinition of the roles of other representative organizations.

In Bulgaria, the transition from communist power was initially even less decisive in the sense that the Bulgarian Socialist Party, a reformed Communist Party, was able to triumph in the first free elections. Elements of the struggle against the old power system were therefore still live issues. That sense of a continuing and clearly-defined struggle delayed the fragmentation experienced in Poland, at the expense of a fragmentation within each of the opposing blocs which, at the time of writing, has still not been fully resolved.

This somewhat ragged process of party formation has to be set against the much stronger continuity in the evolution of the trade unions since the turning-point of 1989, to which we return below. One feature of that contrast, however, is worth presenting in anticipation. Attention has focused on the new parties of the transition. Far less attention has been paid to the way in which the communist parties succeeded in maintaining themselves in being, and even in retaining a remarkably clearly defined social base through their organizational resources, backed up by various strategies aimed at fashioning a new image. They have, however, been at a clear disadvantage in the new order and their political influence has, at least in the initial stages, been limited. The contrast is clear with the old trade unions, which have dominated, in terms of numbers and of potential political influence, the newer creations. The implications of this fact are, needless to say, considerable, even if the elections in Poland in 1993 showed how a backlash against the reforming policies of the new governments, can leave the way open for a post-communist revival.

Explaining the Differences

Clearly, then, the starting points and the courses of transition from communist power differed, but that cannot be the whole explanation for the different courses of party formation, nor indeed can they be imputed to the laxity or severity of electoral laws, which are themselves a consequence of relationships between different political forces within the emerging structure. Most obviously, it cannot explain the differences between the Czech Republic and Slovakia, which brought so much of a common heritage from the past. The suggestion here is that the differences between the countries of eastern Europe can be explained around three 'party-forming' groups of issues. These relate to the means of reconciliation with the communist past, to the ability to formulate and mobilize around a programme of economic reform and to the ability to cope with the decline in living standards caused largely by economic reform policies.[3] In each case, as the discussion that follows indicates, the influence of the different historical backgrounds of the eastern European countries is very clear.

In all cases coping with the past started from a widespread recognition that the communist system had failed, together with an element of anti-Soviet feeling that differed in its intensity across the region. The extent of that failure, and the wider conclusions that could be drawn from it, varied. The clearest-cut case was the Czech Republic. Here the communist period could be seen in unequivocally negative terms. It had meant isolation from the nation's perceived natural home in the mainstream of Europe. It had also meant substantial relative economic decline, which was very plain for all to see once the borders were fully opened in December 1989. There was, moreover, no clash with a national pride which would want to retain some specificity from western Europe. If there were 'heroic' periods in the Czech past – the Hussite movement, the inter-war democracy under Masaryk – they were closely linked to the development of western Europe.

There was, then, no conflict between strident anti-communist rhetoric, national traditions and an economic orientation towards the market and the speediest possible integration into the European Community. Moreover, anti-communist rhetoric had such a wide appeal that it eclipsed other cleavages that the vigorous establishment of market relations might have been expected to engender.[4] In terms of practical policies, it is noteworthy that in none of the other countries considered here has there been so total an attempt to bury the preceding 40 years. The clearest expressions of this are the decisions to return property nationalized after February 1948 and land held in co-operatives to former owners, the laws banning former Communist officials from holding certain posts and other legal measures that can be interpreted as a blanket condemnation of Communist Party members.

Things were not so clear-cut in Poland and Hungary. The communist period had not been a success, but neither did it need to be interpreted as the destruction of an economy that had been built up before. Nor was it easy to condemn so totally a communist power structure that had produced reformers from its own ranks who eventually contributed to the destruction of their own system. Moreover, the alternative of looking to integration into Europe was not so immediately acceptable. Although all influential political forces paid lip service to the slogan of a return to Europe, many were far less whole-hearted than the politicians across most of the political spectrum in the Czech Republic. The preoccupation in both countries with a national destiny, connected in the past with the preservation in those societies of an indigenouos landed gentry class that the Czech Lands lacked, no doubt played an important role here.

Thus in Poland, although there was a tremendous attraction to ideas from western Europe, where so many of the population had relations and personal contacts, there were major political divisions over issues that reflected national pride and pretensions and the country's Roman Catholic heritage. They pointed to the continuation, or in some cases return to, clear differences from the 'normal' situation in western Europe. The most obvious example is the law restricting abortions. In Hungary a major difference between the ruling Hungarian Democratic Forum and the Alliance of Free Democrats concerned the insistence of the former on a return to Hungary's perceived glorious past. This proved to be neither a clear nor a satisfactory basis for the formulation of a strategy for political and economic reform.

In neither Slovakia nor Bulgaria did national traditions point so unequivocally towards a western orientation. In Slovakia, the interwar period was associated with poverty and mass emigration, while rapid economic development was largely a post-war phenomenon. In Bulgaria, too, the communist years had brought significant economic development, for which the communist party could claim credit. Moreover, the links of sentiment between Bulgarians and Russians were strong, resting not so much on a common Slav identity (the Yugoslav experience puts us on our guard against any such conclusion), but on the role of Russia in the liberation of Bulgaria from the 'yoke' of Turkish domination and on a shared Orthodox cultural tradition which was of immense political importance to Bulgaria in its striving to recreate a national identity once the Turk had gone.

The second group of 'party-forming' issues, relating to the ability to formulate a convincing programme for economic reform, appeared to depend on the ability of the group that came to power to act energetically and decisively. Ultimately, all the countries of eastern Europe have moved towards fairly similar economic policies, which are broadly in line with the standard IMF package of 'stabilization' measures worked out for

Latin American countries suffering from high inflation and balance of payments deficits. Particularly where the rejection of the communist past was the strongest, there is an obvious political appeal in being able to present a programme that looks like a dramatic break from the past.

The wiseness of the policies adopted, in terms of effects on the economy, are not the issue here. The point, as mentioned by Gortat and Kloc, is that the 'shock therapy' of the Balcerowicz programme in Poland, starting in January 1990, or the similar measures adopted in Czechoslovakia at the start of 1991, had a very clear political impact.[5] In Poland the political paralysis that followed effectively ruled out further major economic policy initiatives, which further contributed to the declining prestige of politicians and hampered the consolidation of strong political parties around those in government.

In (the then) Czechoslovakia, however, the government was able to press ahead with its novel programme of voucher privatization. This involved every citizen who registered, and the overwhelming majority did. It thus gave the impression that huge changes really were under way. It also, of course, provided an effectively free handout to all participants, ironically from a government that claimed adherence to neo-liberal thinking within which politicians are condemned for courting popularity by precisely such means. Again, the long-term economic impact of the scheme is irrelevant. The point here is its immediate political impact in helping consolidate the dominant position of Václav Klaus's Civic Democratic Party. Other factors, including the low level of Czechoslovak foreign debt and a geographical location and cultural heritage giving excellent opportunities for the development of tourism, were also important in reducing the social costs of the strategy, on which more below.

In the case of Hungary, very similar policies have been adopted to the 'shock therapy' of Poland and Czechoslovakia, but they were not put together in the same sort of package and not presented as a coherent alternative. There was also considerable dithering over privatization, all of which served to increase the impression that the Hungarian government was not acting decisively. The comparison with Czechoslovakia suggests an impact from past national traditions. The Czechoslovak reform was unequivocally based on ideas derived from well-known Western economic theories. There was no attempt to find something specific. The Hungarian Democratic Forum was less eager to embrace that heritage, unlike the opposition Alliance of Free Democrats, which was more oriented towards an international outlook and towards the neo-classical and neo-liberal trends in Western economic thought.

In the case of Bulgaria, as the contribution by Thirkell, Atanasov and Gradev indicates, the UDF made rapid and immediate progress with small privatization, but restructuring and privatizing industry proceeded at a snail's pace. The factors here were not so much the strength of the former communist party, but failures on the part of the governing UDF itself, reflecting the absence of any such consensus as existed in the Czech Republic around the view that ideas from the West could provide a complete solution to the country's problems. The Bulgarian economy was in any case weaker than any of its northern counterparts (see Table 1 below). It had suffered particularly heavily from the loss of Soviet markets and Soviet supplies of energy and raw materials, from a large foreign debt, and from the Gulf War – Iraq being a major debtor to Bulgaria. Sanctions against Serbia, with which Bulgaria complied because of the importance of the western link, further crippled the Bulgarian economy, since all exports northwards, which until then had transited through Serbia, were now restricted to one ferryboat and one bridge across the Danube.

For completeness, it can be added that Slovakia was unable to formulate its own economic reform strategy. The claims that the Czechoslovak reform was worked out in Prague alone are broadly accurate.[6] Whether Slovakia on balance gained or lost in this arrangement is a contentious point. When the two countries finally separated at the start of 1993, Slovakia was not saddled with a significant foreign debt. On the other hand, the fact that tension did end in divorce certainly owes something to the pressures that Slovakia was under as a result of policies devised and applied by the Czech Klaus and his government.

In other words, when the need is for liberalization, privatization and other market-oriented changes, the best kind of leadership comes from the most uncompromininsg supporters of the market. This point need not be accepted in total. There is plenty of scope for asking serious questions about the wisdom of the most vigorous reform strategies that have been adopted, especially in Poland and Czechoslovakia. There could have been a 'social-democratic' alternative, with liberalization supplemented by active state intervention in industry, agriculture and other sectors. The extent of economic decline, as covered below, the political problems that have been engendered by the effects of the chosen reform strategies, including the apparent paralysis of policy-making in some countries, and the possibility of a post-communist revival – whatever that means in a world without a Soviet Union – would seem to justify doubts about the chosen strategy. Nevertheless, in the initial period after the ending of communist power, it was the politicians with the most unequivocal commitment to free market thinking who could inspire confidence by appearing to promise the most decisive break with the past.[7]

A third group of 'party-forming' issues concerns the social costs of reform. These, according to official figures, were substantial in all cases.

Table 1 shows the extent of the fall in GDP and real wages and the levels of unemployment across the countries concerned. Distinguishing between Slovakia and the Czech Republic would show little difference apart from the unemployment figure, which was 2.7 per cent in the Czech Lands and 11.3 per cent in Slovakia in mid-1992.

TABLE 1

THE EXTENT OF ECONOMIC DECLINE IN EASTERN EUROPE BETWEEN 1989 AND 1992

	GDP	Real wages	Unemployment
Bulgaria	52	68	13.1
Czechoslovakia	70	73	5.5
Hungary	82	94	10.1
Poland	83	65	12.6

The first two columns show the 1992 level as a percentage of the 1989 figure. Unemployment is a percentage of the total workforce in mid-1992.

Source: United Nations Economic Commission for Europe.

There are doubts about the accuracy even of these official figures with considerable grounds for suspecting that the declines in output and living standards have been overstated. It would therefore be dangerous to take possible comparisons too seriously. The most obviously suspect case must be the Czech Republic. True, there clearly has been a substantial decline in living standards at least for much of the population. However, the very low level of unemployment partly reflects new growth around a rapidly expanding tourist sector and around firms exporting into the neighbour-ing German market. It is likely that not all of this has been recorded in the official statistics.

Thus the government was able to 'cope' with the social costs of reform within the logic of its general ideological position. The solution was already coming from the opening of international contacts and the inte-gration into western Europe. These benefits might have come from other strategies, too, and they might have involved smaller social costs. Never-theless, the point for now is that a strategy that was in harmony with national traditions, and that was ostensibly based on modern Western ideas, was able to bring enough benefits to give real hope for the future. There was complete harmony between the three groups of 'party-forming' issues, and the Civic Democratic party was able to find a support base among those who had already gained, or could reasonably hope to gain, from the transformation in which it was the leading force.

In Poland it proved much more difficult to incorporate the problem of the social costs of reform into a steadily consolidating political structure.

Indeed, worry that unreasonable sacrifices were being demanded was one of the major factors encouraging Wałęsa to reenter the political arena and to contest the presidential elections in November 1990. This controversy, as in Hungary, appeared to be between those clinging to national traditions and the internationally-oriented intellectuals, who were not impressed by strident Polish nationalism and who were prepared to accept ideas lifted from western European and North American academics. The link-up between the approach more tied to national traditions and discontent over the costs of reform made it impossible for the more cosmopolitan approach to provide consistent leadership in a continued reform strategy. Since, in particular, social costs – most obviously in terms of unemployment, which was perceived as a threat by far more than those actually made redundant – were more obvious than in the Czech Republic, the process of consolidating the supporters of radical economic reform into a party with a solid support base were frustrated.

In the Slovak case the higher level of unemployment indicates that there was less new growth than in the Czech Republic. These higher social costs were one factor destroying any political base for the firmest advocates of Klaus's economic reform strategy. Other factors included the differing assessment of the communist past and a different perception of the benefits of an opening to Europe. Although, as elsewhere, communism was seen as having failed, it could not be seen as having destroyed a pre-existing basis for prosperity. Neither could the failure of communism translate easily into a perceived failure of all left-wing ideas. Indeed, Slovakia seemed to have enjoyed some success only thanks to the post-war state direction of the economy or, even more controversially, during the existence of the wartime Slovak state, which at least had something to offer national pride.

There were, then, very clear reasons in Slovakia for the social costs of reform to encourage, and to link up with, a vaguely defined nationalism which pointed to no particular economic strategy. This proved to be specific enough to set Slovak politics on a somewhat different course from the Czech Republic. Efforts to convert Public Against Violence into a clearly-defined right-wing party, similar to Klaus's Civic Democratic Party, gained very little public sympathy. Instead, a nationalism with little further ideological specification provided the stable ideological base for a major political party, as the machinations of Slovak politics led to the creation of Vladimír Mečiar's Movement for a Democratic Slovakia. Although Slovak governments have actually pursued rather similar economic policies to those adopted in Prague, the different processes of political consolidation between the two parts of the federation clashed so seriously as to lead to the break-up of the federation at the end of 1992.

In Hungary social costs have been spread over a long time period, with economic decline continuing into 1993. They were, however, never a logical stick with which the Alliance of Free Democrats could beat the government. That movement was more likely to look with some admiration to neighbours to the north and to complain that indecisiveness and unimaginative policies were postponing inevitable sacrifices. That, it should be noted, is not an appealing position with which to build a social base beyond internationally oriented intellectuals. Thus the Alliance of Free Democrats can appear to be the clearest of all Hungarian parties on where it stands, but the least clear on who supports it beyond the kind of former opposition intellectuals who formed it.[8]

Social costs in Hungary have therefore had two slightly different effects. The first has been to raise the prospect of a post-communist revival, the re-entry of the Socialist Party into government thus becoming conceivable. The second effect has been to deepen divisions within the Hungarian Democratic Forum as it sought desperately for the means to rebuild some electoral support. There has even been serious consideration of voucher privatization, a method previously ruled out in total but made to seem attractive by its political impact in the Czech Republic.

The social costs of the transition have been particularly heavy in Bulgaria, as a result of the factors noted above – the loss of Soviet markets and energy supplies, the Gulf War and the sanctions against Serbia (see Table 1 above). Dependence on one very unsafe nuclear power plant meant frequent electricity blackouts during the winter of 1991–92. It is of no little interest that in Bulgaria, which is considered to be so peripheral to European developments, these pressures did not lead to populist appeals of the Mečiar, or even Wałęsa kind. Distance from Brussels does, in fact, count for much in this Bulgarian pragmatism. The blame for past misfortunes has been laid at the door as much of a 'Zhivkov clique' as of the communist party itself (the individual Zhivkov being put on trial, whereas in Czechoslovakia 'lustration' was aimed at the party as a whole, Jakeš being left in peace to enjoy his pension), whilst the West as a whole is blamed for present troubles – particularly in the case of the sanctions against Serbia, where Bulgaria, as noted, has paid a high price for playing a game organized by west European governments.

Trade Unions

The position and importance of trade unions within this process of political consolidation can be viewed within a similar framework. An 'ideal type' of stable democracy can be postulated with trade unions independent of both the state and of employers. They could be treated in the political sphere as accepted 'social partners', respecting the results of parliamentary elections, but trying to influence politics through existing political parties. Their political role would, however, be limited to employment-related issues.

This, of course, is not an accurate description of any existing case. It is anyway impossible to define precisely what political issues could be considered as 'legitimate' areas for trade union intervention. Neither are systems of parliamentary democracy so perfect at representing popular feeling and conflicting interests as to rule out the justification for unions to involve themselves more decisively, at least in certain periods, in political issues. There is therefore a very slow learning process during which political power and trade union power have to learn the limits to each other's spheres of activity.

This learning process would appear to be substantially more complicated in eastern Europe, partly because of the lack of clarity in the party-political system, but primarily because of a similar lack of clarity in the normally accepted primary function of trade unions. Their role as representatives of employee interests remains ambiguous amid the massive changes in ownership and organization throughout the economy.

As with the development of party systems, there are some common trends across the area, but there are also substantial variations. One common feature is the claim of high levels of union density, with the successors to the old 'official' unions clearly having the great bulk of union members. The figures claimed are certainly exaggerations, due both to inaccurate claims by union centres and to the acceptance of non-employees, such as pensioners, as members. Figures for 1991 suggest that the main Bulgarian union centre could have over 100 per cent coverage of employees, while the rival Podkrepa organized slightly over ten per cent. In Czechoslovakia, the ČSKOS made claims suggesting up to around 80 per cent coverage. In Hungary the MSzOSz claimed a membership equivalent to around 70 per cent coverage, compared with only three per cent for the Liga. In Poland, the OPZZ unions claimed 57 per cent coverage, leaving Solidarity organizing only around 20 per cent of employees.[9] Evidence from Russia suggests a similar imbalance with the successors of the old official unions clearly still dominant.

There are also in all countries some unions that belong to no centre, but their political impact is minimal. They too are sometimes referred to as 'independent' unions. There is remarkable consistency across the countries of eastern Europe, and even including Russia, in the kinds of employees that they organize, the most effective representing potentially powerful groups such as locomotive drivers, airline pilots and air traffic controllers. In many respects they resemble the trade unions familiar to

Western pluralism, concerned only to use their bargaining power to improve their economic position.

An analysis of trade unions' role in politics during this transitional period could be developed around a synthesis of three broad, but very different and seemingly incompatible, theoretical approaches. The first can be derived from classical Marxism, the second from the 'Oxford' school of industrial relations and the third from the European social-democratic tradition. None of these on its own provides anything approaching a satisfactory framework, but together they offer some points of reference for comparing eastern European trade unions with their namesakes in western Europe.

Within the Marxist framework,[10] all attention is directed onto the role of unions in the revolutionary transformation of society's socio-economic base. There is no attention to their role in the development of political democracy. Moreover, it can be convincingly argued that Marx and Engels provided no consistent position, starting off tending to view trade unions as if they 'ought' to be revolutionary, but gradually moving towards the separation made famous by Lenin between purely economic struggles – meaning here struggles in the workplace – and political or 'class' movements.

Much of subsequent Marxist writing can be seen as an attempt to find the relationship between these two broad kinds of struggle with, for example, Rosa Luxemburg's idea of the 'mass strike', in which protests that are started over economic issues can acquire broader political character. The key point here, and the common thread among Marxist writers, is the assumption that the working class will somehow become the leading force in a political transformation as the champion of a clearly socialist position. Its potential political orientation is predetermined and the political role of trade unions is defined within that context. The trouble, as pointed out long ago by the 'revisionist' Bernstein, is that workers could come to accept that capitalism actually gives them the best chance of the highest possible standard of living. Trade unions can then play a more permanent and specific role within capitalist society. More-over, as support for capitalism seems to be the dominant view in eastern Europe, the classical Marxist approach can have only very limited appeal either as a guide to trade-union activists or as a framework for analysing their activities.

Nevertheless, some analogies are possible at the analytical level even if they relate more to form than to content. Thus social demands were significant in the collapse of communist power, albeit to varying degrees, in all cases except Czechoslovakia. These provided the base for the inde-pendent union centres. In Poland Solidarity continued as a broad umbrella. In Bulgaria social protests provided the basis for the development of the independent Podkrepa. In Hungary the political role of independent unions was less significant, owing to the smaller scale of social protest and the speed with which parties emerged to dominate the political scene. In Russia the independent union centres have failed to play a major role for slightly different reasons.

All the newly-formed independent union centres have faced major problems precisely because the radical reform of a communist system is not in harmony with the social demands usually associated with trade unions. This could even point to a degree of validity for the Marxist position in that an active political role for unions – in the sense of contributing directly to the shaping of the whole political system – becomes highly problematic when their political position is not in harmony with the social demands that they naturally represent. Thus, it has been extremely difficult for the new independent unions to remain trade unions while also adopting a firmly and actively pro-capitalist position. This dilemma has contributed to their becoming a factor *disrupting* the process of party formation. In Poland, Solidarity (the movement) spawned parties, but Solidarity (the trade union) did not allow them scope: this confusion over roles therefore spread into the parties.

Reformed 'old' unions might appear a more likely source of social protest after the collapse of communist power. That, however, has been limited by two important factors. The first relates to the continuation of past habits and practices and is pursued later. The second relates to the old unions' political image in the eyes of much of the public which means that attempts to lead social protest run the risk of being condemned as a bid by failed figures from the past to disrupt reform. Both the OPZZ in Poland and the MSzOSz in Hungary are considered to be linked to the successors to the communist parties and this factor has also been an important constraint on the Czech unions. The experience in Russia appears to be remarkably similar.

The explanation for unions' apparent passivity can be advanced with a consideration of the second possible theoretical approach for the study of unions' role in politics which can be developed out of the 'Oxford' school of industrial relations. The starting point is the classic studies by the Webbs which led them to conclude that the methods used by unions to regulate the terms of employment of their members are the major determinant of other aspects of their behaviour.[11] The approach has been developed by Hugh Clegg into a theory of trade unionism 'under collective bargaining'. He provided comparative evidence across a number of countries suggesting that such variables as union density, union structure, union government, workplace organization, strikes and approaches to industrial democracy could all be explained by differences in collective bargaining. It was also presented as the determinant of political involvement.[12]

Clegg does accept some reservations. It is far from clear what should be treated as cause and what should be seen as effect. Thus the greater predilection of the French unions to take political action could be the cause or the effect of different bargaining structures. The variations in union density across eastern Europe are certainly more likely to be explicable in terms of different historical and political backgrounds, while involvement in wage determination is probably very similar. Thus Poland was affected by the unique experience of the 1980–81 period during which the old, official unions were so completely discredited as to be reduced to relative insignificance. The differences between countries in union density may, however, have important implications in the future for the kinds of bargaining systems that emerge.

Clegg's approach clearly cannot tell the whole story. As long as unions fulfil the basic requirement of protecting their members' interests, leading officials and activists have considerable freedom to take a political stand on issues with only the vaguest of relationships to collective bargaining. They do not have absolute freedom and their ability to retain a credible voice on major issues ultimately depends on their ability to prove, at least from time to time, that they have the backing of the membership. There is therefore a strong tendency for unions, in the interests of maintaining the unity and loyalty of their constituency, to narrow the scope of their political involvement. A dramatic illustration was the Czechoslovak unions' determination to avoid taking any stand on the break-up of the federation.

There seems to have been a greater effort to break free from this kind of constraint by those union organizations more closely associated with reformed communist parties, such as the MSzOSz in Hungary and especially the OPZZ in Poland. There clearly is a degree of freedom for union leaders in their political role, the limits of which they can only learn through experience. Nevertheless, it does seem reasonable to postulate that the role of unions in politics must be influenced, at least to a significant degree, by the key activities that bring them membership.

In eastern Europe, however, the collective bargaining of Clegg and the Webbs is not the unions' main activity. At best, it is taking an embryonic form in a few cases only. There clearly is strong continuity, at least for the reformed 'old' unions, with the 'welfare' role from the past. This assures them of a solid membership base, just as it did under communism, which cannot be rivalled by the new, independent unions. However, as several of the country studies indicate, it indicates a role of passivity both towards major political issues – a tendency reinforced by the ambiguous· political origins of the unions as mentioned above – and towards local managements. Experience in Poland has been particularly revealing, with the OPZZ consistently criticizing government policies at the national level and even contesting parliamentary elections in alliance with the reformed communist Social Democracy of the Polish Republic. It has, however, proved less successful than Solidarity, or other union centres, at mobilizing protest actions. It certainly appears to lack any serious militancy in the workplaces.

Thus, although the reformed 'old' unions have considerable strength derived from their resources and membership, they are constrained both by the need to avoid too close an identification with their political past and by the heritage of past activities. They have no real experience of mass mobilization, having concentrated rather on the welfare role, and have therefore often been seen making threats that they cannot back up.

The implications of these limitations to unions' political activities can be clarified further around the third broad approach which, as mentioned above, can be derived from the traditional, central European social-democratic position. This relates to the argument put by Curt Sørensen, that broad historical research points to the working-class movement as the most consistent fighter for, and best defender of, democracy. This argument has probably been put most clearly and consistently by leading figures in the dominant German trade union federation, the DGB (*Deutscher Gewerkschaftsbund* – DGB), which has continued the German tradition of trying to produce theoretically rigorous programmatic statements. Its origins can be seen in the specific situation of post-war Germany which in some respects has analogies with the societies of eastern Europe as they emerge from communism. German experience provides a useful comparison for eastern Europe at two levels. In the first place, it can provide some insights on the role of unions in the development of democracy, while in the second place the German experience itself has influenced the behaviour of eastern European unions with such widely divergent examples as the Czechoslovak ČSKOS and Poland's Solidarity looking at times to their powerful neighbour for helpful advice.

The first DGB leaders consistently presented themselves as staunch defenders of parliamentary democracy, opposing both Nazism and communism, but insisted that formal, political democracy was not on its own enough. The downfall of the Weimar Republic was seen as stemming from the concentration of economic power into the hands of a small group of men who then used Hitler to destroy political democracy.

The conclusion drawn from this analysis was frequently expressed by Hans Böckler, the DGB's first chairman. The aim, he argued, could not be the restoration of a 'capitalistic society', and in this he was reflecting the very widespread craving for a 'new beginning' rather than a return to the past, which was portrayed as the source of war and misery. Instead, he argued, there should be 'democracy of the economic system', because 'we know by experience that political democracy can never be a lasting thing if we cannot have economic democracy at the same time'.[13]

It is an open question how far trade unions really were important in securing and defending democracy in Germany. In a major study, Andrei Markovits reached the conclusion that they were 'important participants' in the polity through their 'deep commitment to the survival of liberal democracy', through their staunch defence of 'the pluralist order', and through their involvement in a wide range of debates on major political issues. Indeed, he concluded that it would be 'hard to imagine' the German Federal Republic without the presence of the unions. Their responsible attitude, refusal to identify in total with one political party and hence their broad unity were, he suggested, a major change from the ill-fated Weimar Republic.[14]

It is, however, very difficult to *prove* that West German democracy would have developed along very different lines had unions been more like some others in western Europe, with their divisions along political or religious lines or, in some cases, with closer ties to political parties. It may be that their contribution to the development of a welfare system and to industrial democracy was of some significance in making society more stable, and hence in providing a more favourable base for political democracy. It is, however, all really a matter of speculation, just as it is very unclear how far the apparent 'moderation' of the Czech and Slovak union movements, which have to some extent modelled themselves on the DGB, was a cause rather than a consequence and reflection of the apparent relative stability of their countries' political lives.

There is, however, a more practical sense in which German experience may be significant, in that it can be taken, by east European trade union leaders themselves, to confirm the irrelevance of grandiose programmatic pronouncements. In early post-war Germany, all the emphasis was on broad issues, such as economic justice and democratic reform, with very little attention to the mundane issues such as collective bargaining. Markovits's account rather suggests that the DGB was forced to move towards more pragmatic issues after its hopes for a fundamental reform of the capitalist system ran into a dead end.[15] It continued to make pronouncements on a full range of issues affecting society, but its 'radical rhetoric' was accompanied by 'moderate, often demobilizing, action'.[16] More practical emphasis was placed on 'action programmes' which gave top priority to standard trade union concerns, most notably in later years to reductions in the length of the working week. This, it could be argued, is very much where the ČSKOS started with its programmatic document in 1991.

This same trend can be observed in other countries where programmatic statements about transforming society can be left safely on paper. Unions, however, still have plenty of scope for political involvement around issues that are currently of growing importance, such as training, social policy, consumer protection and the environment.[17] Indeed, it could be argued that the retreat from 'ideologically comprehensive' pronouncements could lead to a *greater* political role in so far as it is associated with concentration on issues that unions really can influence.[18] These are not typically the sources of the major political divisions and it is therefore possible for unions to appear more as a typical pressure group, trying to shape policies by influencing political parties.

This, it could be argued, is precisely the logical starting point for the reformed 'old' unions. They clearly could not adopt the kind of programme for economic democracy espoused by the DGB in view of their desperation to appear as loyal supporters of capitalism. Ideas of a 'third way' seem to have been pretty universally rejected, at least for the time being, leaving only an isolated minority clinging to ideas associated with reform communism. Moreover, eastern European unions can feel that, by avoiding any distinct pronouncements on the direction society should be taking, they are following the experience of the more successful unions of western Europe.

They have therefore set about creating tripartite structures and conciliation machinery which, it has been argued, have not grown 'out of a genuine new grassroots movement', but are imposed from above as part of a model derived from foreign experience.[19] This has considerable truth, although it is clear that adopting a model from western Europe itself has considerable appeal for much of the population. Indeed, independent unions, in Hungary, Bulgaria and with less success in Russia, have been pulled in this direction too when they have tried to move towards a more clearly trade union role.

The most notable exception to this trend has been Poland, in which no effort has been made to create tripartite structures, presumably because of the very special relationship between Solidarity, with its pretensions to be much more than a social partner, and the government. Solidarity could hardly, as a trade union, accept a subordinate position to the larger OPZZ within a structure similar to that in the former Czechoslovakia, which in turn effectively left unions as a mere pressure group trying to influence the government. The consequence of this has been a remarkable failure of social dialogue, with Polish governments consulting with employees only when forced to do so by major protests. The recent development of the Enterprise Pact, referred to by Gortat and Kloc, appears as a belated and rather feeble alternative to the attempts at social dialogue in all the other countries.

Conclusion

The importance of trade unions within the transition to democratic politics can be analysed around the three party-forming groups of issues outlined above: the means devised for a reconciliation with the communist past, the ability to formulate and mobilize around a programme of economic reform, and the ability to cope with the decline in living standards caused largely by economic reform policies. Where the transition was associated with social protests, independent union centres could emerge, enjoying high prestige but, Soldarity included, with a small regular membership base in comparison with the formerly official trade unions. They could play an important role in the formation of the new political system, but face a major dilemma over their role once communist power is eliminated. There are a number of possible options and practice has produced various combinations between them.

They could try to develop into genuine trade unions, disentangling themselves from too much direct involvement in politics: that is most logical where the level of social protest remains high, but has proved the most difficult for Solidarity in Poland. Secondly, whilst they have not tried to transform themselves directly into political parties, they can play a role in recruiting elite personnel where the party system is at an early stage of development: this has clearly been a significant factor in all countries with independent union centres, including Russia. Finally, they can play a role in supporting the development of parties, although this seems to come into conflict with a possible role as a trade union and with the heritage of a prominent role during the transition before parties had emerged.

Reformed 'old' unions are of greatest importance where the social element in the overthrow of communist power was the least significant. They typically lack any grandiose ideological pretensions, having abandoned Marxist commitments which anyway had long since ceased to have any real significance, and grass-roots activities imply no particular political orientation. Facing major obstacles to the mobilization of social protest against the effects of economic reform, they are ideally placed to adopt the practices of some of the very experienced western European and North American unions which are cautious of too much involvement in party politics. They could be praised for adopting a responsible attitude, which has contributed to social peace and narrowed the scope for social demagogues. The implication is that they have made a contribution to the development of democratic politics largely by accepting falling living standards without too much protest.

NOTES

1. Attila Ágh, *The Hungarian Party System* (Budapest: Hungarian Center for Democracy Studies Foundation, 1993).
2. Lászlo Kéri, *Between Two Systems* (Budapest: Institute of Political Science of the Hungarian Academy of Sciences, 1992), pp.25–8.
3. For an account of economic developments, see United Nations Economic Commission for Europe, *Economic Bulletin for Europe*, Vol.44 (1992).
4. See Herbert Kitschelt, 'The Formation of Party Systems in East Central Europe', *Politics and Society*, Vol.20, No.1 (1992).
5. See also Martin Myant, *Transforming Socialist Economies: The Case of Poland and Czechoslovakia* (Cheltenham, Edward Elgar, 1993).
6. For an account of the formulation of the Czechoslovak reform strategy, see Myant, *Transforming*.
7. See Martin Myant, 'Problems of Transition in Eastern Europe: Should we Seek Alternatives?', *British Review of Economic Issues*, Vol.15 (1993).
8. Kéri, pp.70–74.
9. Figures calculated from M.Upham (ed.), *Trade Unions of the World 1992–93* (Harlow: Longman, 1993).
10. For a full discussion, see John Kelly, *Trade Unions and Socialist Politics* (London: Verso, 1988).
11. Sidney and Beatrice Webb, *Industrial Democracy* (London: Longmans, 1902), and Sidney and Beatrice Webb, *The History of Trade Unionism 1666–1920* (London: Longmans, 1920).
12. Hugh Clegg, *Trade Unionism under Collective Bargaining* (Oxford: Basil Blackwell, 1976).
13. *Official Report of the Free World Labour Conference and of the First Congress of the International Confederation of Free Trade Unions* (London, 1949), p.115.
14. Andrei S. Markovits, *The Politics of the West German Trade Unions: Strategies of Class and Interest Representation in Growth and Crisis* (Cambridge: Cambridge University Press, 1986), pp.3-5, and 417.
15. Ibid., p.73.
16. Ibid., p.67.
17. Beyme, pp.138–45.
18. Siegfried Mielke and Fritz Vilmar, 'Die Gewerkschaften', in Wolfgang Benz (ed.), *Die Geschichte der Bundesrepublik Deutschland* (4 vols., Frankfurt aM: Fischer Taschenbuch Verlag), Vol.2, pp.85–6.
19. Mihály Csákó, 'Trade Unions and Legislation in the Transition Period: Comments on the Institutional Context', Paper presented to conference 'Parties, Society and Trade Unions in the Transition to Democratic Politics', Budapest, 28 to 31 March 1993.

Index

Ágh, A., 164
Alliance of Free Democrats, 167–8, 172
Association of Industrialists and
    Entrepreneurs, 151
Atanasov, B., 103

Bachrach, P., 29
Balcerowicz, L., 118, 125, 168
Ball, A., 7
Baratz, M.S., 29
Bentley, A., 23
Bernstein, E., 174
Berov, L., 101, 108–9
Bielecki, J.-K., 120
Blackbourn, D., 141–2
Blondel, J., 11–12
Böckler, H., 177
Bogdanov, A., 162
Bonapartism, 39
Borovoy, K., 153
Bruszt, L., 32
Bujak, Z., 120
Bulgarian Socialist Party, 1, 99, 105, 109,
    111–12, 165
Burbulis, G., 157
Business Bloc, 29

Čalfa, M., 66
Catholic Church, 25, 167
Centre Alliance, 120–21
Charter 77, 15
Christian National Union, 121
CITUB (Confederation of Independent
    Trade Unions in Bulgaria), 32, 101–9,
    112–15
Civic Democratic Alliance, 83
Civic Democratic Party, 75–8, 80, 83, 168,
    170
Civic Forum, 15, 62, 72, 75, 163
Civic Movement, 79
Civic Union, 151
Clarke, S., 2
Classes, in transition to democracy, 39–44,
    47
Clegg, H., 175–6
Collective bargaining, 32, 61, 67–8, 93, 140,
    150
Communist Party, 1, 26, 62, 72–3, 87, 99,
    102–3, 107, 134, 136–8, 149, 151, 158,
    164–6
Confederation of Labour, 138

Conservative Party, 9, 13
Corporatism, 35
ČSKOS, 27, 32, 59–84, 173, 177, 179

Dahl, A., 50
Democracy, 37–45, 50–52
Democratic Party of Russia, 137
Democratic Russia, 138
Democratic Union (Poland), 18, 120, 122
Democratic Union (Russia), 137
DGB (German Trade Union
    Confederation), 177–9
Di Palma, G., 45
Dimitrov, F., 31, 101, 107–10
Duverger, M., 9–14, 16

EBRD (European Bank for Reconstruction
    and Development), 31
Economic transformation, 68–75, 105–6,
    118, 128–32, 139–45, 167–72
Edinstvo, 105, 111, 114–15
Eley, G., 41–2
Employers' organisations, 28–9
Engliš, A., 78
Enterprise Pact, 121, 132, 180

Falbr, R., 59–60, 76–7, 79, 80
FNPR (Federation of Independent Trade
    Unions of Russia), 134, 146–55, 157,
    159
Foreign debt, 29–30, 169
Frasyniuk, W., 18
Fukuyama, F., 51

General Agreement
    Bulgaria, 103–5
    Czechoslovakia, 68–72
    Russia, 150–51
Germany
    democracy in, 40–42
    trade unions, 177–9
Gheyselinck, T., 78
Golikov, V., 148
Gorbachev, M.S., 136–7, 141, 146
Gortat, R., 168, 180
Gradev, G., 168
Gramsci, A., 49

Hankiss, E., 46
Hausner, J., 29
Herz, J., 45